Russell Foster Aldwinckle is Emeritus
Professor of Systematic Theology,
McMaster Divinity College, McMaster
University, Hamilton, Ontario, Canada. A
native of England, Professor Aldwinckle
studied at the University of London (B.A.
with honours), at Oxford (B.A. with
honours; M.A.), and at the Université de
Strasbourg (D.Th.). He came to McMaster
Divinity College as Professor of Systematic
Theology in 1947, which post he held until his
emeritus retirement in 1977. In postre-
tirement, Professor Aldwinckle has been
Visiting Professor of Theology at Eastern
Baptist Seminary (1977), the American
Baptist Seminary of the West (1978-1979),
and at Southern Baptist Theological Seminary (1979-1980). He is the author of *Death
in the Secular City* (1973) and *More than
Man: A Study of Christology* (1976).

Jesus—A Savior or the Savior?
Religious Pluralism in Christian Perspective

Jesus—A Savior or the Savior?

Religious Pluralism in Christian Perspective

by
Russell F. Aldwinckle

BIP 88

Mercer University Press

Macon, Ga. 31207

All books published by Mercer University Press are produced
on acid-free paper which exceeds the minimum standards set by the
National Historical Publications and Records Commission.

Library of Congress Cataloging in Publication Data

Aldwinckle, Russell Foster.
  Jesus—a savior or the Savior?

  Bibliography: p. 217.
  Includes index.
  1. Christianity and other religions.   2. Jesus Christ—Person and offices.
I. Title.
BR127.A55   261.2   81-19033
ISBN 0-86554-023-3   AACR2

Contents

Acknowledgments

Permission from the publishers to quote, paraphrase, and/or summarize certain portions of the following publications is hereby gratefully acknowledged.

Brandon, S. G. F. *The Saviour God.* Manchester, England: Manchester University Press, 1963.

Herberg, Will. *Judaism and Modern Man.* New York: Atheneum Publishers, 1970.

Otto, Rudolf. *India's Religion of Grace and Christianity Compared and Contrasted.* London: SCM Press, 1930.

Panikkar, Raimundo. *The Intrareligious Dialogue.* New York: Paulist Press, 1978.

Panikkar, Raimundo. *Myth, Faith and Hermeneutics.* New York: Paulist Press, 1979.

Robinson, H. W. *The Christian Doctrine of Man.* Edinburgh: T. & T. Clark, 1911.

Preface

It may assist the reader to know that this work is a further extension of a previous one entitled *More than Man: A Study in Christology* (Grand Rapids: Eerdmans, 1976). This explains the limited number of books in the present bibliography with special reference to Christology. One of the interesting things to observe, for anyone who has been involved in theological teaching for more than thirty years, is the way in which our Western parochialism has yielded to the pressure both of events and scholarship. It is now impossible to discuss the claims of Christ or of anyone else, except in a global context. The dialogue between the world religions has an extra personal dimension for the present writer in that his sister, a Westerner by birth and nurture, has lived for more than thirty years in the Sri Aurobindo Ashram in Pondichery, India. The dialogue has, therefore, been a private domestic affair as well as a matter of my own increasing knowledge and interest.

After much reading over the years in the psychology, sociology, history, and phenomenology of religion, I became more and more convinced of the necessity to go beyond a science of religion. It became increasingly clear to me that if religion in any form is to survive at all, it will only do so if there continue to exist men and women who have faced the difficult questions of truth-claims and have still dared to make a commitment of faith. One cannot remain permanently in a state of "methodological neutrality" if religion is to remain more than an interesting subject for academic discussion. It has also been my hope to show that one can make such a move without abandoning careful scholarship and the resolute attempt to understand sympathetically what members of other faiths are saying and what their commitment entails. I do not expect the thesis of the present work to be readily accepted by all. I hope, however, that it is a fair statement of the issues. Individual faith is, of course, a personal affair and responsibility. For those who are already Christian this book perhaps may help to strengthen them in the faith they have and the confession they have already made. For those who are not Christian I trust that it may give them some insights as to why Christians believe as they do and perhaps persuade them that more than prejudice and religious imperialism are involved.

My indebtedness to the labors and scholarship of others is obvious and I simply express my gratitude. At this stage I find it difficult to sort out my own thinking from the influences which countless persons have exercised upon my own intellectual and spiritual growth, whether by way of agreement or disagreement. I simply wish to thank the Canada Council and the American Association of Theological Schools for two fellowships in 1959-1960, which gave me the opportunity to begin a serious study of myth, symbol, mysticism, and the history and phenomenology of religion. This research has continued ever since and has provided the impetus to clarify my own convictions.

It is no mere formality to thank again my wife who has lived with one manuscript after another and has patiently endured the isolation in the study which writing imposes. She also typed the manuscript. I would also like to thank the Mercer University Press for making it possible to share my thinking with a wider audience.

Hamilton, Ontario, Canada   Russell F. Aldwinckle

Introduction

In the history of Christian thought, certain issues arise from time to time and become the dominant focus of theological discussion. Historical and cultural situations often determine the nature of Christian discussion at any particular moment. Two major issues seem to be emerging at the present time. One is the question of unity and diversity in the Christian faith and the degree to which theological freedom and diversity can be permitted. The disciplining of Hans Küng and others by the Vatican is a dramatic illustration of this. The main theological charge against him, apart from the infallibility issue, is that he is calling into question the fundamental dogma of the divinity of Christ. This is not an exclusively Catholic issue, for the same question has arisen in many forms of modern Protestantism. The recent impassioned debate about *The Myth of God Incarnate,* edited by John Hick, shows that Protestant theology is experiencing the same tensions. Among Protestants, too, there is renewed tension between the adherents of a view of scriptural authority interpreted in terms of infallibility and inerrancy and those who wish for greater flexibility and openness in the way the Scripture is to be used. Both the conservative and liberal views of scriptural authority also have obvious implications for the Christological question.

The other issue, which is linked with those just mentioned, concerns the attitude of Christians to the great non-Christian religions. Living as we do in the global village created by modern technology, Christianity is no longer confined to a geographically restricted Christendom. The same is true for other faiths. In most Western countries today, sizable ethnic groups are committed to a non-Christian culture and religion. These other religions are no longer mysterious and distant realities on the other side of the world. We meet them daily in individuals whom we know. The study of other religions is no longer a scholarly preserve. Even the non-theological, so-called man in the street can hardly be entirely oblivious to the problem. The trouble in Iran and the taking of the American hostages have awakened the whole world, and the Western world in particular, to the existence and continuing vigor of the Islamic faith.

The fact of religious pluralism is now plain for all to see. The church, or churches, can hardly be content much longer to deal with world religions on a purely political, diplomatic, or sociological level or even as interesting items in the history and phenomenology of religion. Sooner or later, they will have to define their attitude at the deeper level of serious theological agreement or disagreement. Nor can this issue be resolved by sheer assertion or by an absolute refusal to enter into serious conversation. The theological tensions within Christianity itself, brought to light by the ecumenical movement and the World Council of Churches, will seem mild indeed when real, rather than superficial, dialogue begins between adherents of the Christian faith and the other religions. This issue is going to be with us for a long time to come and it is going to occupy the center of the stage. The present work is intended to be a modest contribution to this debate which will be fraught with immense significance for the future peace and harmony of the world community.

The present work is not written from the standpoint of what may be called "methodological neutralism." We are overwhelmed today by the sheer mass of material about religion presented to us by historians, phenomenologists, sociologists, philosophers of religion, psychologists of religion, and so forth. It is academically respectable to be interested in and to do research in the field of religious studies. It is possible, however, to study religion at this level without the author ever disclosing his own evaluation of the truth-claims of the religious faith which he or she is studying. The problem of norms, or whether there are any norms at all in this area, is conveniently bracketed and put on one side. It may be that religious studies or the "scientific" study of religion can be justified solely on the grounds that they widen our intellectual and spiritual horizons and therefore equip us better to adjust to the religious pluralism of our kind of world. Yet it remains an urgent question as to whether the religious experience of mankind tells us anythihg about the nature of reality, ultimate or otherwise, or only gives us an interesting insight into the powers of the creative imagination.

As far as the practicing adherent of any particular faith is concerned, it is safe to say that the great majority hold the faith they do because they believe it to involve a true account of the nature of the cosmos and the human place within it. They may not be very sophisticated intellectually. If challenged, they might find it difficult to articulate or defend effectively the kind of truth which they believe their faith to have. Yet the fact remains that they are believers, men and women of faith, not sociologists, psychologists, or phenomenologists of religion. The matter we propose to examine is the Christian understanding of salvation and the relation which this has to the person of Jesus. What does it mean to be "saved" and why does Christian faith link this so inextricably, as it seems to do, with claims for the unique and indispensable role of Jesus of Nazareth? Can these Christian claims be defended and justified in the light of the religious pluralism which characterizes our world and in view of our increasing awareness of the other religions and their continued vitality? We use the language of salvation deliberately in order to underline the fact that the question transcends what would normally be considered to be a scholarly inquiry. There is something incongruous about a merely academic discussion of salvation. To be saved, if it means anything at all, must mean more than the cool detached acceptance of a set of interesting ideas. While we realize that this same question can be asked from many different perspectives, we have chosen to deal with it from within the Christian faith, which is the only one we can speak about from any measure of firsthand experience.

We anticipate the charge that this is to make prejudice the criterion from the outset. This is a risk that has to be taken. To claim to have at least some experience of what it means to be "saved" seems to some people to be spiritual arrogance plus a claim to be more righteous than anyone else. Yet how extraordinary it would be in any case to write about salvation and admit to having no idea whatsoever on the experiential level of what salvation is all about. The central position which Bernard Lonergan has given to conversion can hardly be gainsaid. It is true that he uses the word *conversion* in a broader sense than that to which we may be accustomed: "By conversion is understood a transformation of the subject and his world."[1] This can take place on the intellectual, moral, and religious levels and all three elements do not need to be inevitably involved at the same time in the experience of any particular individual.

The crucial point, however, is emphasized in the statement that the "threefold conversion is not a set of propositions that a theologian utters but a fundamental and momentous change in the human reality that a theologian is."[2] In this conviction we tackle the question as to what it means to be saved and whether Jesus is not only a savior but also the Savior. To the charge that a Christian cannot even ask the question properly, let alone answer it, without being completely determined by his prejudices (biases or prior judgments), we can only let our attempt speak for itself. At least, in our view, the question cannot be usefully discussed at all within a framework of methodological neutralism without reducing the issue to the level of triviality.

Our prime concern is not to convince those who have already rejected a high doctrine of Incarnation, important as this is. For our part, we believe that the basic thrust of the evolution of dogma in the patristic period was on the right lines in its interpretation of who Jesus was and is. This does not mean that we are committed to the uncritical acceptance of every statement made by a Greek or Latin father. Nor do we think that Chalcedon has put an end to the task of developing a Christology in a language which may be more appropriate to our own age. Nevertheless, we still maintain that the basic intent behind Chalcedon was sound, whatever the inadequacy of the philosophical assumptions or the linguistic tools which were at its disposal.

Starting, therefore, from the Christian confession that Jesus is Lord and Savior in a unique sense, we ask what consequences flow

---

[1]B. Lonergan, *Method in Theology* (London: Darton, Longman & Todd, 1972), p. 130.
[2]Ibid., p. 270.

from this for the Christian attitude to the fact of religious pluralism. It is often assumed that there is only one answer to this, namely that all non-Christians are neither "saved" nor capable of being saved by virtue of their ignorance of the Word made flesh as a unique and unrepeatable historical actuality. It is this often unexamined assumption which we question as an absolute and unchanging implication of the Christian claim for Jesus Christ. Whether we have succeeded in our development of an alternative view will be for the reader, of course, to decide.

Having said this, however, we also wish to deal with our question of salvation in a spirit of openness to the ways in which other faiths have tried to answer the question about salvation. Here again our procedure is somewhat different from that often adopted. Our view is that in trying to relate Christian claims to other faiths, the most difficult and urgent theological problem for Christians concerns the Christian attitude to the continued existence and spiritual vitality of Judaism. Only when we have thought our way honestly through this issue can we turn to the encounter with the non-Christian religions. This seems the appropriate place to comment on the kind of language which we shall use in what follows. We have continued to speak in this book of the non-Christian religions, despite Professor Cantwell Smith's solemn warning that "there is hardly a more fruitful way towards misunderstanding a Muslim, a Hindu or a Buddhist than of thinking of him as a non-Christian."[3] We hope we have taken the warning to heart.

We have also permitted ourselves from time to time the use of the phrase "Christian theism." I am fully aware that this might be regarded as making a very questionable claim. In an age when the fusion of faith and philosophy has been much attacked, when language is frequently heard that the end of theism is near, if not actually here, when claims for a radically new version of theism are widely canvassed, when all the talk is of myth, symbol, story, and even pre-linguistic experience, to talk of Christian theism may seem bold to the point of rashness. I can only confess myself to be unrepentant. I am persuaded that a completely non-conceptualized version of the Christian faith is an

---

[3]Mircea Eliade and J. M. Kitagama, ed., *The History of Religions* (Chicago: University of Chicago Press, 1974), p. 33.

impossiblity. Nor do I think that philosophy can be kept at arm's length, even in talking about such an existentialist theme as salvation. We agree with Professor John E. Smith that "the religion of special occasions is always dependent upon interpretation through the experience and knowledge of general occasions."[4] In my judgment Christian theism is a valid goal for the Christian theologian, however much we may want to improve, or consider ourselves as capable of improving, the kind of theism or theisms bequeathed to us by tradition.

Having said this, however, I would want to say that if there is the possibility of such a thing as a Christian theism, it must arise on the basis of some experience of what it means to be saved. It is my hope to take up later in more detail in another book the subject of Christian theism—that is, the Christian doctrine of God. For the present, we shall concentrate on the theme of salvation in relation to our contemporary world of "gods many and lords many," of countless sects, cults, and so-called new religions and above all hope to clarify what exactly the Christian is claiming when he speaks of Jesus Christ as the power of God unto salvation.

In spite of the criticisms of Ronald Hepburn,[5] we still affirm that unless faith, in some authentic sense, directly grasps the reality of God, then there is in fact nothing to talk about. On this point we agree with Edward Farley that "redemption itself involves direct apprehensions"[6] and that if it does not, we are left only with an inferred God and such a God never saved anyone. We also agree with his further comment that when the community loses its living awareness of the presence of the saving God, no amount of theological or other argument can replace this loss. "If the historical community of faith is corrupt, no Feuerbach is needed to show that its theology is anthropology. God himself will make sure of that."[7] As he correctly observes, "Believing in God simply

---

[4]John E. Smith, *Reason and God* (New Haven: Yale University Press, 1961), p. 263. The meaning of the author's language should be noted. There are two channels or approaches to God. One is through repeatable experience and general knowledge (general occasions). The other is through historical events and their records as preserved and interpreted by a continuing community of faith or church (special occasions).

[5]Ronald Hepburn, *Christianity and Paradox.*

[6]E. Farley, *Ecclesial Man* (Philadelphia: Fortress, 1975), p. 9.

[7]Ibid., p. 12.

does not mean believing in believing in God."⁸ Smith himself made the same point back in 1961 about "the indispensability of direct experience as a ground for belief in God."⁹ The problem of religious pluralism, therefore, is not simply a matter of comparing systems of ideas. Rather it forces us back to the personal issue of how, if at all, I as an individual can be saved and whether I am prepared to stake my existence in personal faith. There are many ways in which this personal commitment can be made. This is, indeed, the theme of this book. Yet even when such a commitment has been made, far-reaching issues are raised. What should be my attitude as a man or woman of faith to men and women of other faiths? While we do not pretend to answer this question from the standpoint of a neutralist methodology, we trust that the seeking of an answer has not been devoid of sympathy and the attempt to understand.

At this point we have made what may seem to some to be rather radical modifications in the traditional eschatology, whether Catholic or Protestant. The reason for these changes lies in our desire to defend the unique saviorhood of Christ while at the same time leaving open the possibility of God's gracious activity in and through the various forms which religion has taken in the experience of the human race. Some may think that this is an impossible undertaking. We hope, however, the attempt is worth making and that the present work will contribute to what must evidently be the continuing discussion of the issues involved. Certainly the Christian faith assures us that the love of God exceeds the measure of man's mind. It is in that confidence that we can face the uncertain and rather bewildering future in hope.

Our last word must be to repeat the warning that this is an essay of exploration rather than a full-scale treatment. The trouble with our chosen theme is that, in the last analysis, it covers everything and requires an interdisciplinary approach and the contribution of many minds. We are well aware of the inadequacy of our treatment of many specific themes on which numerous books have been written and extensive research done. This essay is not a complete systematic theology. This accounts for the lack of detailed biblical exegesis in the major areas of Christology and Soteriology, not to mention others.

---

⁸Ibid., p. 15.

⁹Smith, *Reason and God*, p. 179.

There is perhaps a value, however, in a brief treatment which seeks to clarify what the basic issues are and helps us to avoid the common error of failing to see the forest for the trees. If at times our stance seems to be dogmatic in the bad sense of the word, we can only plead the limitation of our purpose as a contribution to a wider debate. Nor has our intention been a full-fledged defense of the Christian faith vis-à-vis the unbeliever. Assuming the Christian experience of salvation to be a valid and true experience of the grace of God in the Christian sense, we have tried to discover what implications follow for our attitude to and our evaluation of the major non-Christian religions. If the atheist or the agnostic feel left out in this discussion, we can only plead for patience until we take up again at a later date the problem of belief and unbelief and see what can be said for Christian theism as a whole in relation to the total human experience.

Meanwhile, it is clear that the Christian community has to resolve certain basic issues about its own attitudes to men and women of other faiths before it can speak with conviction to those who, for one reason or another, find any idea of faith problematic. This conviction has guided our researches and has imposed the necessary limitations which have already been noted.

Chapter One

Salvation and Many Religions

What is salvation and how far is the experience of "being saved" dependent, if at all, upon a relationship to a specific person? We wish to discuss the question of religious pluralism from a distinctively Christian perspective, that is, from the point of view of those who claim that Jesus Christ is not only a savior but the Savior in a normative and final sense. There are, of course, some who will object that this is to beg all the important questions from the start. Yet one has to begin somewhere. If one begins with the history and phenomenology of religion and brackets the question of norms and refuses to make value judgments, then, of course, the question of uniqueness, finality, or normativeness will not arise. This, however, is to eliminate from the study of religion all those issues which make such a study interesting and challenging for most people. It is to reduce such a study to an academic enterprise and no more.

We do not question the legitimacy of a "scientific" study of religion which deliberately refuses to ask about the truth or validity of the religious experiences of mankind. Nevertheless, we believe even more strongly that it is necessary to go beyond a phenomenologyof religion and ask the questions which all serious persons will sooner or later ask. We are using the world *phenomenology* to indicate the "attempt at value-free descriptions in religion." We also note that Smart himself is not content with such a narrow definition for he wishes to have a description which is value-rich yet "aspectual, polymethodic, pluralistic and without clear boundaries."[1] Smart, however, also clearly distinguishes his view from doing theology which is the articulating of a faith. In this sense, our study of salvation will be theological but in the spirit of Smart's own remark: "I am far from claiming that the study of religion is the most important thing to be undertaken in connection with religion. Being a saint is more important."[2] The word *saint* is too ambiguous for us, but in as far as it connotes a reference to the actual practice of religion and its experiential side, we gladly accept it. For Smart and his view of the scientific study of religion, theology is part of the phenomenon to be understood, but from what vantage point is a question that cries out to be handled. Whether a particular theology can be true and consequently needed to interpret and assess the scientific study of religion must be left an open question at this stage and not pre-judged.

If one decides to do this, then it is obvious that one cannot begin in a vacuum. One can only start from a point in one's own experience where it is sincerely believed that the ultimate meaning of human existence has been disclosed, even if that disclosure is only partial and even spoken of as "baffling reflections in a mirror." If religion is not a serious and compelling factor in one's own experience, then it is hardly likely that an understanding of the faith of others will be very profound, if intelligible at all. While it may be true that "the man who knows only one religion knows none" (Max Müller), it is also true, as Eichrodt comments, that "the man who knows the religion of the Old Testament knows many."[3] The Christian would want to add the New Testament and make a similar claim for it. For this reason, we have chosen to speak about salvation because it is difficult to reduce such a theme merely to an analysis of ideas.

The existential dimension of salvation is obvious. It must have practical and experiential consequences for the total human existence of the one who claims that he or she knows what it is to "be saved." To

---

[1]Ninian Smart, *The Science of Religion and the Sociology of Knowledge* (Princeton: Princeton University Press, 1973), p. 21.

[2]Ibid., p. 8.

[3]W. Eichrodt, trans. J. A. Baker, *Theology of the Old Testament*, vol. I (Philadelphia: Westminster Press and London: S.C.M., 1961), p. 25.

have no interest in or firsthand knowledge of what salvation means on this level must surely preclude any hope of understanding the basic concern of all the major religions and indeed the minor ones, if one can make such a judgment or classification. We believe that such a starting point is legitimate and that one must start with religion as experienced. This means, of course, that one has to start within a specific religious tradition. The issue then becomes whether such a starting point is so rigid as to make it impossible to be open and to learn from others who do not begin at the same point. This matter can hardly be settled a priori at the start of the investigation. We, therefore, begin from the Christian experience of Jesus Christ as the Savior and hope to test it as fairly as we can in the context of the religious pluralism which all agree to be a fact of our contemporary situation.

Even to adopt such a point of departure is to find oneself in the midst of some of the most passionately debated issues which agitate all branches of the Christian church today. We note the perennial question concerning the exact nature of the authority which is claimed for the canonical Scriptures. To this must be added the recent concentration on the Christological issues and the attack upon the historic doctrine of the Incarnation. Is this latter the only or the necessary implication of and development from the New Testament witness to the fact and significance of Jesus? If the Jewish and Christian Scriptures are no longer authoritative without further question, then why not start with the Vedas or the Upanishads or the Gita or the Buddhist Tripitika or the Koran or for that matter, with the Old Testament without the New Testament? Or why not start with mystical experience claimed as a universal phenomenon from which specific symbolizations of its meaning in particular traditions have been reduced to a secondary place? On the second count, if the doctrine of the Incarnation is no longer viable, then can any exclusive claim for Jesus as Lord and Savior be still affirmed? If a negative answer is given to this question, then what doctrine of God emerges from a global syncretism of all forms of religious experience? This is assuming that we are not content to be humanists and wish to retain the God-concept or the idea of the transcendent in some meaningful sense.

We do not wish to foreclose at this stage the legitimate discussion of these important issues. However, once again, they cannot or ought not to be settled prior to the discussion of the actual way in which

Christians believe themselves to have been saved. As a matter of method, we agree that simple appeal to sheer authority is not the most promising starting point. We shall not, therefore, begin with an appeal to an infallible and inerrant Scripture or an infallible magisterium of the church. These issues will have to be resolved in the light of our investigation as a whole. It would appear to be the case that countless Christians, who disagree on the answers to the above issues, would still wish to give to Jesus a unique centrality in relation to what they believe themselves to have experienced of Jesus' power to save. The experiential dimension of the Christian faith will be our point of departure, even though it is realized that the term *experience* may appear to be vague and ambiguous. It is hoped that clarification of the meaning of this term will be achieved as we proceed.

The crucial question, therefore, for the Christian theist is whether he can still make out a case for the normative status of Jesus Christ in the absence of an infallible Scripture and in view of the confusing diversity and multiplicity of human intuitions as to the nature of transcendent Reality. It is difficult to see how this position could be defended on the level of philosophical speculation alone. At some point an appeal to experience will have to be made. We, therefore, now propose to examine the Christian doctrine of salvation to see if the impact of Jesus Christ on human beings and history has been such as to warrant the special claims made for him. This requires two things. First, to show that Jesus Christ has made a difference in ways which can be experientially tested. The second is to justify the Christian interpretation of that difference as unique and normative for the way we think of the divine activity in the affairs of mankind.

The third requirement is to show that the religious pluralism either of the past or the present is no legitimate basis for rejecting completely the possiblity of a final and normative disclosure. It can, of course, be argued that this appeal to historical events and persons is not an answer either to the question of factuality or normativeness. G. W. H. Lampe, for example, tells us that "persons, like events, are not in themselves revelatory of God."[4] They may become the focus of revelation under certain circumstances but this depends on how they are interpreted. Interpretations, however, are conditioned by the

---

[4]G. W. H. Lampe, *God as Spirit* (Oxford: Oxford University Press, 1977), p. 105.

personal character, temperament, and disposition of the subject of the revelation and this depends in turn on the presuppositions he or she brings to the task. This seems to imply that there is some kind of neutral fact which has no meaning until it is put there by some interpreter, whether the person who has the experience or someone else who interprets it. This means that the issue of normativeness depends on the validity of the interpretation but on this view this cannot be the result of a straightforward historical investigation. It is obvious, of course, that revelation, as far as we humans are concerned, cannot have any specific meaning until someone has received it. The disclosure, in this case God's activity, must be apprehended and, in part at least, understood and interpreted by someone.

As Austin Farrer says: "If we do not believe that the same God who moved St. Paul can move us to understand what he moved St. Paul to say, then (once again) it isn't much use our bothering about St. Paul's writings. 'God is His own interpreter and He will make it plain'. "[5] Thus, if we are to arrive at a norm, what is required is some assurance both as to the historical actuality and the way in which it is interpreted. Pannenberg has advanced the thesis that event, meaning, and interpretation do not have to be separated in this way. Meaning and interpretation are given in and with the event or the person. This is a difficult idea but it is dictated by the following considerations:

1. Christian faith does depend upon historical actualities—where "historical" means "scientific" investigation of the past.

2. The events and persons decisive for Christian faith did not take place in a ghetto of a special redemptive history but in the context of universal history.

3. The prejudgments or basic assumptions which govern historical research do not have to be imprisoned within an anthropocentric world-view.

4. The historian's own interpretation of the past, governed by the principle of analogy based on the historian's present understanding, does not require the omnipotence of analogy or the consequence that all events must be comprehended as if they conform to some uniform and universal pattern.

[5]A. Farrer, *Interpretation and Belief* (London: S.P.C.K., 1966), p. 11.

5. The historian and the theologian are interested in the individual, particular, and contingent. The question, therefore, as to whether a particular event is unique and without parallel is not to be decided by the blanket application of the universal homogeneity of all events. The resurrection of Jesus may not fit into any pattern of similiarity based on analogy from present experience. Is it, thereby, to be rejected out of hand?

6. This means that the object of faith cannot remain untouched by the results of historical and critical research but it also means that the latter is not bound irrevocably to the omnipotence of analogy in making truly historical judgments. Some events may be unique in the strongest sense and may bear a meaning intrinsic to those events. The historical actuality contains both and the event-intepretation is not simply the reading in by the historian of his own personal meanings upon a neutral and merely factual succession of meaningless events.[6]

We shall return to these basic issues later. They are mentioned now to assure the reader that our pursuit of the norm is not naive and that we do not assume that the question of pluralism can simply be reduced to a conflict of merely subjective interpretations on the part of different historians and theologians, whether we are thinking of Christianity or any other major religion in the history of mankind. The issue of pluralism must be raised, therefore, in the context of the Christian understanding of salvation. Is there a sense in which a relationship to Jesus Christ as saving can be affirmed in a sense in which this would not be true if we are talking of Buddha, Plato, or Mohammed? If this claim is being made, then what meaning does "saving" have in this connection and what is the experimental basis for such a claim? We are not concerned at the moment with the assertion of a secular humanism that whatever salvation means, it must be something capable of being achieved by man himself, depending on resources already resident in human nature as such and only waiting to be tapped. This solves the problem by eliminating any appeal to God or the transcendent.

---

[6]W. Pannenberg, *Basic Questions in Theology,* vol. I (Philadelphia: Fortress Press, 1970), pp. 39ff.

Our concern is rather, granted that a saving divine activity is both possible and actual, is this activity mediated solely and exclusively through one particular person, or perhaps a special selection of persons? In the latter case, how do we justify our selection? It is, of course, possible to argue that there was and is a saving divine activity manifested in Jesus of Nazareth but that there are, or may be, many other media for that same saving activity. The scandal is not so much that God, however defined, "saves" but that he saves exclusively through this one Jesus of Nazareth. Is this intolerable arrogance? It is this specific challenge of pluralism which a Christian theism has to try and meet.

In dealing with this issue, we contend that the Christian cannot handle it only on the level of differing theological concepts and ideas, important as these may turn out to be. We sometimes hear such phrases as *saving knowledge* and *saving belief.* What do knowledge and belief involve when such language is used? Does it mean that salvation not only implies but requires certain specific theological affirmations, or the making of a choice between different world-views? For example, does one have to make a choice between theism, pantheism, panentheism, atheism, agnosticism, and so forth before one can be saved? This claim has been made in the course of Christian history. The Quicumque Vult (or so-called Athanasian creed) says that whosoever would be saved, before all things it is needful that he hold the Catholic Faith, which faith except a man have kept whole and undefiled, without doubt he shall perish eternally . . . this is the Catholic Faith, which except a man have faithfully and steadfastly believed he cannot be saved.[7] It is clear from the above that whatever salvation means, it cannot be had apart from an intellectual commitment to certain theological dogmas or creedal affirmations.

There is a widespread distrust today, even in some Christian circles, of this close linking of theological dogma and salvation. The distrust extends not only to the religious exclusivism of the Athanasian creed but also to the classically formulated doctrine of Incarnation. We see this in *The Myth of God Incarnate,*[8] as well as in the works of such process theologians as John B. Cobb, Jr., and David

---

[7]A.E. Burn, *The Athanasian Creed* (London: Rivington's, 1930), pp. 4-6.
[8]John Hick, ed., *The Myth of God Incarnate* (London: S. C. M., 1977).

Griffin.[9] However, we find a similar reaction in such writers as G. W. H. Lampe who appears to have a more positive appreciation of the classical theological heritage than might appear to be the case with, for example, Maurice Wiles.[10] Lampe wants to develop a positive view of salvation in Jesus Christ but not necessarily one that is tied to specific dogmas: "It is not the case that the idea of the Incarnation of the Second Person of the Godhead is required by belief in a saving work of God, centered and focused in Jesus Christ, which has done for man that which he could not have done for himself."[11] Also, "in order, then, to interpret God's saving work in Jesus, we do not need the model of a descent of a pre-existent divine person into the world."[12]

Lampe himself is concerned to develop the thesis of the continuity of God's work in creation and redemption, conceived as a universal divine saving activity through the Spirit of God. It is clear that Jesus has a prominent, perhaps central role in this but certainly not an exclusive role. If salvation is to be divorced from theological dogma, it is necessary to ask how far this is to be carried. What exactly is salvation if it is not linked to specific doctrines? The other question is whether one can talk meaningfully about salvation without at least a minimum of "interpretation" and is such interpretation possible without at least some theological concepts which imply doctrinal affirmations, however undeveloped or restricted in scope?

Most Christians would in fact admit that salvation is not to be equated simply with certain theological beliefs. If these latter are taken to mean the giving of some kind of intellectual or mental assent to Christian truths, divorced from personal commitment and practical obedience to the will of God, then such an assent is not salvation. This is confirmed by what biblical scholarship has been saying for a long time about the broader implications of "knowledge" both in the Old and New Testaments.[13] What, then, is salvation and what kind of knowledge, if any, is involved in the experience of being saved? We

---

[9]David Griffin, *A Process Christology* (Philadelphia: Westminster, 1973); J. B. Cobb, Jr., *Christ in a Pluralistic Age* (Philadelphia: Westminster, 1967).

[10]Maurice Wiles, *The Remaking of Christian Doctrine* (London: S. C. M., 1974).

[11]Lampe, *God as Spirit.*

[12]Ibid., pp. 22, 33.

[13]C. H. Dodd, *The Bible and the Greeks* (London: Hodder & Stoughton, 1935), pp. 70ff.; J. Barr, *Old and New in Interpretation* (London: S. C. M., 1966).

shall try to deal with this question first from within the biblical and the Christian context. The question will then be asked as to whether salvation, in this Christian sense, is only available to Christians or whether it is possible to be saved in the Christian sense apart from the acceptance of the Christian faith. Only after this investigation is made will it be possible to assess the relation of the Christian experience of salvation to the religious pluralism which has always characterized the global human community.

We today, of course, are much more acutely conscious of the challenge which this situation offers, not only to the exclusive claim of Christianity but also to the exclusive claim of any religion, past or present. The scandal of the Christian claim is that appeal is made, not simply to a normative Christ-principle, of which Jesus may be taken to be one possible, if all-important manifestation. Nor is it an appeal to a specific set of teachings or doctrines which can be detached from the teacher. In both of these cases, a thoroughgoing pluralism could be adopted without falling into inherent contradiction in principle. Hans Küng has told us that what distinguishes Christianity from other religions is not its symbolic, theological, or metaphysical concepts but the simple fact of Jesus. It is this emphasis on the historical actuality of Jesus of Nazareth and the importance of our relationship to him for our salvation which constitutes the stumbling block for many Christians to the adoption of a thoroughgoing pluralism. With these questions in mind, we now turn our attention to the biblical understanding of salvation. This is necessary both because of the authority of the canonical Scripture for most Christians and because Jesus was a Jew who can hardly be understood apart from the Old Testament tradition, life, and witness from which he came.

What, then, does salvation mean, first in the Old Testament and then in the New? In order to avoid missing the forest for the trees, we shall take the risk of summarizing those elements of the Old Testament faith and tradition which are germane to our present discussion. If one defined salvation in general terms as a right relationship to God which results in certain blessings for men and women, obviously some idea of the nature of God, to whom we are so related, is involved. Yet where does this concept of God come from? In turning to the Old Testament, therefore, we are turning to the specific history of a particular people who believed that God has made known his will to them in and through their tempestuous history. In the light of this history,   .

salvation could be equated with a right relationship to Yahweh which involved obedient faithfulness to his will on the part of Israel as a whole as well as of the individual Jew. According to the degree of Israel's faithfulness to the covenant, God would sustain them and bless them, in fact "save" them. This general interpretation of Hebrew and Jewish history raises its own special set of questions.

Did the Jew always think of the will of Yahweh in the same way or did this change in the course of and under the pressure of historical events? If this latter was the case, then what it means for Yahweh to save would itself undergo modification. There might then be more than one view of salvation. If there is a pluralism of the concepts of salvation in the Old Testament, then it would have to be asked whether all these ideas could be coherently synthesized in one general concept of salvation, or whether some ideas of salvation must be taken as more normative and "true" than others. In answering this kind of question, two methods of approach could be adopted. The question of salvation can be asked strictly within the Old Testament tradition itself or in the later developments of Rabbinic Judaism right through to modern Judaism. In this case, whatever definition of salvation was adopted would not be related in any way to Jesus of Nazareth except by ignoring him as relevant to the specific Jewish answer to the question what it means to be saved. On the other hand, one could approach the question from the Christian perspective, in which case, whatever salvation might mean in the Old Testament or in later Judaism, it would be regarded as in some way incomplete apart from the relationship to Jesus as Messiah, Lord, and Savior. The problem could then become: In what sense can the Jew, at any period of his history, be said to be "saved," or is he only partially saved, or saved only by anticipation, or possibly not saved at all? And is the Jew in any different position than the Hindu, the Buddhist, or the Muslim when it comes to a saving relationship to Jesus Christ?

It is obvious that at this stage the issue of pluralism is anything but an academic question. Claims and counterclaims, involving powerful emotions, are involved. Because of this, the temptation is great to resolve the issue by denying any authoritative norms in this area. Salvation or ways of salvation are as numerous as the religions of mankind and the proper attitude is to accept them all with a good grace and agree to a charitable coexistence, the only practical alternative to continued religious strife and the odium theologicum. One could, of course, reject all religions and their offers of salvation as aberrations and seek refuge in a humanism from which every reference to a transcendent Reality has been ruthlessly excised. We shall not at present consider this alternative.

Salvation in the Old Testament and Later Judaism

After this preamble, we now turn to the Old Testament view of salvation but in order to achieve some measure of clarity, it will be considered under the following headings:

- Salvation as fellowship and communion with Yahweh.
- Salvation as deliverance and liberation from hostile powers—for example, the Egyptian pharaoh and death and the devil.
- Salvation as the resolution of the problem of guilt through forgiveness and restoration to divine fellowship.
- Salvation as confident trust in and knowledge of the steadfast love of God.
- Salvation in and through the offering of an adequate sacrifice.

The word *salvation* itself, which is of Latin origin (*salvere*—to be well or in good health; *salvus*—sound, well, in good health, safe) tells us little except as a warning against making theological deductions from the etymology of words taken out of context. Certain key terms appear in the Old Testament which are basic for our understanding of what being saved meant to the Jew. These are *mishpat* (judgment), *hesedth* (lovingkindness or steadfast love), and *tsedheq* (righteousness). As the human judge or *shophet* makes a judgment, so the divine Judge gives his judgments to his covenant people. This is the realm where his covenant love or *hesedth* is operative. His judgments are his way of indicating his demands upon his people. They are not given primarily for condemnation but in order to guide the people of Israel that in trusting obedience, they may enjoy Yahweh's steadfast love and the blessings he is anxious to give them. The Torah contains the judgments of the great divine Judge (Ex. 24:3). Yahweh's *mishpat*, however, is not the same as the very imperfect justice which societies of sinful men partially achieve. His *mishpat* is righteous (Gen. 18:15; Isa. 40: 27-28), and since the Creator of all the earth is just, he will be true to himself and administer perfect justice. The essence of Yahweh's *mishpat* is contained in the Decalogue or Ten Commandments (Ex. 31:18; Deut. 4:13), obedience to which is required for health and well-being of the people of Israel at every level of their personal and corporate existence.

If Yahweh must punish, he does so to bring them back into line, into obedience to his will which is the basis of their true prosperity. The righteousness of Yahweh (*tsedheq*), the proper reflection of which in human conduct is *tsedeqah*, means more than simply being good in the usual rather pedestrian sense of "moral," especially as later views of morality have sometimes tended to think of the moral as either conformity to conventional rules or as involving only a part of human life. The root *ts-d-q* means to be right in the sense of "normal," but man's condition, because of rebellion, is far from normal. He is a sinner, in opposition to the will of Yahweh. God's righteousness is not only telling man what is right but the act whereby Yahweh puts him right, that is, puts right one who is in the wrong and who, as a consequence, is suffering and needs to be helped and saved. Righteousness can thus be used as the equivalent of salvation or deliverance from whatever evil is oppressing the people of Israel or the individual Israelite. Thus, because Yahweh is a righteous God, he is also a God who saves. The root of the word to save (*y-sh*) originally bears the sense of wide or spacious. Hence in the Hiphil to give width and breadth to, hence to liberate from what is narrow and oppressive, therefore to "save."

The Hiphil participle *moshia* is the common noun for Savior. The same root lies behind the name Joshua in the Old Testament and Jesus in the New Testament. When Yahweh delivers or saves his people from different kinds of bondage or oppression, his supreme gift to them is *shalom*, a term with much richer meaning than peace, which is the usual English translation. It can mean tranquility of mind, contentment, confidence, or assurance for the individual (Isa. 32:17). For the psalmist, it could mean the material security of the community (Ps. 69:32); for Jeremiah, it could mean true friendship (Jer. 20:10), that is, ideal right relations between men and women living in harmony. It can also mean physical health (Gen. 43:27) or general welfare (2 Kings 10:13). The verbal root again conveys the idea of being whole or sound, hence to make whole, to restore, or to complete. "It is in Isaiah 40-55 more than anywhere else in the Old Testament that Yahweh's essential character as the Savior God is emphasized."[14]

---

[14]F. F. Bruce, *'Our God and Saviour': A Recurring Biblical Pattern.* Cf. *The Saviour God,* S. G. F. Brandon (Manchester University Press, 1963), pp. 51ff.

He is His people's gō'el, their kinsman-redeemer. He alone is Yahweh and "beside me there is no savior" (Isa. 43:11). So also:

A righteous God and a Savior (*saddîq* and *môsia*) there is none besides me (Isa. 45:21).

Perhaps we can now attempt a brief summary of what is involved in the Old Testament understanding of salvation. It is assumed, of course, that since the Exodus and the Ten Commandments, the will of Yahweh is known with sufficient clarity to be the basis of the ordered community of the life of Israel and the guidance of the conduct of the individual within the covenant community. To be saved is to be delivered from enemies without and sin within, to experience Yahweh's righteousness not simply as punishment but also as expressive of Yahweh's desire to deliver and rescue. He manifests his righteousness precisely in saving or delivering the humble and the afflicted and in particular his afflicted chosen people, the people of Israel. This saving purpose may sometimes have to be carried out through suffering (see the Servant Songs of Isaiah 40—66) but eventual deliverance is certain because Yahweh is both powerful and righteous.

At this stage of Old Testament history, there is no tendency to suggest, as does a modern Jew like Richard L. Rubenstein in *After Auschwitz*, that Yahweh can no longer be counted upon to bring about real deliverance. The Hitler holocaust, according to Rubenstein, was of such a magnitude as to call in question the confidence of a Second Isaiah. For the Old Testament, however, the hope of Yahweh's deliverance from oppression and suffering remains strong, whatever the corporate or individual disasters. Salvation, then, is the blessing of living in a right relation to Yahweh—whose righteousness can be trusted, whose love is steadfast, and who will eventually save and deliver, however dark the present. In a moment we shall consider in more detail what exactly it is from which Yahweh delivers. We pause, however, to ask about the nature of this relationship to Yahweh from the point of view of the inner life of the individual Israelite.

When today we use such language as fellowship or communion with God, we tend to think of some kind of inner experience which we may loosely describe as spiritual: repentance, faith, trust, assurance of God's presence, an inner awareness of being forgiven, perhaps an especially vivid sense of union with God. Was this also true for the Hebrew and the Jew of the Old Testament? Was Yahweh's saving action reflected in a personal experience, and if so, of what kind? We ask the question because it has been frequently asserted that the Old Testament view of salvation is not related to what has been called mystical experience. The Old Testament emphasis is on Yahweh's deliverance from specific forms of this-worldly oppression (for example, slavery in Egypt) or from physical death and suffering. This, it is said, does not reflect a mystical way of dealing with these problems. The giving of the Law authoritatively "from above," the external requirements of the sacrificial system, the rules and regulations of the Torah and the later scribal commentary upon it: all these have been taken to indicate either the lack or unimportance of the "inner life" from the point of view of the Old Testament and later Judaism. But this is a one-sided and unfair assessment both of the Old Testament and of Judaism.

At the least we must say with T. W. Manson that "it is clear that we are unjust if we represent Judaism as being indifferent to the motives for action. It also lays great stress on the necessity of doing the command for the right reasons."[15] Whether we can go further and find in Judaism something that can properly be called mystical depends upon our definition of mysticism. The word is notoriously ambiguous. Certainly there is little or no evidence as to the existence in the Old Testament of what has been called absorptionist mysticism. There was too strong a sense of Yahweh's distinction as Creator from the created order and as a Person incapable of absorption into the immanent energies of nature.[16] Nor was there a tendency to an ascetic discipline which aimed at out-of-the-body experiences or ecstatic union with Yahweh with a consequent lack of conscious individuality and self-control. These elements may appear from time to time in the Old Testament or in the Qumran communities[17] but they are not dominant and they are not characteristic features of the relationship to Yahweh.

It would, however, be wrong to deduce from this that the inner experience of Yahweh's presence is either absent or unimportant in the life of the devout and obedient Jew. An analysis of the role of the Word

---

[15]T. W. Manson, *Ethics and the Gospel* (London: S. C. M., 1960), p. 43.

[16]H. W. Robinson, *Inspiration and Revelation in the Old Testament* (Oxford: Oxford University Press, 1946), p. 21.

[17]Hans Küng, *On Being a Christian* (New York: Pocket Books, 1978), pp. 149-150; 194-201.

or Wisdom of Yahweh, and particularly of the Spirit, make it clear that the objectifying or hypostasizing of these concepts did not rule out the individual, inner experience of Yahweh's Word, his indwelling Wisdom, and the presence of the Spirit. For the moment, we may accept Dr. Lampe's judgment that the Spirit in the Old Testament is the personal activity of Yahweh and that Wisdom-Spirit is virtually equivalent to the grace of God.[18] They indwell the soul or spirit of man and parallel Jeremiah's hope of a new law written by Yahweh in the heart of the whole community of Israel.[19] It is unfair, therefore, to think of salvation in the Old Testament as a reference to some kind of external deliverance to the exclusion of any inward experience of Yahweh's presence in and to the individual. This needs to be said in view of the emphasis of some contemporary exponents of Liberation Theology who regard the Exodus as the only or the most important model for the understanding of salvation as deliverance in the Old Testament. There is another dimension to the Jewish experience to which the Exodus model does not do justice.

Salvation as Deliverance from External Hostile Powers
Having said this, however, it has to be admitted that salvation as deliverance from external hostile powers does play an important part. Indeed, in the early historical stages of Israel's history, a savior was one who could deliver from the tangible enemies with whom Israel was in conflict. Yahweh was mighty in battle and he raised up deliverers in this sense (see Ex. 14:30; 1 Sam. 10:19). God's right arm is strong enough to obtain salvation, not as an inward experience but as victory over earthly enemies and the consequent blessings of security and freedom from harassment by such enemies. Again, Yahweh's power to deliver in this concrete sense never disappeared either in the Old Testament or the intertestamental period or indeed in Judaism up to the formation of the modern state of Israel.

The enemies of Israel were not only political oppressors like the Egyptians, the Babylonians, or the Romans; death also was an enemy, for it was the destruction of life and life was the supreme gift of Yahweh. Thus to be delivered from the pit—that is, to be brought back

[18]Lampe, *God as Spirit,* pp. 49ff.
[19]Jeremiah 31:31ff.

from the brink of physical death—was a signal expression of Yahweh's power and ability to save. For most of the Old Testament, deliverance from death is not linked with a life after death. Rather it is Yahweh's act in postponing or deferring the departure to Sheol, from which the Jew shrank as being no real life at all, even if he continued in Sheol as a shade (*rephaim*). Even if we accept Professor Gundry's thesis about the duality of the Old Testament view of man, as opposed to the widely accepted "holistic" view and the implication of this view that the shades in Sheol were not devoid of consciousness and activity, it was still the case, as he admits, that the activity was minimal and not such as to make life in Sheol an attractive prospect for the Jew.[20] Salvation in the Old Testament, therefore, does not mean primarily deliverance into a life after death. Salvation is basically the knowing of the goodness of Yahweh in the land of the living. In some cases the individual's confidence in Yahweh may have carried the assurance that even death cannot separate from Yahweh:

> Whom have I in heaven but Thee?
> And having Thee, I desire nothing else on earth.
> Though heart and body fail
> Yet God is my possession for ever (Ps. 73:25-26).

Here we may be near the idea of life after death as a positive existence with Yahweh, a life worth the having. Yet this conclusion is not clearly and unambiguously drawn by the psalmist in terms of a formal doctrine of the after life. This agnosticism about life after death is attractive to some modern Christian theologians who feel compelled, in the context of modern scientific views, to deny that dead men live again.[21]

In a few passages in the Old Testament, however, we begin to discern the first anticipations of a doctrine of resurrection. In the inter-testamental period, this becomes a fully developed doctrine in the Pharisaic tradition. Salvation could then, at this stage, be interpreted as involving the guarantee of resurrection at the end of the age when

---

[20]R. H. Gundry, *Soma in Biblical Theology* (London: Cambridge University Press, 1976), pp. 130-31.

[21]G. Kaufman, *Systematic Theology in Historicist Perspective* (New York: Scribner's, 1968), p. XV and 426. (For a fuller discussion of Kaufman's position cf. R.F. Aldwinckle, *Death in the Secular City,* ch. 3.)

history reaches its consummation. Salvation as deliverance from present enemies and oppressors still continues; apocalyptic works, however, envisage this, not as the result of political and military action in the usual sense but as the result of some special, supernatural, and dramatic manifestation of God's power at some point in the future. Even so, the rule of God is still seen as established on a transformed and renewed earth and not as relegated to a "time" beyond history altogether. One further point deserves to be mentioned, namely salvation, not simply as deliverance from earthly enemies but from cosmic evil powers.

Again, the concept of Satan or the devil as a wholly evil power is not fully developed in the Old Testament itself, but only in the period between the Testaments. Certainly we find demonology in the Old Testament and, therefore, the idea of deliverance from disease and other disorders which have been caused by such hostile and evil spirits.[22] Salvation from the power of the devil as intrinsically evil awaits the post-exilic era and in particular the post-Old Testament period and is found again in the New Testament.

Salvation as the Resolution of the Problem of Guilt Through Forgiveness and Restoration to Divine Fellowship

The problem of sin and guilt arises in the Old Testament because Yahweh is a holy and righteous God and man is held responsible for deviation from the commands of the covenant God. Yahweh is steadfast love but his love is not simply a kindly feeling devoid of moral quality. He makes ethical demands of his people and his love is expressed in the divine insistence that the covenant people shall reflect his righteousness and holiness, not only in a proper attitude to Yahweh but also in the relationships which obtain between people in the covenant community. Despite this strong emphasis on relationships in community and the corresponding duties and obligations involved, there is no hint in the Old Testament that the righteous demands of Yahweh can be explained away merely in terms of social pressures in the manner of Freud's superego. Yahweh's righteousness is not a projection of social demands, though it involves them. Rather the latter is a reflection of Yahweh's righteousness, which is a powerful force not reducible to psychology and sociology.

---

[22]Edward Langton, *Essentials of Demonology* (London: Epworth, 1949).

The problem of guilt arises, therefore, not only as a psychological sense of guilt but as a matter of objective status before God. Man is guilty before Yahweh, whatever his moods, feelings, or psychological awareness may be. Because this is so, salvation, as deliverance from guilt, demands not only a change of the human attitude but also an act of God which will change man's status from that of a disobedient rebel to one who is accepted, forgiven, and restored to his proper status of trusting obedience within the divinely-given covenant. How does the Old Testament conceive this to be effected and what does Yahweh do to help bring it about? Despite the strong emphasis in Christian theology on an historical "fall" of man, and despite the presence of Genesis 3, it is not clear that the Old Testament has a developed doctrine of the "fall" in this sense. Once again we have to go to the period between the Testaments for the later Jewish theological answers to the question as to how sin originated and how man came to be the alienated rebel that he is.[23] The Old Testament understanding of sin and guilt is thus developed without any explicit theological explanation of sin in terms of the Fall. Certainly Genesis 3 puts disobedience in the center of the picture but this is by no means the same as the later elaborate doctrines as to the state of Adam before and after the Fall.

Sin in the Old Testament is classified by Wheeler Robinson under the following categories:

1. Deviation from the right way of which hatā' is the significant term with the meaning of missing the mark or goal. This tells us little about the precise nature of the deviation apart from the context.

2. The changed status (guilt) of the agent rāshā' suggests the forensic meaning of 'pronounce guilty' (Exodus 22:8) while the adjective describes the guilty as opposed to the innocent (Deut. 25:2) asham also implies guilt. Other terms like 'āwōn and hātā' easily pass over to imply guilt.

3. Rebellion against a superior or unfaithfulness to an agreement (Pasha'). This yields a more positive idea of sin as rebellion (cf.

---

[23]N.P. Williams, *Doctrines of the Fall and of Original Sin* (London: Longmans, Green & Co., 1927).

Job 34:37). "He added rebellion (pesha') unto his sin". Where the fear of the Lord is, there is pesha' ,that is, impiety or godlessness in the form of rebellion against Yahweh, the superior and final authority.

4. Some characterization of the quality of the act. There are many Hebrew terms to denote sin and its consequences e.g. badness, violence, destructiveness, trouble, worthlessness, vanity, folly, senselessness. Rā'āh covers all kinds of evils.[24]

Granted that sin is impiety in the sense of rebellion against Yahweh's authority and that this is in fact the human situation, how does Yahweh deal with it and how does this fit into the general concept of salvation? Here must be noted the transition from moral responsibility, as applicable mainly to the group or Israel as a corporate entity, to the individual, such as we find in Jeremiah and Ezekiel. There are two basic ways in which Yahweh deals with the situation of human rebellion. One is to demand a change of attitude on the part of the rebellious. This is repentance in the sense of *shub* (turn or return), that is, to turn back to Yahweh in obedience. When this takes place, Yahweh's lovingkindness (mercy or steadfast love) comes into play. As we have seen, it could be rendered grace, except that grace does not suggest those elements of loyalty, moral obligation, and social bond which the Hebrew *hesedth* connotes. Yahweh not only is gracious but also is linked to Israel in a bond of faithful and unbreakable loyalty, provided Israel keeps her part of the bargain (Jer. 31:2,3). Repentance, therefore, is not only being sorry about sin and its consequences but also is a new resolution and direction. To reject Yahweh's steadfast love is not only to commit a moral fault, but also is to have a churlish ingratitude in the face of Yahweh's faithfulness and loyalty and love (see Psalm 51 as the classic passage as to what repentance means in the Old Testament). Thus the contrast of spirit and flesh, holiness and sin, grace and repentance are resolved by action from Yahweh's side, whom to know is to love, as he is the Redeemer. We may now define salvation, not only as deliverance from external enemies (whether the foes of Israel, the power of demons, or the last enemy, death) or from sin as deviation from the will of Yahweh with all

---

[24]H. W. Robinson, *The Christian Doctrine of Man* (Edinburgh: T & T Clark, 1911), pp. 43ff; *Inspiration and Revelation in the Old Testament* (London: Clarendon Press, Oxford, 1946), pp. 55ff.

its fateful consequences. Salvation is now confident trust in the knowledge of Yahweh's love (*hesedth*) with the *shalom* which this gives in face of life's trials as well as in the valley of the shadow of death.

Salvation Through the Offering of an Adequate Sacrifice

So far it seems that, although Yahweh demonstrates his loyalty to Israel in action, the responsibility for turning again to him after rebellion appears to rest fairly and squarely on man himself. He must respond and in some way the initiative must come from the manward side too, even though Yahweh has acted with a view to eliciting that response. Yet two practical questions remain. How could the devout Jew be sure that he had offered a sufficient and adequate repentance to Yahweh? The deeper his awareness became of the holiness and righteousness of God, not only as an outward conformity to external law but also as a matter of inner intent, of the heart, the more difficult, if not impossible, it seemed to meet the divine requirement of repentance. But where was such help to come from? Historically, it seems as if the sacrificial system developed in part to meet this need. Not that the Jew regarded the system as created by man. Rather it was a gracious provision of Yahweh himself to enable the rebellious sinner to approach the holy God in confidence and be assured of acceptance rather than rejection.

Wheeler Robinson asserts that sacrifice was an indispensable part of Israel's religious life from beginning to end. As we shall see later, Israel was not unique in offering sacrifices. If there was anything distinctive about it, it was because of its relationship to Yahweh and his covenant with Israel which has already been considered. Inasmuch as sacrifice was a way of establishing or renewing the covenant from the human side, it is the distinctiveness of the covenant from the Godward side which gives a special character to Jewish sacrifice which it did not have elsewhere and in other religions. Whatever criticisms may be made of the sacrificial system and its inadequacy, whether viewed from the angle of a later enlightened humanism or from the perspective of a "higher" concept of sacrifice due to the life and death of Jesus, it would be unfair and historically inaccurate to treat it as if it dispensed with repentance and conversion or with obedience to the other commands of Yahweh in the Torah. The elaborate sacrificial system of later Judaism cannot be attributed to Moses in detail. It was the result of a long and complex historical development, with important and new developments taking place during the Exile and afterwards. It is also impossible to discover a coherent and consistent interpretation of every aspect of sacrifice so beloved of systematic theologians centuries later.

In the light of our brief survey, is it possible to say in broad terms what it meant to the Old Testament Jew to be saved? We believe an answer is possible in the following way:

1. Salvation meant to live in trustful obedience to Yahweh and to be a loyal member of the covenant community for whom Yahweh had provided guidance in the authoritative Torah. Such obedience entailed conformity to a complex set of rules, regulations, ethical principles interpreted as divine commands, sacrificial rituals, and later synagogue worship. It would be unfair to regard this requirement as merely an external imposition by Yahweh upon his people. Christians have sometimes seen it this way because of their strong reaction against legalism. Yet looked at from within the covenant community, the legalistic system was not seen by the devout Jew merely as an alien and external requirement. His delight was in the Law of the Lord. There is a spiritual inwardness, even in later Judaism, which has been overlooked by unsympathetic observers, both Christian and non-Christian.

2. Faith as trust in Yahweh and his promises meant that Yahweh's grace, loyalty, and lovingkindness would bless his people. What kind of blessings were expected? If we look at the history of Israel from the earliest times, we see a great diversity in this respect. Salvation as divine blessing could mean deliverance from Israel's enemies, from demons and disease, from going down into the pit or Sheol. It could also mean long life, numerous children, wealth, and prosperity. More inwardly, however, it could mean knowledge of Yahweh's grace (*hesedth*), forgiveness of sin, the *shalom* that comes from knowing Yahweh's promises can be trusted for the future even in the shadow of death. In the later post-exilic and intertestamental period, it could mean the assurance of the resurrection at the end of the age and the assurance of ultimate deliverance from oppression and suffering in the present age. The kingdom of Yahweh would no longer be a restored Davidic earthly kingdom or an earthly utopia in the

future, although millenial expectations had their role. An eternal kingdom, beyond the frustrations of historical existence, would one day replace any temporary earthly blessing. Needless to say, the precise•meaning of salvation depends on the degree of importance given to these various elements or any particular combination of them. The basic and underlying theme, however, is the faithfulness and trustworthiness of Yahweh if his people are loyal to the basic provisions laid down for them in the Torah and the covenant community.

The above is, of course, a general description and does not take into account the grappling with the problem of undeserved or so-called innocent suffering from the book of Job up to Rubenstein's *After Auschwitz* at the present day. The latter is radical theology in the sense that it questions whether it is really possible after the holocaust for the modern Jew to trust Yahweh's faithfulness and justice, not to mention his mercy and grace. However urgent and painful this issue, we shall assume that Rubenstein's position is not typical or representative, even of modern Jüdaism. Before we leave this question of what salvation means for the Jew, we turn briefly to a consideration of this issue by a modern Jew.[25] Will Herberg sees a radical difference between what he calls Greco-Oriental spirituality and the Hebraic world-outlook. While both of these affirm some absolute reality as ultimate, they differ fundamentally in what they say about that reality. The following lists are the present writer's summary of the sixth chapter of Herberg's book, showing the contrasting ideas characteristic of the Hebrew and Greco-Oriental approaches to the nature of transcendent reality.[26]

Hebraic

1. God is not a metaphysical principle or an impersonal force but a living Will, endowed with personality, that is, a Transcendent Person who created the universe and cannot be identified with it.

2. The empirical world is real and significant, though dependent on God as Creator. Strikes a this-worldly note. No depreciation of this world in favor of a timeless world of pure being.

---

[25]W. Herberg, *Judaism and Modern Man* (New York: Atheneum, 1970).
[26]Ibid., p. 91.

3. Man is a dynamic unity, which does not exclude distinction between the natural and spiritual dimension of human life. This distinction is not between body and soul as good and evil. Body and "soul" are God's creation and therefore good.

4. Personality and individuality basic. Man can hear God's Word and respond. The world is neither evil nor unreal. The basic evil is alienation from God. Man's proper condition is fellowship with God in faith and obedience. Self-absolutization in rebellion against God is sin. Salvation is repentance and reconciliation, not the denial of personality but its enhancement.

5. Salvation is reconciliation with God for life and for the world. No such thing as self-salvation.

6. The man of the Bible hears and obeys. Ethics central and ultimate. God transcends ethical categories, as he does all others, but man does not transcend them. The moral life is not left behind at any stage of the spiritual life.

7. Not escape from life but its fulfillment. Transworldly and transhistorical vision. Notion of the End. The whole man fulfilled in the resurrection of the dead.

8. The "I" is not given up, only the self-asserting impulse. Salvation is faith, repentance, forgiveness. Moral action the ultimate duty of man.

Greco-Oriental.

1. Ultimate reality is some primal, impersonal force. "All" is God, that is, pantheism.

2. The empirical world as illusion induced by the shifting flux of sensory experience. Life and history, as temporal processes, hopelessly infected with the irrational and the unreal. Salvation is true knowledge breaking through the veil of illusion.

3. Body-soul dualism. Matter/body is evil. Mind/reason is good. Body the prison house of the soul (Plato).

4. Salvation is freedom from error and illusion. Individuality condemned as source of craving and greed. Tendency to absorption in the All-Soul.

5. What shall I do to be saved? Fragment of the All-Soul must return to the divine Whole.

6. The Good Life is contemplation and freedom from attachment to the empirical world. Mystic or philosopher "sees and enjoys." Beyond Good and Evil. Goal transcends ethics.

7. Fulfillment beyond immediate life. Liberation of the soul from time and empirical existence.

8. No sense of sin and guilt. Evil is separateness from the All and associated with the Body. Salvation an achievement of the individual for himself and by himself.

Salvation, then, as we have previously noted is a relationship to God conceived as personal will. Herberg is fully aware of the modern criticism of the emphasis on God as "Person" as sheer anthropomorphism. He admits that we can only speak of such a "Person" in symbols and that the symbolical language is analogical, not literal.[27] There is both the inevitable paradox and the inadequacy of human language. All the same, anthropomorphic, better anthropopathic, language about God cannot be eliminated. "The God of Hebraic religion is either a living, acting, 'feeling' God or he is nothing."[28]

One further point needs to be noted, although we do not intend to go into detail now: namely the relationship of salvation, as Judaism conceives it, to ethics. First, life cannot be separated into secular and sacred. No area of life falls outside God's jurisdiction. Ethics is integral to the Jewish understanding of the demands which God makes. Conscience is not simply the Freudian superego or the reflection of social pressures. It is a mark of original perfection in sinful man and points back to the divine order of creation and the image of God in

---

[27]Hans Küng, *On Being a Christian* (New York: Doubleday, 1976). It is interesting to note the agreement of both Jew and Catholic Christian on this point. "God is certainly not Person as man is person" says Küng, but he is not less but more than Person. The suggestion of impersonal must be avoided and with proper safeguards we might speak of transpersonal or superpersonal (Küng, p. 303). The point is that both agree that while the personal symbols of biblical language are analogies, the personal aspect must not be reduced to the impersonal.

[28]Herberg, *Judaism and Modern Man,* p. 61.

man.[29] Ethical obligation is rooted in man's freedom to obey or disobey God. Thus, the root of wrongdoing and moral evil is not the evil body but idolatry, the essence of which is the making of finite things, and especially man himself, into an Absolute and consequently the refusal of the sovereignty of God and his Law. "Idolatry is the absolutization of the relative."[30] This strong emphasis on Law calls for further comment. Says Herberg: "Jewish ethics is an ethic of law: but beyond that there is an ethic of love."[31]

In view of the oft-repeated criticism of Judaism, particularly by Christians in the Reformation tradition, special attention should be directed to the points made by Herberg.

1. Humility is central to Jewish ethics, not self-righteousness as a boasting of human ethical achievement apart from dependence upon God.

2. Jewish emphasis on Law is not on mere external conformity to imposed rule as against Kavanah, disposition of the heart or direction of the will.[32] Impulse and action, inwardness and externality are organically related but they are not the same thing.[33]

3. Law is not to be opposed to grace. "Consciousness of sin and assurance of grace are the two great motive powers of religion" (Solomon Schechter).[34] Salvation, therefore, is a relation of the self in faith to a larger whole beyond the self. This larger whole, however, is not a pantheistic World-Soul or an impersonal force but the living God, a superpersonal but not an impersonal reality. Repentance, 'turning' (*teshubah*), and grace are correlative aspects of this divine-human relationship. The Jewish emphasis on Law is not a form of self-salvation achieved solely by human effort. "The Pharisaic position tries to hold the balance between man's duty to strive to earn pardon and his inability to attain it without God's gracious gift of it" (Israel Abrahams).[35] "Salvation

[29]Ibid., p. 91.
[30]Ibid., p. 95.
[31]Ibid., p. 106.
[32]Manson, *Ethics and the Gospel,* pp. 38-39.
[33]Herberg, *Judaism and Modern Man,* p. 102.
[34]Ibid., p. 115.
[35]Ibid., p. 123.

is of repentance and faith, for faith is at bottom right relation to God and that is salvation."[36]

Last but not least, salvation—individual and social, vertical or horizontal—is oriented to eternity. Eternity is not escape from but the fulfillment of time, as contrasted with the Greco-Oriental spirituality already considered. Salvation is the redemption of all history through its consummation in the eternal kingdom of God.

Much more could be said, but perhaps enough has been indicated to give a reasonably fair idea of what salvation means from the Jewish point of view. Herberg may not be entirely typical in all of the personal opinions he expresses. Judaism seems to have as many theological diversities as Christianity. Nevertheless, the basic outline seems to be clear enough. We began this investigation, it will be remembered, in order to clarify the issue of religious pluralism. The question was raised concerning the possibility of finding some kind of norm which might be considered the authoritative basis for judgment and evaluation. In the case of Judaism, it appears that the norm is to be found in a certain understanding of the character of God and his relationship, through creation and redemption, to men and women as fashioned in his image. Despite the great importance given to certain historical figures—especially Moses, the prophets, the priesthood, and the wise men—it does not appear as if the Jewish view of salvation depends solely or exclusively on one man or any particular group of men. Yahweh works through a particular people and specific individuals. Yet above all particularities stands the sovereignty of the one God, holy, righteous, gracious, and faithful to those who observe the requirements of the covenant.

It was only after completing this section that there came into the author's hands E. P. Sanders' new book, so relevant to the theme we have been considering.[37] It would be presumptuous to offer detailed comment on points of detail by someone who makes no claim to rabbinic scholarship. Nevertheless, what Sanders has to say is so important in relation to our question that something must be said about it. We repeat again that our concern is with the issue of pluralism, and in dealing with this we have been obliged to ask how the

---

[36]Ibid.
[37]E. P. Sanders, *Paul and Palestinian Judaism* (London: S. C. M., 1977).

Jew understands salvation as a preliminary to asking what the New Testament says on the same theme. It is obvious that by putting it in this way, we are revealing a Christian perspective and Christian assumptions. Indeed, our interest is primarily directed to finding an answer to the question as to whether salvation offered in the New Testament is distinct from that offered in Judaism and if there are differences, precisely what are those differences?

At this point, we take note of the objections made by Sanders against such an approach. He believes that this evaluation of Judaism from a Christian perspective has resulted in many serious distortions of the facts. The reason for this is that Christian scholars see Judaism through Christian eyes and bring to its evaluation criteria taken from their Christian understanding of salvation and particularly the centrality of Jesus in relation to this. The assumption, open or hidden, in this approach is that Judaism is incomplete, unfinished, merely a stage on the way to something else, namely Christianity. This is illustrated in particular by the sharp antithesis between Judaism as a religion of legalistic works-righteousness and the Pauline doctrine of justification by faith and the emphasis on grace rather than works as the basis of salvation rooted in faith alone.

For this, Sanders wishes to substitute what he calls a "holistic comparison of patterns in religion." In other words, Judaism is to be seen and evaluated in and for itself, not simply as a preparation for something else, for example, Pauline Christianity. After all, whatever Christians think, Judaism is not an historical anachronism but a continuing reality. This being so, Christians must admit the possibility that Judaism and Christianity may both be valid ways of salvation on their own terms. To make exclusive claims for one over against the other is both to contradict the facts and sin against an open, sensitive, and loving attitude to those of another religion. On this issue at least, religious pluralism is justified as a theological principle insofar as salvation is possible to the Jew and the Christian in the context of their own religion and faith without any implication that the one must be converted to the faith of the other in order to be "saved." If this point is conceded, the further question can be raised as to whether the principle should be extended to some or all of the other religions.

At this point, we also note that Judaism is often as exclusivist in regard to the other religions as Christianity is often charged with being. We have already seen Herberg's sharp contrast between Greco-

Oriental spirituality and the basic tenets of Judaism. It has been customary in recent times to talk of the Judeo-Christian tradition as contrasted with other religions. This too poses problems of interpretation. Does it mean that Judaism is seen as only anticipatory of Christianity, a view which Sanders questions, or does it mean that Judaism and Christianity, holistically interpreted in Sanders' sense, represent a view of salvation which, though distinct in several ways, yet have enough in common to justify contrasting the Judeo-Christian tradition with other traditions? This is an issue to which we shall have to return. We shall, however, first look at the issue of salvation in the New Testament context and relate this to our previous discussion of the Old Testament and later Jewish thought on the subject.

Chapter Two

Judaism and New Testament Salvation

The issue of pluralism becomes most acute in the Western world, as we have seen, in the relationship of Judaism and Christianity. When pluralism is under consideration, it is more often discussed in relation to non-Semitic religion, namely what Herberg called Greco-Oriental spirituality. Hinduism, Buddhism, Shintoism, Confucianism, Taoism, Mysticism, as a universal phenomenon, are usually given the central place in any discussion of pluralism. Sometimes an appeal is made, as we have seen, to the Judeo-Christian tradition as over against all the others. Only recently has there developed a genuine theological dialogue between modern Judaism and Christian theology. The problems here are enormous, mainly because of the way in which Jews have been treated in so-called Christian societies. This has made it extremely difficult to isolate and discuss fundamental issues apart from historical and contemporary painful memories. The issue of religious pluralism on a world scale has made this more difficult.

If, for example, Christians are going to retain their emphasis on the centrality of Jesus Christ for salvation, and on a specific doctrine of incarnation, then what does this mean not only for a Christian understanding of the Old Testament but of rabbinic and contemporary Judaism? If, as is obviously the case, Jesus is not central to salvation to Judaism, then is the Jew "saved"? If the answer to this is yes, then the logical consequence would appear to be the abandonment by Christians of the central and indispensable role of Jesus for salvation. This means a frank repudiation of any Christian attempt to convert the Jew. The latter will be, and indeed, is saved through his obedience to the will of God as made known through his Judaism without any necessary relationship to Jesus Christ. If, on the other hand, we say that the Jew is saved through his Judaism but not wholly saved or fully saved, then what precisely is it that the Jew lacks which the Christian has? In the eighteenth century, Semler regarded the Old Testament as the book of a different religion. The discontinuity was absolute. Christianity needed to be purged completely of its Jewish origins.[1] Toynbee seems to come close to saying precisely this in our own day. We realize that this is a sensitive issue indeed. Nevertheless, the issue is of such central importance that it cannot be avoided. It is very unlikely that Christians can deal effectively with religious pluralism on a world scale until they have rethought their attitude to the Judaism out of which, historically, the Christian faith has come.

Before we try to deal with these basic issues, we shall consider first what salvation means in the New Testament and where it differs from what we discovered in our previous consideration of the Old Testament and later Judaism. The first point to emphasize is that Jesus was a Jew and that he took for granted the Old Testament understanding of God both in relation to creation and redemption. Creation, covenant, holiness, righteousness, love (*hesedth*), the fatherhood of God, faith, repentance, sin, guilt, grace, the kingdom of God: all these basic Jewish ideas are found in the teaching of Jesus. We cannot make sense of the ministry of Jesus apart from these ideas. Jesus' radical criticism of some aspects of the Judaism of his day in no way alters this fact. Jesus saw himself as the agent of the fulfillment of God's age-old purpose for mankind mediated through Israel. This rediscovery of the Jewishness of Jesus has led to interesting developments.

One is the willingness on the part of some Jewish scholars to see Jesus no longer as an alien but one of them, to claim him as a 'brother' and to give him an honored place in the long line of Jewish prophets and teachers. An example would be in Martin Buber's noteworthy

---

[1]W. Pannenberg, *Theology and the Philosophy of Science* (London: Darton, Longman & Todd, 1976), p. 383.

words written in 1950. "From my youth onwards I have found in Jesus my great brother. . . . I am more than ever certain that a great place belongs to him in Israel's history of faith and that this place cannot be described by any of the usual categories."[2] It should also be noted that while Buber admits the importance for him of trying to understand how and why Christianity understands Jesus as God and Savior, he also declares with equal firmness that "we will never recognize Jesus as the Messiah come, for this would contradict the deepest meaning of our Messianic passion."[3] He also seems to speak as if the basic difference between the Jewish messianic hope and the Christian faith is that the former still knows the world to be unredeemed, while the latter speaks as if the world has already been redeemed. Buber points to "the bloody body of our people" as proof that the world is at present unredeemed. Yet to put it in this way is highly misleading.

It is true that the Christian faith believes that the redeeming grace of the sovereign God has already been liberated into present history through the death and resurrection of Jesus. The redemptive power of God is active in our world, all appearances to the contrary. Yet Christians from the New Testament onwards have always known that the present world is not yet the kingdom of God and of his Christ in the fullest sense possible. How could they think this in the face of the cross, not to mention the New Testament insistence that the kingdom in its totality is still to come at the parousia of the risen Jesus. Whether Buber intended his words to be taken in that sense, the impression given is that Christians are insensitive and unfeeling because they do not see the agony of the present world, and the historical agony of the Jews in particular. Whatever the deficiencies in Christian attitudes and actions, it must be said that, for Christian faith, redemption is both present fact and future consummation.

It also has to be said, however, that the more Judaism accepts Jesus as one of its own, the more it will be compelled to come to terms with the criticism which Jesus leveled against some aspects of Judaism. This could lead to a reform of Judaism from within on the basis of self-criticism initiated by Jesus as a member of the covenant community.

---

[2]M. Buber, *Two Types of Faith* (New York: Macmillan, 1961), p. 12.

[3]Cited by Maurice Friedman, *Martin Buber: The Life of Dialogue* (Chicago: University of Chicago Press, 1955), p. 279.

There is no reason why this in principle should not take place without Judaism conceding anything to Christian claims about messiahship or the more precise doctrinal claim that Jesus was "truly God." It also needs to be said here that all criticism of Judaism is not to be taken as anti-Semitic or even anti-Judaistic. After all, the severest critics of some aspects of Jewish religion and practice were themselves Jews, whether the prophets or Jesus himself. While it is understandable that Jews might be quick to see in all criticism a hidden anti-Semitism, this cannot be taken as universally valid in the light of the above facts. There is both criticism and criticism. Neither Jesus nor Paul were anti-Semitic. They were obviously deeply bound to their own people, despite their forthright challenge to some aspects of the Judaism they encountered. Jesus' weeping over Jerusalem and Paul's willingness to be cast off for his brethren's sake surely witness to this.

There are tendencies, however, in some recent biblical scholarship which, if accepted as valid, would throw quite a new light on ancient questions. If, for example, it became widely accepted in Christian circles that Jesus did not in fact make a specific claim to messiahship, then this would remove one basic source of theological conflict. This, however, would then confront Christians with the question as to whether they could continue to defend a unique incarnation of God, even if Jesus made no claim to messiahship. Since the early church soon came to the conclusion that the category of messiahship did not express adequately all that Christian faith wanted to claim for Jesus, there seems no reason why the modern Christian should not live with the ambiguous results of biblical scholarship on this point. If, for other reasons, it was felt necessary to abandon the doctrine of the Incarnation, then the most that could be claimed would be that Jesus was the "decisive" but not the exclusive divine instrument of salvation. A notable number of Christian theologians, though certainly not all and not the majority, seem to have come already to this conclusion, for example, John Hick, David Griffin, J. B. Cobb, Jr., perhaps Norman Pittenger, Maurice Wiles, and other contributors to *The Myth of God Incarnate.*

In broad terms, it may be said that the difference between the Jewish and the Christian views of the nature of salvation is to be found in the special relationship to Jesus which lies at the heart of the Christian faith. The designation of Jesus as "God" and "Savior" belongs to the later New Testament writings. In Titus 2:13, Christians are to wait "for the appearing of the glory of our great God and Savior Jesus Christ." *Theos* and *Soter* seem to belong together in this context. Second Peter 1:1 mentions the "righteousness of our God and Savior Jesus Christ." The fact that in the Greek text of both passages the two substantives "God" and "Savior" come under the regimen of a single definite article strongly suggests that one and the same person is being denoted as being both God and Savior, the Savior God.[4] Four other passages in 2 Peter refer to "our Lord and Savior Jesus Christ" (2 Pet. 1:11; 2:20; 3:2,18). A characteristic expression of the Pastoral epistles is "God and Savior" (1 Tim.1:1; 2:3; Titus 1:3; 2:10; 3:4) where the reference is probably "God the Father." It is notable that the designation Savior, applied either to God or Christ, occurs fifteen times in the Pastoral epistles and 2 Peter as against nine times in the remaining books of the New Testament. The noun *soteria* (salvation) is quite differently distributed. Why this emphasis on the personal substantive in the later writings?

F. F. Bruce suggests that it is a reaction against the claims being made, especially in the second half of the first century, to the other *Theoi soteres* and in particular the Roman Emperor.[5] On the other hand, the title was hardly an innovation. The infancy narratives exult in "God my Savior" (Luke 1:47) and proclaim the "birth of a Savior who is Christ the Lord" (Luke 2:11). The term has its roots in Old Testament usage which uses Savior both for Yahweh and for the King. of Israel. Theologically, this involves the claim of the later New Testament writings that Jesus is *the* Savior in a manner which distinguishes him from other "saving" figures, and that this saving role of Jesus is linked to his unique role as God's Son and representative. Certainly, from the New Testament onwards, Christian devotion has used the noun Savior in what can only be called an exclusive sense.

As far as this bears on our discussion of religious pluralism, certain questions can now be asked:

1. Did Jesus himself make this exclusive claim to be *the* Savior as contrasted with other expressions of Yahweh's saving activity in the history of Israel?

---

[4] F. F. Bruce, *Our God and Saviour: A Recurring Biblical Pattern;* S. G. F. Brandon, *The Saviour God,* pp. 51ff.

[5] Ibid., p. 52.

2. If he did make such a claim, was it the equivalent in Jesus' understanding of the later claim of the church as to his "divinity"?
3. If he did not make such exclusive claims, does this mean that later Christian claims are unjustified?
4. In the light of the answers given to these questions, what can we deduce from Jesus' teaching and action as to the past role of the people of Israel in God's saving purpose for mankind and their future role in the working out of that saving purpose?
5. The last and most difficult question is: What did Jesus bring in the way of salvation which was not already available in the Judaism of his day? On this latter issue, Jews and Christians are divided, but it is not always clear as to where the precise differences are to be located.

We shall now make some general comments on these issues without a detailed consideration of each, which limitation of space forbids.

Jesus appears to have accepted without question the fact of Yahweh's saving activity in the history of Israel. What, then, was distinctive of his own proclamation? It appears to have been his insistence on the nearness and indeed the present reality of the kingdom. This was no longer a far-off divine event to coincide with the end of history and the final consummation of the kingdom. The "signs" of the near approach of the kingdom were already evident in his own ministry. To the question whether his contemporaries should look for another deliverer, he points them to the signs which fulfill the prophetic anticipations (Luke 11:20; Matt. 13:16; 11:6). The framework of Jesus' thinking is apocalyptic and he proclaims "the proleptic presence of the future Kingdom of God."[6] If this were all, it would not separate Jesus in any fundamental theological sense from Judaism. To say that God's saving activity was already operative now and that the full splendor of the kingdom was soon to be fully manifest was certainly a significant fresh emphasis but not a fundamental departure from the main line of Jewish hopes and expectations.

The crucial issue, however, is how Jesus understood his own role in relation to the imminent kingdom. Was he in his person central to the

---

[6]R. H. Fuller, *The Foundations of New Testament Christology* (London: Lutterworth, 1965), p. 122.

proclamation in a way which involved an exclusive claim for which no parallel could be found in the history of the Jews up to that point? Further, did such a claim involve the further implication that Jesus believed himself to be the Messiah and, therefore, the fulfillment of all Israel's hopes? Furthermore, did he see himself as a universal Savior for all men and women everywhere, whether Jew or Gentile?

There seems little doubt that Jesus spoke with authority in a way which impressed his contemporaries. The saying, "Truly, I say to you," means that Jesus pledges his whole person behind the truth of his proclamation. The exorcisms and healings are his work and show the proleptic presence of the kingdom. Those who listened to him were told: "Blessed are the ears which hear what you hear" (Matt. 13:16). On one occasion at least, he could call men and women directly to himself: "Come unto me all you that labour and are heavy laden and I will give you rest" (Matt. 11:28). He called for a decision for or against his person. He relativized the authority of the sabbath by subjecting it to the more overriding claims of mercy and compassion. Yet this is not without precedent. The rabbis taught that the sabbath is "delivered into the hand of man (to break it when necessary) and not man into the power of the Sabbath."[7] "Danger to life annuls the Sabbath and one sabbath may be violated to save many."[8] More offensive to Jewish ears would have been "Moses said unto you . . . but I say unto you."[9] Even this could be interpreted as a prophetic challenge to a deeper, fuller, and more radical fulfillment of the intent and spirit of the Torah rather than the putting of himself on some kind of equality with Yahweh.

We may note here the general thesis of Pannenberg to the effect that for the God of Israel to become the God of all mankind, the idea of the totality of history as the revelation of God must be developed. Yet if the full meaning of history and the complete confirmation of the deity of Yahweh can only be shown when history is complete, then how can a specific event within history be treated as having absolute meaning as revelation?[10] Whereas the whole of Judaism expected the decisive, saving, self-revelation of Yahweh in the eschatological future,[11] the answer to the above question could only be given if within

---

[7]Herberg, *Judaism and Modern Man,* p. 293.
[8]Ibid., p. 293.
[9]Ibid.
[10]W. Pannenberg, ed., *Revelation as History* (New York: Macmillan, 1968), p. 17.
[11]Ibid., p. 59.

history itself the end becomes present and the significance of the whole of history is given proleptically in an event within history. This, in fact, according to Pannenberg, is implicit in the fate of Jesus, the claims he made, and the reality of the resurrection. The latter is now an event within history and not simply an expectation of the general resurrection of the dead at the end of history.

Jesus' unique self-consciousness involved the claim that he was the one to proclaim the imminence of the end and God's final offer of salvation. Because of this, he was able to challenge the rabbinic way of thinking and set the authority of his "I" against the authority of the Torah.[12] Thus discipleship of Jesus determines a person's relationship to the final, eschatological salvation. Christian confidence that the end-event has come in the person of Jesus is justified by God's raising Jesus from the dead, even now, in the midst of history.

However, the self-revelation of God to the biblical witnesses is not a theophany, a direct manifestation of God in human form, but is given indirectly through the historical acts of God. These acts are public in the sense of facts which people can know of through the use of their normal faculties, even though they do not necessarily believe. The universal revelation of the deity of God, that is, his Godhead for all men everywhere in all time and space, is not given in the history of Israel but is given in the fate of Jesus.[13] The end of history is already seen within history and hence Jesus is a real foretaste of the end, that is, of the final sovereignty of God over the whole of mankind. This revelation in the fate of Jesus is still indirect, for God can remain hidden for some, even in the death and resurrection of Jesus. Nevertheless, the fate of Jesus does "reveal" the deity of the God of Israel, but not as an isolated event. The event of Jesus Christ is in fact the fulfillment in time of the history of God with Israel. The Christian claim for a final revelation of the universal deity of Israel's God for all mankind is thus not a mere cancellation of Judaism but a genuine fulfillment of what God has already been doing and purposing in his dealings with the covenant people. The Jew can thereby find his true fulfillment as a Jew in the proleptic reality of God's final sovereignty in the fate of Jesus and his death and resurrection.

Nevertheless, some explanation is needed to account for the conflict between Jesus and the Jewish authorities of his day. Even

---

[12]Ibid., p. 70.
[13]Ibid., p. 139.

though the common people heard him gladly, there also seems to have been both political and theological objections to him on the part of the scribes and Pharisees, even if this cannot be taken to mean that Jesus condemned whole groups of people out of hand. Despite the justifiable objection of Judaism today against the treatment of all Jews, of whatever historical period, as corporately guilty of deicide, the fact of real conflict between Jesus and the Judaism of his day is a historical fact. No resolution of the problem of anti-Semitism, which has disfigured the history of Christianity, can alter this fact.

The question is: What was the root cause of this conflict? Was it because he was a disturber of the peace and the delicate political balance of power between the Roman occupying power and the Jewish authorities? Was it a matter of theological principle because he rejected the authority and centrality of the Torah? Or was it because of claims concerning his own person and status which were interpreted as blasphemy? Yet would the claim to be the Messiah in itself have been enough to convict him of blasphemy in the eyes of the Jews? To claim that the age-old messianic claim of Israel was at last fulfilled would have been startling and no doubt dangerous to established authorities. Was it in itself tantamount to a denial of the role of the covenant people in the saving purpose of God? Would a Jew who accepted Jesus as Messiah have had to reject his Judaism on fundamental theological grounds? "The Jewish Christians' recognition of Jesus as Messiah did not conflict with Pharisaic orthodoxy."[14]

The difficulty in answering some of these questions springs from the uncertainty which modern biblical scholarship has injected into the debate as to exactly what it was that Jesus claimed. Even if we leave the question of his claim to some form of messiahship undecided for lack of conclusive and consistent evidence in the Gospels, it could be affirmed, as it is by Fuller, that "In Jesus as he understood himself, there is an immediate confrontation with God's presence and His very Self," offering judgment and salvation.[15] If this is not merely a reading into the Gospel material from a Christian perspective, then it could be affirmed that Jesus was in fact the Savior of the world, whether he claimed to be the Messiah or not. Again Fuller: "While he asserted no

[14]G. F. Moore, *Judaism in the First Centuries of the Christian Era,* vol. 1 (Cambridge, MA: Oxford University Press, 1927-1930), p. 90.
[15]Fuller, *Foundations,* p. 106.

explicit Messianic claim and displayed no direct Messianic consciousness, he was certainly conscious of a unique Sonship to which he was privileged to admit others through his eschatological ministry."[16] In this case, the traditional messianic concept, whether interpreted politically or more spiritually, becomes theologically secondary. The central issue now becomes the unique Sonship of Jesus. In this case, the implication would be that the right relationship to Yahweh, which as we have seen, is the basic Jewish idea of salvation, is now established, not through loyalty to the historic Torah, but through loyalty and obedience to Jesus in whom the saving purpose of God in Israel has now reached its consummation.

The fundamental idea of the covenant people and the Law must now be superseded by the claim of this Jesus which is now the divinely appointed way to salvation and the blessedness of the eternal kingdom still awaiting its full consummation but nevertheless a reality now in the "new Israel" which Jesus has established. On this view, the historically indispensable role of Israel in the early stages of the *Heilsgeschichte* has now ceased and the further development and fulfillment of the God of Israel's saving purpose must now take place through this Jesus, the Son in a final and definitive sense. This would imply that for Jesus himself, historic Judaism has now been superseded by a reconstituted Israel, the distinctive feature of which would be loyalty to Jesus himself as its Head and Lord. Jews may reject this claim as preposterous or even blasphemous. They can hardly regard it as anti-Semitic, since Jesus the Jew, on this view, sees himself as the head of a new Israel, startlingly different in some ways from historic Judaism but certainly in direct continuity with it.

The above position is basically the attitude taken by the majority of Christians from New Testament times. The difficulty is that it leaves the Jews after the time of Jesus in a kind of limbo. Judaism has now fulfilled the role assigned to it and is no longer needed. The logic of this would seem to require the disappearance of Judaism as such in the period between the coming of Jesus and the final kingdom which Jesus inaugurated. Salvation henceforth is in and through him alone. This leaves Jews in the Christian period with only two options: Either to become Christians or to merge themselves in society at large and surrender their existence as the covenant people living in obedience to

[16]Ibid., p. 115.

the Torah. This was in fact the opinion of Arnold Toynbee when he spoke of Judaism as a fossil or a back-number.[17]

Toynbee does not appear to be saying that Jews must now become orthodox Christians. If they did, of course, then they would be absorbed into the Christian fellowship and lose their Jewish identity as such. They would still have some kind of identity as Jewish Christians in the loose general sense in which we now speak of American Christians or African Christians. Toynbee sees the basic tension within Judaism itself. Jews must choose between the preexilic "national God" of which Toynbee obviously does not think very highly, and the worship of the one true God—the absolute spiritual Reality in its Personal Aspect,[18] attained by Deutero-Isaiah and carried to its logical universalism by Jesus. The Jews, he says, have yet to make up their minds between these two incompatible alternatives.[19] We have seen that Pannenberg resolves this same problem of the tension between exclusive Jewish claims and the universal God of all mankind by seeing the fate of Jesus as the proleptic manifestation of the deity of Israel's God in a universal sense. This is not the destruction of Israel's God, however, but the proper fulfillment of faith in Him. This does involve, nevertheless, the need for the recognition by Jews of the truly universal implications of what Yahweh has been seeking to accomplish through their special destiny and history, and Jesus is central to this understanding. In any case, a national religious community, Jewish or non-Jewish, is now a historical anachronism and must in the end be willing to sacrifice its national identity in the world community. The Jew, of course, can always maintain that empirical Christianity, that is, Christianity in its various historical developments, is just as much characterized by national and indeed racial exclusiveness as was historic Israel. This is indeed true. Despite the intentions and views of Jesus, Christianity is not a truly universal religion because loyalty to Jesus has been distorted by national, racist, sociological, and cultural exclusivism. If these could be removed or overcome, would the Jew still feel that he would lose his identity in any worthwhile sense by acknowledging the lordship of Jesus and entering the Christian

---

[17]A. Toynbee, *A Study of History,* vol. 1 (New York: Oxford University Press, 1964), p. 479.

[18]Ibid., p. 487.

[19]Ibid., p. 488.

family? It must be admitted that this presupposes a radical transformation of Christianity, at least as radical, if not more so, than the transformation of Judaism which Jesus himself had demanded of his people.

We shall have to return to these fundamental issues later. For the time being, we desire to reach, if we can, a more precise understanding of what Christians mean when they talk of Jesus Christ as the Savior. This is a basic theological question which takes us beyond the New Testament witness to the more formally developed orthodoxy of later centuries. The crucial question in this context would be: Does the claim that Jesus is the unique Savior depend upon this later Christological orthodoxy? Could Jesus be the unique Savior, even in Pannenberg's sense, without necessarily being the "truly God" of Chalcedon or interpreted in terms of the myth of the Incarnation, to use the language of the authors of a recent book.[20] We can hardly attempt an answer to these questions until we have decided how Jesus saves, what he saves us from, and how important is his Person in relation to this saving activity.

---

[20]John Hick, *The Myth of God Incarnate* (Philadelphia: Westminster, 1977), cf. ch. 1 by Maurice Wiles.

Chapter Three

Jesus: A Savior or the Savior?

In the previous chapters we have been concerned with the issue of religious pluralism in relation to the Jewish understanding of what it means to be saved and in relation to a modern defense of a specific Christian theism. The fact of religious pluralism, in the sense of the phenomenology of religion, is not our prime concern. Rather it is the challenge which it poses as to whether there are any normative events or persons by which we can measure and point to revelatory and redeeming acts. The Jew would say yes to this and point to Exodus, Covenant, and Torah. Christian faith assumes also a positive answer in relation to the life, death, and resurrection of Jesus of Nazareth. In considering the issue of religious pluralism in this sense, Christians have tended in the past to concentrate on the major non-Christian religions such as Hinduism, Buddhism, Islam, and so forth. They have tended to forget that the issue is most acute in relation to the continued existence and vitality of the Jewish people as the contemporary manifestation of the people of the covenant in the modern period.

Islam has also proved to be something of an embarrassment to Christians, a fact of which we are vividly aware today. That a major religion should emerge and endure after the coming of Christ poses a quite different set of problems from those which existed prior to the Christian revelation. We have tried to take up this delicate issue between Judaism and Christianity in our previous asking as to the sense in which the Jew as Jew can be said to be "saved," whether in the Old Testament or in later Judaism. We should note again in passing that a religious pluralism, which relativizes all religions, is as much a threat to Judaism as to Christianity. Exodus-Sinai is not more normative than is Jesus Christ for such a pluralism.

We now put the same question about salvation to the New Testament and the later developments of the Christian faith. In what sense is the Christian "saved" and to what extent is this a salvation distinct from, or more normative than, the salvation which the Jew believes has been graciously provided for him through the Torah and the redeeming acts of Yahweh in Jewish history? Furthermore, is the Christian "saved" in a sense which would not be true for the Hindu, the Buddhist, or the Muslim? If a Christian is asked in what sense Jesus is the Savior in a way which makes him the measure of all other saviors, the answer has often been given, as we have seen, in terms of authoritative doctrine. He is *the* Savior because the Bible says so and as the Bible is divinely inspired, then the claim must be valid. Or Jesus is the Savior because the church has declared him to be "truly man and truly God." This is divinely attested truth given to the church. It, therefore, follows that there can only be one God and Savior and that is Jesus Christ, the God-man.

There is a proper and responsible appeal to both Scripture and tradition, as we shall see, but it is obvious that this answer to the question of Jesus' saviorhood rests simply on the basis of an authoritative assumption. Our thesis will be that this assumption has to be tested and defended by an appeal to experience. The unquestioned appeal to authority does not do justice to the subleties of the Christian theological tradition nor does it give sufficient weight to the way in which the great thinkers of the Christian tradition have themselves appealed to experience rather than to sheer authority as such. When we penetrate beneath the authoritative forms of the faith, we discover again and again a pragmatic element, not in the precise sense of William James' philosophy, but in the sense of an appeal to experience in a broad empirical sense.

Jesus is the Savior because he saves men and women both by present power and future hope. In the actual business of living and dying, he rescues men and women from the threats of meaninglessness, sinfulness, alienation, and death. If the unique saviorhood of Jesus is to be retained in the context of a global religious pluralism with its competing religious claims, it is obvious that some attempt must be made to show that Jesus has done this on the level of experience and not simply by dogmatic pronouncement. This is not to say that the dogmas are invalid, still less that a "liberal" Jesus, stripped of all dogma, is a viable alternative to the historic faith.[1]

It is, however, to say that the dogmas are rooted in a life-transforming experience in the first place. As T. R. Glover said many years ago, the early Christians out-thought, out-lived, and out-died the pagan world.[2] If this had not been substantially true, the dogmas would never have taken hold and Jesus would have remained only another interesting historical figure and the founder of another Jewish sect. He would not have become the center of another world religion which involved a radical break with the Judaism in which he was nurtured. How, then, did Jesus come to be able to "save" in a way which had such far-reaching consequences? We can seek an answer to this question in several ways:

1. There was an intrinsic quality of character and personality which drew men and women to him in utter devotion, trust, and love. This, of course, is not itself such a unique phenomenon. We know many examples from history of the magnetic power of an outstanding personality to elicit the devotion of countless followers. There readily come to mind such diverse figures as Gotama the Buddha, Mohammed, Hitler, Gandhi, and Karl Marx. To grade Jesus only on this level, we would have to credit him with an extraordinary power to sway and capture the imagination and loyalty of men and women. Even if Jesus were not the God-man of orthodox Christian faith, he could hardly be reduced to an ordinary or insignificant figure. This is why one is always puzzled by Karl Barth's remarks about Jesus as an ordinary rabbi.

2. Or we can emphasize the nature of his teaching rather than the charismatic quality of his personality, to use the word charismatic in Weber's sense rather than the apostle Paul's.[3] In

---

[1]See the discussion of this issue in R. F. Aldwinckle, *More than Man: A Study in Christology* (Grand Rapids: Eerdmanns, 1976).

[2]T. R. Glover, *The Jesus of History* (London: S.C.M., 1948).

[3]Reinhart Bendix, *Max Weber: An Intellectual Portrait* (New York: Doubleday, 1962), ch. 10.

this case, we would, presumably, have to try and show that Jesus' teaching was more original, nobler, truer, and capable of more fruitful application than the teaching of other outstanding philosophers and religious persons. Of course, it could be properly urged that in this case, Jesus would not strictly be the Savior but the best Teacher that ever was, and that the two things are not the same. The use and application of the teaching would still be the responsibility of men and women. On this view, Jesus, as Kierkegaard once said, would be only a greater Plato. Or, like Gotama, it would be his Dharma or his doctrine rather than his Person which would be the normative factor.

3. Without any disparagement of the teaching of Jesus, firmly anchored in Judaism, it could be affirmed that it was not so much what Jesus said but what he did. Actions speak louder than words. This may not seem at first much different from the position expressed above, but it does stress an important point. Here we have a charismatic leader and teacher whose teaching is perfectly expressed and lived out, even at the cost of the sacrifice of life itself. The plausibility of this thesis runs into some difficulties if one accepts a more radical biblical criticism. As Denis Nineham asks in *The Myth of God Incarnate*, do we have enough well-substantiated and detailed historical knowledge of Jesus of Nazareth to be able to talk with confidence of his unique moral and spritual perfection, once all dogma has been stripped away.[4] Here again, we do not have to capitulate to a radical and unwarranted historical scepticism nor need we deny that there emerges from the Gospels a figure of impressive moral integrity and spiritual power. Nevertheless, none of the three positions just outlined seems to be an adequate basis for any claim as to the unique saviorhood of Jesus. Jesus becomes, not the answer to religious pluralism, but only another aspect of the same problem.

4. Is there any other possible position to take? Certainly, if Jesus was and is what the creeds of the church assert, then he is unique in a much more fundamental sense. The question now concerns the experiential basis of the fundamental theological claims. Will Herberg remarks that "Exodus-Sinai is, for the Jew, the

---

[4] John Hick, ed., *The Myth of God Incarnate*, pp. 186ff.

interpretive center of redemptive history, as Calvary is for the Christian."⁵ We, therefore, turn to the cross to see if we can find the clue to the nature and significance of God's saving activity in Jesus. Why is this death in particular central for the salvation of the whole human race?

Before we rush in with pat theological answers, we still need to ask another prior question. Do we need to be saved and if so, from what? It seems rather pointless to present Jesus as the answer to questions which we are not even asking or the resolver of problems which we do not acknowledge that we have. In what sense, then, has Jesus made a fundamental difference in regard to suffering, error, sin, and death as well as making possible a life more abundant than any other figure in history? By a difference here is not meant simply a new way of thinking about things, though that is included, but rather a difference at the practical level where men and women have to meet these threats and cope with them. Again, on the surface, it is not easy to see how he has done this.

Has Jesus saved us from suffering? In one obvious sense, he has not. Christians continue to suffer in the flesh: bodily weakness, disease, injury through accident, mental disorder, nervous breakdown, mental strain of one kind or another, the sorrow of bereavement, and so forth. Christians are not saved here in the sense of rendered immune to all these things. Despite the claims of faith-healers, this statement must stand. Nor is it acceptable to say that all Christians who are not miraculously healed or "saved" from these things in the present owe their tragic fate to lack of faith or importunate prayer. We need only remember in passing the apostle Paul's thorn in the flesh.

Has Jesus saved us from death? Again, in the obvious sense, the answer is no. Men and women continue to die a biological death as they did in New Testament times. It is appointed unto men once to die (Heb. 9:27), and there seems no evidence that this law has been cancelled since the coming of Jesus.

Has Jesus saved us from inadequate knowledge of God? Again no: We only see baffling reflections in a mirror now.

Has Jesus saved us from sin? At this point, many Christians would

---

⁵Herberg, *Judaism and Modern Man,* p. 251.

hazard a more positive answer. What Jesus did for us on the cross has guaranteed the forgiveness of God and given us assurance against his punishment or final separation from God. Furthermore, by a living relationship to Jesus Christ crucified and risen, we mysteriously receive the power to live without fear and anxiety, to rest in the love of God, and in part, at least, to reflect such love and forgiveness to at least some of our neighbors. Liberation theologians might also claim that Jesus gives us the strength to fight against unjust and oppressive political and economic structures. Yet it is obvious here also that the Christian believer is not wholly saved here and now from the power and reality of sin. Sin may have been overcome "in principle" but in the struggle of daily living, the Christian knows that the battle against the "Old Adam" is still real, even if his faith gives him the confidence that he will not finally capitulate to the enemy. With Paul, we press on but we have not yet finally attained. (See Phil. 3:12.)

It seems, therefore, that Jesus has not saved us from suffering, death, error, and sin in any straightforward sense. The Christian still has to live and cope with the first three. Even in the case of sin, apart from those who hold to the reality of Christian perfection here and now, and even they have to make some important qualifications, the Christian still has to do battle, even if the believer has the confidence that the grace of God will guarantee ultimate and final victory. If the Christian is going to substantiate his claim that Jesus is the Savior, then it needs to be shown that he has done something decisive on our behalf which we could not do for ourselves and that he has made a decisive and major difference to the way we live our lives and die our deaths. What exactly is this something which Jesus and no one else has done or could do? In what follows we shall be concerned chiefly with the answer which Christian faith gives to this question. How this is related to claims made by other religions will be deferred for later consideration.

One of the criticisms often made against the classic claims for Jesus, whether the two-nature God-man of Chalcedon, or the affirmation of the unique saviorhood, is that this makes him a stranger or an alien breaking into this world from the "outside." Jesus Christ is a kind of celestial divinity from outer space with no real roots in the mundane history of which the rest of us are an integral part. His unique saviorhood removes him so far from ordinary human existence that, despite the formal emphasis of the creeds on his true humanity, in fact he is not man at all but deity in human disguise. Whether this is a fair characterization of the creedal, theological, and devotional tradition of Christianity is for the moment beside the point. That such docetism, openly confessed or only implied, has played a significant role in Christian history can hardly be denied. The consequence in our own day has been to play down the discontinuity between Jesus and the history which preceded him. The renewed awareness of his Jewishness and the depth of his roots in Israel's history has only strengthened this tendency. In recent Christian theology, we need only cite such scholars as J. A. T. Robinson, G. W. H. Lampe, and Wolfhart Pannenberg, to name only three.

Robinson starts from the premise that "if Jesus as the Christ is to be our man, he must be one of us: *totus in nostris*, completely part of our world."[6] Dr. Lampe warns us against overemphasizing the radical break with the past involved in the appearance of Jesus. The emphasis should be on the continuity of God's creative work in the process of cosmic evolution: "We should try to set the process of the Christ-event within the perspective of a continuous process of which we can discern neither the beginning nor the end and to avoid the idea that in Christ God has broken into that process in which he is always immanent and radically altered his own relationship to his human creation."[7] Without at present going into detail about Pannenberg's theology as such, he can be classed with the above two scholars in the sense that he too does not believe that the revelation of God can be sought and found in the isolated person of Jesus.[8] "History is the most comprehensive horizon of Christian theology. All theological questions and answers are meaningful only within the framework of the history which God has with humanity and through humanity with his whole creation."[9] Any doctrine of the Incarnation, therefore, must be judged on the basis of Jesus' connection with Israel's history of promise.[10] It is noteworthy also that John B. Cobb, Jr., in his recent book[11] begins with the universal Logos acting in revelation and

[6]J. A. T. Robinson, *The Human Face of God* (London: S. C. M.; Philadelphia: Westminster, 1973), p. 38.

[7]G. W. H. Lampe, *God As Spirit*, 1977.

[8]W. Pannenberg, *Basic Questions in Theology* (Philadelphia: Fortress Press, 1971), 1:67.

[9]Ibid., p. 15.

[10]Ibid., p. 25.

[11]J. B. Cobb, Jr., *Christ in a Pluralistic Age* (Philadelphia: Westminster, 1967).

redemption throughout the whole of history. Jesus of Nazareth is a particularly powerful and effective actualization of the saving activity of God through his creative Logos. He nowhere suggests that Jesus is the only or exclusive mediation of that saving activity.

In the light of these comments, any claim to a "unique" saviorhood of Jesus would have to be developed in the context of universal history and on the assumption that in some sense God's saving activity was at work in that history, even prior to the coming of Jesus. As all these scholars admit, the basic theological question then becomes: What is there about the saving activity of Jesus which is distinctive and peculiar to him? Or put another way, in what sense, if any, is Jesus now normative, that is, final in significance and authority for an understanding of how God works "savingly" in the whole of history and will work in the future and what are the implications of this for the attitude of Christians to Jews and to the other world religions? We have seen that there is good reason to believe, even on the basis of the most radical New Testament criticism, that Jesus saw himself as acting in the name of the God of Israel to summon men and women to repentance, faith, and obedience to the will of God mediated through the past history of Israel and now confronting the present generation with a final offer of salvation before the end of the age and the eschatological denouement of the divinely established kingdom of God.

There also appear to be strong grounds for the assertion that Jesus saw this crucial decision for and against God to be closely, indeed decisively linked, with their attitude towards his own Person, whether in acceptance or rejection. There seems to be no basis for thinking that Jesus denied or questioned the reality of God's saving action in the history of Israel which preceded his own ministry. If this is so, then Judaism's witness to the character and activity of God would remain valid. What, then, was new and decisive about the life and death of Jesus other than his proclamation of the imminent kingdom and God's final offer of salvation through him as the eschatological prophet? Would the Jew, who has responded to the offer of God's salvation through the Torah, not be "saved," even if he did not recognize God's last appeal in and through Jesus? The New Testament appears to say no to this question, at least as far as the Jewish contemporaries of Jesus were concerned. The decisive question for the New Testament is not obedience to the Torah but to Jesus: "There is no other name under heaven whereby men must be saved" (Acts 4:12).

If the New Testament followers of Jesus had been asked what the decisive difference was, it seems certain that they would have said the resurrection. The bearing of this "event" on the claim that Jesus is the Son, or the Savior, or the Lord obviously depends on the way we understand the resurrection. In order to justify the claim that God vindicated Jesus by raising him from the dead—thus showing him to be the victor over sin, suffering, and death—some conviction as to the reality of his triumph would seem to be required. If Jesus rose from the dead "bodily" and is alive now for evermore "after death," then it could be plausibly argued that this makes Jesus unique. Nothing comparable for any other religious leader can in fact be found. This would reinforce the claim that Jesus is the Savior in a way quite unparalleled and enable the Christian to confront religious pluralism in the confidence that no other religious leader or teacher could possibly be given the same status. "I would submit that if, at this point, we fall back into a dichotomy of inward and outward, making the resurrection only an event in the internal spiritual history of the disciples and not an event in the history of Jesus and of the world, then we abandon the possiblity of claiming that Jesus is the clue to history."[12]

If, however, the resurrection of Jesus is demythologized or reinterpreted in such a way as to eliminate the possibility of his being alive with God on the other side of death, then the resurrection ceases to be evidence in the same way for the normative character of the saving activity of God in Jesus. If Jesus was raised from the dead as an historical event which has already occurred rather than a waiting for the general resurrection at the end of the age, then vis-à-vis historic Judaism, a radically new manifestation of the power of Israel's God has now taken place. Again there is no precedent in the history of Israel for such an event as the resurrection, except perhaps the translation of Elijah. Judaism, therefore, has rejected not only the Christian affirmation of the messiahship of Jesus but also his resurrection.

This apparently clear-cut difference between Judaism and Christianity takes on another appearance, however, in the light of the

---

[12]Lesslie Newbigin, *The Finality of Christ* (London: S.C.M., 1969), p. 85.

way some biblical scholars have dealt with the resurrection. If the resurrection is only one way of interpreting the significance of the cross (Bultmann); if dead men, even Jesus, cannot live again after death (Kaufman); if it only symbolizes a psychological change in the disciples (vision and hallucination theories and Tillich's restorationism); if it only symbolizes the power of God in the future to transform earthly society into the kingdom of God here on earth (some theologies of hope, perhaps Moltmann himself, and some forms of liberation theology); if the resurrection is to be identified completely with the presence of Jesus in and to the believing community (Peter Hodgson and G. W. H. Lampe); if the resurrection only expresses the recovered existential courage of the disciples and the banishment of fear and anxiety in relation to their future: then in all these interpretations the resurrection can no longer be cited as evidence for an objective victory of Jesus over the power of death. Jesus, of course, can still be cited as the mysterious source of the transformation of human lives. This, however, is not something distinctively new in the history of religions. It is considerably less decisive evidence of the unique lordship and saviorhood of Jesus than what may be called the classical or traditional view of the resurrection.

As long as Christians have the historical and theological nerve to affirm the resurrection in the sense given to it by Newbigin, there is a uniqueness about God's action in Jesus which cannot be paralleled elsewhere, either in Judaism or in the non-Christian religions.

The above remarks are relevant also to the suggestions made by Schillebeeckx in his recent book *Jesus*.[13] He desires to substitute the idea of exaltation for resurrection. The advantage of this from his point of view is that one is freed from making the resurrection dependent either on the empty tomb or on supernaturally given veridical visions. "But with or without resurrection, in no way does the affirmation of belief in Jesus' being taken up into heaven depend on a possible empty tomb or on appearances: both these last presuppose belief in Jesus' assumption into heaven after his death, whether after a sojourn in the realm of the dead or 'from off the cross'."[14] Exaltation, that is the return of Jesus to God in triumph, becomes an expression of

---

[13]E. Schillebeeckx, *Jesus* (New York: Seabury, 1978), pp. 516ff.
[14]Ibid., p. 538.

faith, rooted in a conversion experience of some kind. This faith is the source of the confidence that Jesus is alive with God and that God has vindicated both his mission and his person. This idea seems to require some kind of psychological miracle after the shock of the crucifixion but at least it does not seem to involve such a radical breach of the natural order and its regular patterns as the traditional view of the "bodily" resurrection of Jesus. At least, so Schillebeeckx seems to think.

To the degree that this view is accepted, no straightforward appeal to the resurrection of Jesus can be made in defense of the unique saviorhood. If one wants to hold to this latter view, the grounds for it would have to be found elsewhere.

All this in no way implies that the hope of victory over death is absent either from later Judaism or from the non-Christian religions. The Jewish anticipation of the general resurrection at the end of the age or the Greek view of immortality both imply a confidence in some real (that is, ultimate) victory over death. Neither of these positions resembles the radical, secular this-worldliness which is supposed to characterize our era. Nevertheless, there is a difference between Jewish and Platonic hopes and the conviction that death and victory over it have been demonstrated in historical actuality. Certainly, as we have seen, the Christian lives by faith and hope, too, and victory over death in the full sense is still in the future for the believer. Yet Christian hope takes on a different quality of assurance and confidence because God has raised Jesus from the dead. Of course, if Jesus be not raised, the Christian is in exactly the same position as the Jew and the Platonist, and many today would say exactly that. Yet Christian faith has always been persuaded that this is not the case because of a unique and unparalleled act of God in raising Jesus from the dead.

Yet it is also the case that the cross, considered as a separate event distinct from but not separated from the resurrection, has also been given a special, indeed, a unique role for the reconciliation of men and women with God. In what sense can this be defended in the context of religious pluralism on a world scale? As we have already seen, the reality of God's forgiveness, in response to human penitence, faith, and obedience, can hardly be questioned as a central emphasis in the Old Testament and later Judaism. Few Christians would be willing to deny outright to the Jew any experience of divine forgiveness. In this case, what more, if anything, is needed? What sort of forgiveness has been secured through the death of Jesus which the Jew could not already have through obedience to the Torah? As far as the non-Christians are concerned, is the situation anything different in principle? Are Hinduism and Buddhism totally devoid of the notions of grace and divine forgiveness? And if these ideas are dependent on some concept of sin from which men and women need to be delivered, then are these other religions also devoid of the knowledge of sin in the sense which a Christian would give to this term? If they are devoid of such knowledge, then can we speak of forgiveness?

Our contention so far has been that if Jesus was really raised from the dead through the power of God, then this is a fact of decisive importance in any claims for his uniqueness and finality in relation to the human situation. Yet even this does not do full justice to the whole gospel. It is also the case that the cross, considered as a separate event distinct from but not divorced from the resurrection, has also been given a special—indeed, unique—role in the reconciliation of men and women with God. Yet can this once-for-all death be given this status when placed in the widest possible context? Why the death of Jesus rather than the death of Socrates or of Mahatma Gandhi? Can any such distinction be made between these deaths? The scandal of particularity seems even more scandalous here than in the case of the resurrection. From the New Testament onwards, it can hardly be doubted that the majority of Christians have taken Acts 4:12 as an affirmation about Jesus Christ as universal Lord and Savior and this, of course, has included both the death and the resurrection. "There is no salvation in anyone else at all, for there is no other name under heaven granted to men by which we may receive salvation"(Acts 4:12, NEB).

J. A. T. Robinson has argued that this has been a misleading and unfortunately exclusive interpretation of the text. He contends that the context is not that of comparative religion but of faith healing.[15] We must certainly agree that the writer of Acts did not have in mind Hinduism, Buddhism, and so forth. On the other hand, he can hardly have been unaware of the extraordinary mixture of religious faiths and cults in the world of his day. The issue in Acts 4:12, according to Robinson, is not an exclusive claim for the saving power of Jesus over

[15]J. A. T. Robinson, *Truth Is Two-Eyed* (London: S. C. M., 1979).

all other possible saviors. It is rather a question of the source of his healing power and whether the apostles are working miracles of healing through some innate divine power of their own. It may be admitted that this is a possible exegesis but one wonders why such sweeping language had to be used if it were only a question of whether Jesus received his power from God or from some other source.

The words "no other name under heaven" certainly seem to suggest a universality in the claim, even if the universality is limited to the world and the religions which came within the horizon of the author of Acts at that time. However, even if we concede Dr. Robinson's point, that does not solve the larger issue. The answer to this does not depend on finding a text or texts which set the claim to Jesus' unique saviorhood in antithesis to all the other religions of which we have such an increased and detailed knowledge today. The question is whether the power of Jesus to save can in fact be paralleled elsewhere, whether in the ancient world or now.

We have also claimed that the attempt to defend the "decisiveness" of Jesus apart from any doctrine of the Incarnation is doomed to failure. There is nothing sacrosanct about a word and Farmer's "inhistorization" might well be substituted for incarnation. It all depends on how the language is used and what we intend to mean by it. The heart of the matter is that Christian faith has claimed that in Jesus we meet not only a prophet, a proxy, an ambassador, a messenger from God, but God personally and savingly active in a unique way and here again the cross is central. Unique here means that no other person in human history can be substituted for Jesus or can accomplish or has accomplished what he did.

Furthermore, we have contended that this uniqueness, one without an equal, resides not only in what Jesus said, but also in what he did and what God did in and through him. The debate about divinity is not only an intellectual problem about natures, important as this may be for any well-rounded understanding of who Jesus was and is.[16] It must also be concerned about salvation at the point where particular individual men and women experience the power of salvation.

We have also maintained that salvation in the New Testament

---

[16]For a discussion of the functional-ontological debate in Christology, see R. F. Aldwinckle, *More than Man,* pp. 54ff.; and R. H. Fuller, *The Foundations of New Testament Christology* (London: Lutterworth, 1965), pp. 247ff.

means not only a restored right relationship to God in a general sense but specifically a deliverance from death, suffering, error, or obscured vision as well as from sin. This deliverance is experienced both here and now and in the future when God's purpose is consummated for the individual, for mankind as a whole and indeed for the total cosmic process. In technical language, it is proleptic and eschatological in the realized purpose of God. The death of Jesus is not only a temporal manifestation of the love of God in a man but also a divine action which has permanently changed the status of all men and women before God, whether their attitude is one of faith and commitment or of unbelief and rejection.

In addition, the resurrection signifies a real victory over death in the sense that Jesus lives after death and that he genuinely and really, in his divine-human person, communicated with his disciples from beyond physical death. All alternative explanations of this event of resurrection (hallucinations, visions, veridical or not, the restoration of faith after the crucifixion through a psychological miracle in the disciples, and so forth) fail to do justice to the New Testament records and the sense of joy and victory which pervades all the documents. In other words, we wish to defend a strong sense both of incarnation and of uniqueness.

What does all this imply for the significance of the death of Jesus? Here again we can try to resolve the problem by interpreting the death of Jesus as a vivid illustration of the fact that the sin of man causes God to suffer and that God has further reacted by showing through the death of this man Jesus his participation in the suffering which our sin has produced. This view would give great importance to the death of Jesus but not as the indispensable condition of our salvation, or at least of the salvation of the whole race, past, present, and future. Some would contend, of course, that it is a worthier conception of God to see the unity of the divine and human as a universal feature of the whole of history rather than as an exceptional and isolated achievement of one man. "Is not an incarnation of God from eternity a truer one than an incarnation limited to a point of time?"[17] This question of Strauss seems to be an influential factor in the attempts of G. W. H. Lampe,

---

[17]David Strauss, *The Life of Jesus Critically Examined.* Trans. M. Evans (New York, 1860), 2:895.

Don Cupitt, and others to develop a Spirit-Christology which does not need to make what they call exclusive claims for Christ. It also seems to be a powerful influence on many of the contributors to *The Myth of God Incarnate* and its sequels.

There is no space in this brief study for a survey of all the various theories or models of the atonement which have occurred in Christian history. Yet there seems little doubt that for most Christians, the death of Christ has been seen as effecting an objective change between God and the human race as well as a subjective change in the believer who opens himself or herself in faith to the power and grace of God who brought about this change. Professor George Rupp, in his fascinating study of Christological typologies and their implications for our attitudes to other faiths, has argued powerfully for accepting the collapse of the former absolute dualism between God and the world, the supernatural and the natural.[18] We are told we can no longer take such a dualism seriously nor can we develop a doctrine of salvation which depends on a human hope for a transhistorical fulfillment of human destiny beyond this space-time world. On this view, we cannot speak of the cross as a once-for-all saving event rooted in God's eternal decree as explanatory of what the death of Christ has accomplished.

Rupp's processive Christology is strongly oriented towards a revised Hegelianism. He raises the question as to whether God can exist as self-conscious independently of those finite centers of consciousness which are integral to the ongoing cosmic process. His answer to this appears to be no. God cannot exist or be self-conscious in this sense. Christian trinitarian doctrine has, of course, always denied this and insisted on the reality of the triune God apart from the world, although not unrelated to it. We are not surprised, therefore, when he admits that "the most promising Western resources available to contemporary theology for conceptualizing the universal teleological process are the philosophies of Hegel and Whitehead."[19] At least, we know where we stand.

It is interesting to compare Rupp's judgment on this issue with the

---

[18]G. Rupp, *Christologies and Cultures* (The Hague: Mouton, 1974), p. 198; *Beyond Existentialism and Zen* (New York: Oxford University Press, 1979), p. 29.

[19]Rupp, *Beyond Existentialism and Zen* (New York: Oxford Univeristy Press, 1979), p. 29.

opinion of another distinguished Hegel scholar.[20] "The ordinary believer," says Taylor, "then as now cannot escape the feeling that the sense of his faith is being radically if subtly altered. This in spite of Hegel's protestations of orthodoxy."[21] He goes on to say that the instinct of Christian piety is dead right on this point. "In Hegel's system, God cannot give to man—neither in creation nor in revelation nor in salvation through sending His Son."[22] Again, "lacking the idea of God as giver, Hegel cannot accommodate the relations of God and man as they must be for Christian faith. He has no place for grace in the properly Christian sense."[23] He admits as valid Karl Barth's claim that "Hegel, in making the dialectical method of logic the essential nature of God, made impossible the knowledge of the actual dialectic of grace, which has its foundation in the freedom of God."[24]

Barth's essay on Hegel is remarkably sympathetic in many ways despite this final strong adverse judgment on the Hegelian philosophy as a whole. We realize that the debate about the right reading and interpretation of Hegel will no doubt continue. Nevertheless, in the light of this diversity of opinion among Hegel scholars,[25] we are more confident to question Rupp's judgment that the philosophies of Hegel and Whitehead provide the most useful conceptuality for doing Christian theology in the future. We shall not try to justify a similar judgment in regard to Whitehead but refer the reader to recent discussions of process philosophy.[26]

Yet despite this claimed irrevocable collapse of the ancient dualism, there is, however, no possibility for the modern world to return to the primitive orientation to a single cosmos to which we are organically related through myth and rite. The only way for us is to find God, in a revised meaning of that term, in the ongoing natural and

[20]Charles Taylor, *Hegel* (London and New York: Cambridge University Press, 1977).

[21]Ibid., p. 492.

[22]Ibid., p. 493.

[23]Ibid.

[24]Karl Barth, *From Rousseau to Ritschl* (London: S.C.M., 1959), p. 304.

[25]An interesting and penetrating discussion of Hegel's philosophy in relation to Christology may also be noted in James Yerkes, *The Christology of Hegel,* AAR Dissertation Series 23 (Chico, CA: Scholars Press, 1978).

[26]R. F. Aldwinckle, *More than Man,* pp. 270ff; Colin E. Gunton, *Becoming and Being* (New York: Oxford University Press, 1978), part one.

historical process. Samsara is nirvana. In Western terms, God's being is not only expressed in the process. It is the process. Pannenberg's statement about "the identity of God's being with the coming of the Kingdom" is apparently quoted with approval.[27] Pannenberg's concept of an eschatological ontology has difficulties of its own into which we shall not enter here.

Rupp's comment, however, is that "in reference to life on earth the kingdom or rule of God and therefore God Himself is a yet to be fully attained destiny."[28] Is this any advance on the idea of a growing and developing God of which we had many examples in the nineteenth century and early in the twentieth?[29] It is clear that if these are the premises from which we start, the uniqueness and finality of Jesus can only be affirmed, if affirmed at all, in a very attenuated sense. The very notion of a distinctive and unique act of God is ruled out because God as an infinite, personal, and self-conscious agent, prior to the emergence of the world-process, has been abandoned. Religious pluralism must, therefore, remain as a permanent element of an ongoing process which has neither beginning nor end. God can neither will the Incarnation nor some future fulfillment of his purpose, for such would imply a conscious purpose envisaged before the world was and pursued through a divine activity which is constant in its purpose but infinitely adaptable to changes introduced into the process by acts of human freedom. In the last analysis, we are on our own and God becomes a "lure," not the Almighty Creator and Redeemer who can realize his goal when heaven and earth have passed away.

Of course, this is a dualism in the sense previously defined. Whether it has finally collapsed is by no means a self-evident truth. It might just be that beyond the process, there is and always has been and always will be the eternal God and Father of our Lord Jesus Christ, not Aristotle's *thinking upon thought* or Hegel's *Begriff*. At least we believe that the problem of religious pluralism cannot be satisfactory handled by invoking assumptions which get rid of the living and transcendent God from the start.[30]

---

[27]Ibid.

[28]Rupp, *Christologies and Cultures,* p. 198.

[29]H. P. Owen, *Concepts of Deity* (London: Macmillan, 1971), pp. 49ff.

[30]In view of the somewhat sweeping statements in the last paragraph, further brief comment would seem to be in order. Despite the frequent assertions about the "end of theism," the fact remains that theism, like Charles II, remains an unconscionable time

It follows from Rupp's basic assumptions that the death of Christ can in no way be interpreted as a once-for-all divine act effective for the reconciliation of God and man both in time and eternity. We shall have to see the death solely as the means by which certain values are created and continue to shape the ongoing historical process. This may be the only option to modern enlightenment, but it is certainly far removed from the way in which most Christians have envisaged the significance of the death of Jesus.

In striking contrast to Rupp is the point of view expressed by Geoffrey Wainwright in a recent, fresh approach to systematic theology in relation to worship, doctrine, and life.[31] He correctly points out that "the most characteristic function of Christ in Christian worship, then, is understood to be mediation: he mediates human worship to God and he mediates salvation from God to humanity."[32] The more closely God is involved in the total Christ-event, the more urgent becomes the questions as to whether God could die in the death of Jesus, whether God is impassible, and whether Jesus is the only Mediator of salvation in the sense ascribed to this role in Christian worship. We confine ourselves here simply to the question about the death of Jesus. Wainwright again correctly observed that John Hick, in putting God at the center and questioning Jesus' role as unique mediator, also eliminates at the same time the unique significance of his death. "It is noticeable that Hick's own view of humanity, sin and salvation does not appear to require an 'objective' work of redemption

a-dying. Nor is the present climate of opinion as one-sided as many suppose. The following list of books is indicative of a decided trend against Hegelian and processive views. (See the bibliography for publishing information.)

A. Farrer, *Finite and Infinite; Faith and Speculation.*

H. P. Owen, *The Christian Knowledge of God; Concepts of Deity.*

R. Swinburne, *The Coherence of Theism; The Existence of God.*

C. Stead, *Divine Substance.*

Colin E. Gunton, *Becoming and Being.*

J. Macquarrie, *Thinking about God.*

Macquarrie is obviously concerned to incorporate processive elements into his theism but it is still theism. It is more difficult to classify John Hick in view of later developments in his thinking, but even he seems unwilling to abandon entirely the idea of God as existent and truly transcendent as personal agent to the natural and historical process. It is clear that the end is not yet and the last word has not been said.

[31] Rupp, *Christologies,* p. 195.

[32] G. Wainwright, *Doxology* (New York: Oxford University Press, 1980).

after the manner of most theories of the atonement in Christian theology."[33]

It is possible for Hick, as Wainwright observes, to retain an Abelardian view of the atonement and to insist on God's loving participation in human existence to the point of complete self-giving and death. This gives us a Jesus whose death is unique in the sense of giving us an actualized paradigm of unselfish love which in turn is seen as the love of God. However unique and central the death of Christ becomes on this view for human salvation as the growth of faith in and responsive love to God, it is not an objective divine act which changes once-for-all the God-man relationship apart from the subjective change which takes place in the individual believer. This understanding of atonement would retain uniqueness in a limited sense, a uniqueness which transcends the "exclusive-inclusive or culture-bound imperialist alternatives."[34] It would also allow some version of "anonymous Christianity" which we shall discuss in more detail later.

The crucial question now is whether this view expresses all that Christians have believed about the death of Jesus as the all-sufficient ground of our salvation and the divinely provided condition for our forgiveness and reconciliation. Can the so-called "objective" models of atonement, as set forth by the ransom theories (Aulen) or satisfaction theologies (Anselm) or substitution (Luther and Calvin) be restated in such a way as to meet the objections often made and yet retain the uniqueness of the death of Jesus as an objective divine act through which the demands of God's holiness and the expression of God's self-giving love have both been adequately actualized in the death of this Jesus? This depends on the way in which the "objective" aspects of the atonement are understood.

F. W. Dillistone concludes "that no strictly penal theory of the atonement can be expected to carry conviction in the world of the twentieth century."[35] He has in mind the way in which certain concepts of law and guilt dominate the framework of Calvin's theology. T. W.

---

[33] Ibid., p. 66.

[34] Ibid., p. 68.

[35] F. W. Dillistone, *The Christian Understanding of Atonement* (London: Nisbet, 1968), p. 214.

Manson has criticized the juridical theories for watering down the idea of repentance and, therefore, requiring conditions other than repentance for receiving the free forgiveness of God.[36] "It is rather that for Judaism repentance is something which man ought to do: For Christianity it is something which man can do, because Christ has made it possible."[37] Or again: "God does not acquit the guilty, he issues an amnesty or free pardon."[38]

We agree that the Pauline doctrine of justification does in fact transcend merely juridical categories. Nevertheless, all this does not really face the issue as to whether God ever punishes or whether there is a penal element in the death of Jesus. It is true that the New Testament never speaks in so many words of God punishing Jesus. This, however, still leaves open the question as to whether God in Christ freely chooses to participate, not only in our human existence but himself bears the punishment which justly follows human sin. This does not mean that all human suffering is penal, but it does imply that some suffering is and that Jesus' identification with that situation is God's own identification with that situation. Any adequate doctrine of atonement must avoid at all costs a dualism in the divine nature which identifies the principle of holiness and justice with God the Father and love with Jesus as the Son. We must hold to Vincent Taylor's statement that "In no saying of His [Jesus] is there any suggestion of opposition or antagonism; His will and that of the Father are one."[39]

It follows from all this that the uniqueness of the death of Jesus will depend upon the reality of God's action and presence in Jesus. In technical language Incarnation and Soteriology cannot be separated. Nor can Soteriology be developed in independence of the doctrine of Incarnation. Whether Jesus' action, including his death, was saving depends on how we consider the relation of Jesus to the Father and therefore, in the last analysis, on how we think of his person. A radical revision of some aspects of the juridical theories of the atonement does not necessarily require the abandonment of the doctrine of the Incarnation and of the unique saving power of both the death and the

---

[36]T. W. Manson, *On Paul and John* (London: S. C. M., 1963).
[37]Ibid., p. 56.
[38]Ibid.
[39]Vincent Taylor, *Jesus and His Sacrifice* (London: Macmillan, 1937), p. 256.

resurrection of Jesus. If we approach this question from the perspective of Christian worship and experience, there would seem to be no question as to where the majority of Christians have stood on this issue. We shall explore later the implications of all this for the attitude of Christians to the men and women of other faiths and of other religious traditions.

Chapter Four

Christian Faith and Human Nature: A False Diagnosis?

We have considered the unique saviorhood of Jesus as Christian faith discerns it and have also argued that it depends not only upon what Jesus said but what he did, and the most important action of all was the setting of his face to go to Jerusalem. The cross is an integral and indispensable element in the saving work of God on the basis of which we are restored to a right relationship with God both in time and eternity. Whatever view we hold of the cross and its significance, it is also clear that to present the crucified Jesus as the unique Savior is to assume that human beings need to be saved and in a specific sense. Sin and guilt need to be dealt with, and not only by persons on the human interpersonal level but by God. Only if this is both possible and actual can we be delivered from self-centeredness, that freedom which is perfect bondage, into the glorious freedom of the children of God. This emphasis on the cross does not mean, of course, that the death of Jesus can be isolated from his life as a whole or from the resurrection which follows it. Nevertheless, the death of Jesus has always been understood by Christians as an integral element of the divine action by which we are saved.

What, then, shall we say to Don Cupitt's suggestion that Christian anthropology is a time-conditioned and, therefore, relative diagnosis of the human situation?[1] He is rejecting the whole sin-redemption scheme of Christian thinking, whether Protestant or Catholic, though he reserves his more vigorous condemnation for Protestant anthropology. The whole idea of man as a sinner, impotent to save himself because of the bondage of the will, seems to be repugnant to him. Apart from his personal feelings, however, his main objection is that this is a culturally-conditioned diagnosis of the human situation and human need and therefore cannot be invoked as true for men and women in other situations or in the context of other cultures and religions. Any attempt to present Christ as a universal Savior, on the basis of this kind of anthropology, is doomed to failure from the start. The cure simply does not apply where the "disease" does not exist.

It is important to recognize that Cupitt is not only attacking the theological forms which the bibilical doctrine of sin has taken and which the church later developed in a variety of ways. He is not concerned with questions such as: Was there a historic fall and in what sense? How is sin transmitted and what effect has it had on the image of God in man? He is not for or against Augustinianism or the Reformation recovery of Augustinian insights, and so forth. These questions seem to be peripheral to his main charge. What really annoys him is the suggestion that man cannot save himself apart from justification by faith in Christ. This, according to Cupitt, excludes all non-Christians from the possiblity of salvation and this is the real rock of offense. Although he makes only a passing reference to modern Protestant theologians, he is obviously not partial to revised versions of the traditional anthropology which still leave intact the basic assumption that the human situation everywhere shows men and women to be impotent to gain salvation, whether in or outside Christ.

The substitution of alienation and estrangement or separation from the "ground of his being" for the old-fashioned language of sin seems no more congenial to Cupitt. Paul may have said "We have all sinned and fallen short of the glory of God" but this is a culturally-conditioned statement. In a Buddhist or Hindu or other religious context, it makes no sense. Is this, in fact, so? What are the empirical facts of human experience or are these value-laden and, therefore, not facts at all except from a Christian perspective? We are back with a certain kind of relativism which denies the plausibility of any universal

---

[1]D. Cupitt, *The Leap of Reason* (London: Sheldon Press, 1976), p. 125.

statements about the human situation or human nature as such. Can one penetrate beneath the religious language to certain aspects of human existence to which the religious metaphors point? Is phenomenology any help here? Is the concept of sin absent from the non-Christian religions?

Cupitt is presumably not denying the empirical facts of the sad and tragic story of mankind. Violence, strife, injustice, hatred, insensitivity to moral values, falsehood and double-talk, bondage to uncontrolled passion and sheer materialism, not as a philosophical doctrine but as a day to day ignoring of spiritual values, all this is a part of the human story which it would in fact be difficult to ignore. Cupitt would appear to be denying, therefore, a particular interpretation of this state of affairs in terms of sin, original or actual or both. No doubt he would regard the very language of sin as value-charged and therefore suspect.

Now again, it has to be admitted that if sin is defined religiously, not only as moral evil but as the breach of a personal relationship with a holy and loving God in the Judeo-Christian sense, then where such a view of God is absent, such a definition of sin would make no sense. This would appear to be the case, for example, in regard to Hinayana Buddhism. If salvation is defined as the restoration of a right relationship with such a God, then one could hardly speak of salvation in this sense in a context from which such an idea of God is absent. The question then becomes whether a Christian should be willing to accept a thoroughgoing relativism in the field of anthropology as well as in the areas of Christology or of differing views as to the nature of the transcendent, the ultimate reality, the ground of our being or whatever other language we care to use about the final mystery.

Should the Christian give up any attempt to bring the non-Christian to an awareness of sin in the biblical sense? In putting it this way, many assumptions are being made. For example, the claim is implied by those who give a negative answer that the Christian view of sin is quite unintelligible outside the Judeo-Christian context. One could always reply to this kind of charge by citing the evidence of the way in which the Christian gospel has shown its power to win adherents from all historical and cultural situations.[2] This may not

---

[2] Kenneth Scott Latourette's monumental *History of Christianity* could be mentioned in this connection.

convince those who are persuaded on other grounds that the Christian diagnosis of the human situation is relative, time-conditioned, and of only limited application. It does show, however, that there is no built-in impossiblity in other cultures and religions to the acceptance of the Christian gospel and its diagnosis of the human situation and the fundamental needs of human beings as such. Nor again can it be taken for granted that the idea of divine grace is completely meaningless outside the Christian context. We shall discuss this issue later in regard to the specific case of what Otto calls "India's religion of grace." To answer the questions which Cupitt raises, the following issues must be faced:

1. Is there a distinctively Christian analysis of human existence and is it relevant to the human situation in any time and place?
2. How do we escape from a relativism which forbids truth-claims in relation to specific theological analyses or to once-for-all unrepeatable historical events?

It is obvious that these issues have a direct bearing upon Christology and the claims which Christians make for Jesus Christ. For the present, however, we shall leave that issue on one side and concentrate upon the Christian doctrine of man/woman and its diagnosis of the human situation and our fundamental needs.

It is again obvious that if we look at this matter from the broadest historical perspective, there is in fact not one doctrine of man/woman which is identical in all religions and cultures any more than there is one concept of God. Throughout the history of Christianity until the eighteenth century, it was assumed that the Jewish-Christian anthropology was indeed a description and an interpretation of the human situation as such. Individual thinkers here and there might have been aware of the wider issues but the main stream of the tradition was in no doubt that it was speaking about man/woman as such. The only non-Christian religion, with which Christianity came into direct contact, was Islam and that was a Semitic faith. There was no radical break, therefore, with the Hebrew and Semitic anthropology, whatever new elements Christianity might want to add to this. Only after the Enlightenment and in the nineteenth century in particular did Christian thinkers and others become vividly and existentially aware, not only of differing views of the universe and of the transcendent but also of radically different views of the nature of human existence.[3] This is the situation in which we find ourselves at the present time.

It is clear that if we are to make claims for Jesus as *the* Savior, we need to be able to show enough empirical evidence to back the further claim that men and women need to be saved. Further, they need to be saved in the specific sense which this word has in the Christian context, that is, victory over sin, suffering, and death on the basis of a restored right relationship to God where again the concept of God is interpreted in the light of his reality and presence in Jesus Christ. To show this, however, is difficult to achieve as Christian anthropology cannot be treated as an isolated and separate matter. It only makes sense against a Christian view of nature, man, and God and the relationships which obtain between them. We seem to be back where we began. Non-Christians have to be convinced of the basic truth of the Christian faith as a whole before they can know and understand exactly from what and to what they need to be saved. This, however, it will be objected, is to lead us back to the exclusiveness and arrogance of the Christian claim that Jesus is the way, the truth, and the life. As Father Copleston admits: "Still, it seems to be true that there is indeed a sense in which the 'meaning' of the language of faith eludes the man who stands quite outside the relevant form of life or area of human experience."[4]

Now in one sense we must admit that Christian faith makes no complete sense in isolated bits and pieces. It is a coherent whole and involves a total view of the whole and of human existence within it. Everything is interpreted within the context of that framework. Not that this is peculiar to Christianity. It is true of all the major religions and philosophies which have won the allegiance of any considerable number of people. Yet even if one starts from Christian presuppositions, it is not ruled out from the start that non-Christians may be brought to see the force of the Christian analysis of the human predicament, even if the Christian answer to it is rejected. If, for example, the effect of sin has damaged the image of God in man, as formal Christian doctrine asserts, then the effects of this must be evident in the universal human situation. Can this, however, be

---

[3]Cf. E. R. Sharpe, *Comparative Religion* (London: Duckworth, 1975), for a very useful survey of the nineteenth century developments.

[4]F. C. Copleston, *Philosophers and Philosophies* (New York: Harper & Row), p. 53.

substantiated and to what kind of evidence would one point?

Against this attempt comes a serious objection, this time from the side of the Christian tradition itself. Karl Barth insisted that there is no way in which we can arrive at a doctrine of man which is universally relevant and true by an empirical investigation of actual human nature. The result could only be a plurality of anthropologies, a multitude of different, competing, and often contradictory doctrines of human existence. There are, in fact, Hindu, Buddhist, Chinese, Platonic, Aristotelian, Postivistic, Kierkegaardian, and atheistic existentialist doctrines of man, to name only a few. Nor is there any way of deciding between these views, says Barth, by a simple appeal to what is called empirical evidence. The only way we could decide between them would be if we had a normative and trustworthy knowledge of what it means to be truly human. For Barth, of course, this is only to be found in Jesus Christ where we can concretely discern, not only divinity, but human existence as God intended it to be. With this norm in hand, we can proceed to evaluate the other views. Without it, we are completely at sea and the answer to the question, *What is man?* is made impossible because of a radical relativism which infects all our ad hoc choices. One can understand that this solution might be attractive to many Christians. Once again, however, it will cut no ice with those who do not start from Christian faith.

As against this Barthian solution, there are some, including Christian thinkers, who believe that an analysis of the human situation based on a phenomenology of human existence, does in fact reveal certain universal features of such existence. Is this, in fact, so and what are these universal features?

We have already observed how all thinkers, Christian or not, tend to universalize their understanding of human nature and existence on the basis of their own experience of what it means to be human. Plato and Aristotle did not consider themselves to be talking only about Greek human nature but of the human situation as such. The Stoics thought they were addressing persons as members of a world-community, however limited that world might appear to be from a modern perspective. To come nearer home, it is clear that Heidegger does not see himself as offering simply an analysis of German *Dasein* but of human *Dasein* as such. Presumably the analysis of Gotama the Buddha was conceived by him and his followers as a description of what is true for all men and women everywhere, and not simply of

Hindus in North India in the fifth century B.C. And so on almost ad infinitum. This, of course, it may be said, is nothing more than proof of the inveterate provincialism of all of us, the unfortunate tendency to assume that what is true and valid for us is so for everybody. Nor can we deny a large element of truth in this. Nevertheless, we may ask whether these thinkers ever broke out of their "absolute presuppositions" of their cultural situation to a glimpse of at least some truths about the human situation which are universally valid?

Before we address ourselves to these questions, it should be said in passing that it is not self-evident that the plurality of anthropologies leaves us with nothing but an arbitrary choice based only on personal preference and prejudice. This is as unacceptable as the view that the plurality of views about the Transcendent (or God) can never be resolved except on the basis of a personal *blik*.* Just as all views of God are not equally capable of integrating our total experience in a meaningful and coherent way, so not all different anthropologies can appeal to the same range of evidence. Even without the Christological norm, some views of God and some anthropologies can be dismissed as so partial and one-sided as to be quite unfitted to be taken seriously, whether as an account of God or man. It is important, therefore, to keep our options open at this point.

Yet is it possible to discover what the universal elements are? To deal with all the implications of these questions would demand an encyclopedic knowledge of history beyond the competence of one man or woman or any group of men or women. We shall, however, take the risk and see what results. The reader is reminded again that we are basically concerned with Cupitt's charge that the Christian analysis of man as a sinner in need of redemption is time-conditioned and only relatively true. In short, it is valid for Christians but not necessarily for anyone else. Now it might, of course, be argued that the universal validity of a certain analysis of human existence does not necessarily mean that every person must be fully aware and self-conscious about it. It might be, for example, that a Buddhist, who does not work with the idea of a holy and loving personal God and could not use the language of sin against such a God, might in fact recognize that the Christian analysis of the human person in bondage to sin does point to

---

Blik, a word coined by R. M. Hare, designates an unverifiable and unfalsifiable interpretation on one's experience (ed.).

certain recognizable factors in his own experience. In this case, the Christian view would not be wholly unintelligible to him, even if the Christian solution is forbidden to him because of the more powerful presuppositions under which he has been religiously nurtured. John Hick's comparison of the concept of karma and the Christian view does show, not identity of viewpoint, but certainly some significant resemblances.[5]

Cupitt's charge that Christian anthropology is time-conditioned and culturally relative could, of course, be applied to all other views of man/woman which have been developed in the course of history. Yet the charge has been rejected, not only by Christians but by scientific accounts of the evolution and nature of man. Strict Darwinists would no doubt insist that their account of human evolution is a statement about what is actually the case, not simply a theory relative to Darwin's own personal viewpoint or to Western culture in the nineteenth century and later. Marx, Nietzsche, and Freud all present their views as an objective account of what is the case and universally true for all human existence wherever it is found.

Freud traces the Oedipus complex, not only to elements in the biography of the individual but to the primal slaying of the father which was a real event in the past and which has affected all succeeding generations of men and women. However mythical the form, there is no reason to doubt that Freud saw the "myth" as expressing a fact and its universal significance. Jung's archetypes make no sense apart from the assumption of a collective unconscious which is universal in its terms of reference. We realize that it is possible to dismiss all these as only time-conditioned, therefore relative, and consequently not the truth about the human situation as such. The British scientist Sir Peter Medawa has criticized Freudianism as an astounding intellectual confidence-trick.

That some scientific views are as socially conditioned and culturally relative as some religious views is not to be gainsaid. The point to be stressed at the moment is that the Christian diagnosis of the human situation is not peculiar in being time-conditioned and influenced by its cultural context. If, however, the Christian view is dismissed as wholly and totally conditioned in this way, then there is

---

[5]John Hick, *Death and Eternal Life* (London: Collins, 1979), pp. 343ff.

no reason why all other attempted descriptions of the human situation should not be so dismissed on the same grounds. We have rejected such complete relativism on the grounds that it destroys the very notion of truth with all the serious consequences which this entails both for science and religion, indeed, for every aspect of so-called knowledge.

We come back to our original question as to whether there are universal features of human existence as such and whether these features include what we would call sin and the bondage of the will. We admit that biology and Freudian psychology draw our attention to the nature and characteristic features of human existence in at least some of its aspects, without swallowing uncritically any particular scientific or psychological theory. Darwin and Freud may very well have not said the last word about even man's physical and psychological development, not to mention the intellectual, moral, and spiritual aspects of that same existence. It would seem self-evident that all human beings have a physical body. Nor would we question some of Heidegger's phenomenological descriptions. Man is finite, contingent, and mortal and the human person does seem to be distinguished by the fact that he or she is aware of this *Sein zum Tode,* or movement towards death. We are on more controversial ground when we begin to use such language as *body* and *soul,* or *body, mind,* and *spirit.* Is this distinction applicable to and characteristic of all human beings? Is there any evidence that man is a unity in duality and that there is a non-physical component in the human individual? It is not necessary for us to trace the centuries-old debate between idealism and realism, or between spiritualism and materialism of one kind or another, or between various forms of behaviorism crude or refined, or between freedom and rigid determinism. Our view is that mind or soul cannot be reduced to physical process pure and simple, and that more is involved than simply the use of two different kinds of language to talk of physical and mental events. In our view this position has been convincingly defended in recent years.[6]

Obviously the appeal to the relativity of all points of view does not enable us to deal with the kind of issues we have raised. In any case, it seems to be the case that thinkers divide on some of these issues

---

[6]C. A. Campbell, *On Selfhood and Godhood* (London: Allen & Unwin, 1957); Austin Farrer, *Finite and Infinite* (London: Westminster, D'acre Press, 1943); *The Freedom of the Will* (London: Adam & Charles Black, 1958); H. D. Lewis, *The Elusive Mind* (London: Allen & Unwin, 1969).

irrespective of their cultural and historical situation. The question then becomes the kind of evidence to which various sides in the dispute can appeal and how persuasive that evidence is. That man possesses real, if limited freedom, and that this admission entails the meaningful use of such language as responsibility, disobedience, transgression, stain, moral evil, guilt, punishment, and so forth, would be conceded by many in all cultures and among the representatives of all religions. On this issue, if man is a free and responsible being, a wide consensus, if not unanimity, of opinion exists.[7] There is also far more agreement in regard to basic moral values between all the religions than many would admit who wish to place all moral claims in a merely relativistic context.[8] So far, then, there would appear to be little substance in Cupitt's claim that Christian anthropology can make no sense to people conditioned by another cultural and religious situation.

It may be that the Christian understanding of sin depends on the fact of God in Christ for its full appreciation. It is also a fact, as John E. Smith contends, that "there is a religious dimension of human experience which belongs to human life as such in the universe. It belongs to life itself to ask the question of God and to experience the need for the ultimate power and purpose which unifies the self and perserves it from the destructiveness of self-indulgence and the chaos of many competing possibilities when they are without the constraint of an ultimate purpose."[9] Also it is true, as J. A. Baker insists, that to claim Jesus as Savior can carry no conviction except to those "who are willing to be fools of love" and to admit with all its costly consequences the fact that "sacrificial love is the highest of all values, the only thing which has a just claim to be the absolute and universal law of life. If I cannot accept this, then the whole affair remains an irrelevant enigma."[10] Who would dare to say that any human being anywhere, irrespective of his cultural and religious situation, is congenitally incapable of coming to this point? This seems to be denied by the evidence as well as by the fact that people can change their religion and

[7]S. Radhakrishan and P. T. Raju, eds., *The Concept of Man: A Study in Comparitive Philosophy* (London: Allen and Unwin, 1960).

[8]A. Schweitzer, *Christianity and the Religions of the World* (London: Allen & Unwin, 1923).

[9]John E. Smith, *Reason and God*, p. 269.

[10]J. A. Baker, *The Foolishness of God* (London: Collins, Fontana, 1975), p. 415.

enter a quite different cultural and religious context than the one in which they were nurtured.

Even if we can make a good case against a thoroughgoing relativism, this does not dispose of all our problems. The Christian analysis of the human situation implies that it is possible to speak of "human nature" as something which all human beings share. It also seems to imply that, however plastic such a nature is, there is an underlying identity which remains unchanged throughout its various modifications. Only if this is in some sense the case does it seem possible to claim universality for the distortion of that nature by sin. Yet it is precisely this claim that there is a universal human nature which has been so vigorously challenged in recent days. Biology, psychology, and sociology have all raised doubts about it.

Sartre, in his well known "existence precedes essence" has also defended the view that the human being is not born with a fixed and unchanging nature. Man is what he becomes through his free acts and each man may choose to become something very different from his neighbor. It can, of course, be objected to Sartre that the possession of such freedom is in fact a universal feature of all human existence. To that extent, perhaps, it can be maintained that there is a universal human nature whose characteristic feature is freedom, however different the results of the exercise of that freedom.

Certainly, if we consider the study of mankind by scientists of various disciplines, not to mention linguistics and the humanities, it is clear that the issue of a "human nature" is by no means settled. Even a predominantly scientific account can use the phrase "human nature" in its title.[11] In the sphere of linguistics, for example, one of the most interesting developments have been Chomsky's emphasis on the specific difference between human language and nature because of the former's creativity.[12] Against the Watsonian behaviorism, which dispensed with consciousness and mind as necessary presuppositions for the study of human behavior, we find Chomsky postulating a grammar which is an autonomous system of transformations "generated by a certain number of patterns and structures which constitute the *innate framework* of the human mind."[13] If language is

[11]J. Benthall, ed., *The Limits of Human Nature* (New York: E. P. Dutton & Co., 1974).
[12]Ibid., p. 37.
[13]Ibid.

unique to the human being in this sense, then we are not far removed from a universal human nature, especially when we remember the importance of language in the development of the different cultures of mankind.

On the other side, however, we have to put the immense variety and diversity of the cultural and linguistic products of this so-called human nature. World-views, religions, cultural patterns of all kinds are to be found. Berger and Luckman can talk of the "Social Construction of Reality."[14] The basic thesis here is the contention that the way we experience "reality" and "see" reality is socially conditioned. As this bears on our interest, it implies that "reality" for the Buddhist is something very different than "reality" for the Christian. Does this mean that we are left only with a number of different "realities"? Furthermore, does this mean that we must abandon altogether the idea of a Reality or one Reality which is variously experienced but which in some sense is One? Can we any longer speak of God, nature, or human nature as if they were given realties with definable characteristics? Or are we left with a sheer plurality of gods, natures, and human natures? If this were the case, it would, of course, immensely strengthen Cupitt's contentions which have already been examined.

In the case of Peter Berger and his work, such radical pluralism is not the last word for the sociology of knowledge. There is for him a common and public world apprehended through the inter-subjectivity which is the foundation of social and cultural patterns. The door at least is left open for the apprehension of a "reality" which transcends the socially-conditioned "realities" of any particular culture or individual within that culture.[15]

Can we, then, speak of a human nature which transcends the various socially-conditioned forms which human nature takes? At least in some quarters, the pendulum seems to be swinging back to a cautious yes to this question. John Casey, for example, in a stimulating essay, appears to be returning to an earlier view when he says, "It may then be that there are certain unchanging values which have their base in an unchanging human nature."[16] This can only mean that human

[14]P. Berger and Thomas Luckman, *The Social Construction of Reality* (New York: Doubleday, 1966).

[15]P. Berger, *A Rumour of Angels* (Allen Lane: Penguin, 1969).

[16]Benthall, *Limits of Human Nature,* pp. 74ff. and 90.

nature is not infinitely plastic and that it is possible to impose a priori limits upon human nature.[17] Human nature is the realm of thought, intention, and desire, involving the whole range of emotions and the dispositions to rational action we describe as virtues and vices.

It would take too long and require a different kind of book to defend these contentions in detail. The important point for the moment is that the attempt on the part of Christians to analyze human nature and human existence as such is an undertaking which cannot be dismissed by an appeal to scientific studies, as misguided or impossible. True, the concept of sin introduces complications which depend upon a specific view of God in relation to the created order. Arthur Koestler, for example, can agree that "something might have gone wrong in the evolution of our species."[18] He remains unimpressed by the claim that all personal and social evil stems from the selfish, agressive tendencies in human nature. He calls this a "dusty answer" as an explanation as to why human history has taken the course it has.[19] Surprisingly enough, he finds the cause of human ills, not in an excess of aggression but of devotion. Men fight and kill, not because they are as individuals innately aggressive. They fight for words, that is, myths and symbols which the social group adopts and to which the individual feels a passionate loyalty which leads to collective aggression. It is because man is a belief-accepting animal that he can kill his own kind with such abandon.

Koestler finds the clue to the tragic history of mankind, not in the misuse of freedom or in what Christians call sin, but in a physiological aberration. After all, evolution is a story of trial and error and of misfired experiments. The unprecedented expansion of the human brain in the second half of the Pleistocene Age has resulted in a physiological imbalance: "The result seems to be that the recently evolved structures in the human brain—the neocortex—did not become properly integrated with, or coordinated with, the ancient structures on which they were superimposed with such unseemly haste."[20] As he puts it, as he himself admits, in a rather crude way, evolution has left a few screws loose somewhere between the neocortex

---

[17]Ibid., p. 90.
[18]Ibid., p. 51.
[19]Ibid.
[20]Ibid., p. 56.

and the brain-stem. The idea is original, interesting, and intriguing but hardly convincing. If it were true, it would mean that the future of the human race depends on our ability to effect a physiological change in the structure of the brain. We may have to wait a long time for that.

Over against Koestler's thesis must be set the deep conviction of all the major religions that the root of the human problem is not to be found in physiology but in the will. This is not to deny the far-reaching influence of the body as a physical organism on human behavior. There is more to human nature, however, than physiology, and Christian anthropology is not alone in insisting on this.

The rock of offense, however, is not to be found in these general statements about the human situation which a Christian anthropology shares with many non-Christian anthropologies. The real scandal for Cupitt is the doctrine of sin, the bondage of the will and the necessity for an external Savior to secure human release from this bondage. This is made even more scandalous by the Christian claim that Jesus is the only one who is able to bring about this deliverance. Again, Cupitt would no doubt claim that it is possible to accept Jesus as the saving paradigm of sacrificial love without all the theological impediments of sin, original and otherwise, the bondage of the will, and immoral substitutionary theories of the atonement. We shall take up these issues in our next chapter on Salvation and Atonement. Meanwhile, we defend the right of Christian anthropology to talk about human nature in a universal sense, however diverse the religious and cultural expressions of that nature.

So far in this chapter we have been concerned mainly with criticisms of Christian anthropology and the claim that it is an accurate diagnosis of the human situation with universal application. For the convenience of the reader, we shall now sum up what we believe to be the basic features of a Christian anthropology. It is evident that some of these features are capable of more than one interpretation and this has proved to be the case in the history of Christian thought. All we would claim now is that in some form these features will appear in any anthropology which can claim to be Christian in its basic understanding and concern.

1. Pantheism is rejected and the distinction between Creator and creature is affirmed as both biblical and more philosophically acceptable.

2. The birth of the human being is not explained by reference to a drama of a preexistent fall, as developed by Origen in the second century, and by N. P. Williams in more recent times.[21] Nor did the main Christian tradition ever accept the Platonic view of the preexistence of the soul. The position of Origen in the second century on this point is almost unique. Birth into bodily existence is good and willed by the Creator-God. Birth is not an evil and a misfortune but a gift of God. There is no reincarnation in the Orphic, Hindu, and Buddhist senses.

3. While the Bible stresses the psychosomatic wholeness of the human being, this is not to be understood in a modern behavioristic sense, or as implying that mental life can be wholly reduced to the physical process.

4. Matter and the body are good as God's creation. The misuse of freedom and the entrance of sin do not mean that the body is intrinsically evil.

5. It follows that salvation is not deliverance from the physical body as such. It is the gift of the gracious God who justifies, that is, accepts as righteous those who commit themselves to faith in Jesus Christ. Persons do not save themselves but the response to the grace of God is truly our own response. Our wills are ours to make them Thine.

6. The Christian understanding of God and salvation implies a certain view of history as the arena for the working out of the divine purpose. Persons have, as Kierkegaard affirmed, a fundamental ethical responsibility in regard to their present conduct and eternal destiny.

7. The eschatological dimension is integral to the Christian faith and hope. The eternal destiny of human beings is not a mystical absorption into the Godhead but a blessed existence after death in which selfishness is overcome by the grace of God but individuality preserved.

While some of the above features perhaps could be accepted by a non-Christian theist or even a humanist, it is clear that a Christian anthropology is distinctive in that it presupposes a special understanding of nature, Man, and God and their relationships. The further implications of this will be discussed in the later chapters.

---

[21]N. P. Williams, *Doctrines of the Fall and of Original Sin* (London: Longmans, Green & Co., 1927).

Chapter Five

Why This Particular Death?

We take up again the question of the saving significance of the death of Jesus. In what sense is God's action in the death of Jesus sufficiently unique as a basis for the claim that Jesus is the Savior in a way which cannot be claimed for any other historical figure? We have already noted that the death cannot be separated from the life or from the resurrection. The centrality of the cross, in Christian devotion and atonement theories, does, however, justify a special concentration on the significance of the death. As will be evident, the problem of religious pluralism is still with us.

We have rejected Don Cupitt's thesis that the Christian analysis of the human situation in terms of sin and redemption is only a relative and culturally-conditioned one. All the major religions have offered salvation in some sense, that is, deliverance from some flaw in empirical human existence which prevents human beings from achieving the goal of a meaningful and blessed existence. It is also true that the nature of the flaw is diagnosed differently, whether it be ignorance (*avidya*) in the Hindu and Buddhist traditions or the notion of sin as deviation from the will of a holy, righteous, and loving God, as in Judaism and Christianity. It has also been admitted that the Christian understanding of sin presupposes a particular view of God

and his relation to the created order and that Hinduism and Buddhism
do not interpret the basic flaw in the same way.

On the other hand, it does not follow from this that the Christian
analysis of the human situation must be meaningless to the non-
Christian or that the non-Christian is inherently incapable of grasping
the idea of God which underlies such an analysis.

Let us now turn to the question as to how the death of Jesus is
saving and in what sense. We are also asking about the nature of
salvation, not as an intellectual answer to the problem of theodicy but
on the practical level of what it means to be saved. How is the death of
Jesus related to this latter issue? The problem of evil presupposes the
reality of evil in its many forms as actually experienced by all human
beings. These may be listed as finitude, suffering, the inevitability of
death, the universal experience of conflict between what we are and
what we feel ourselves called to be.

This raises the further question of our identity as human beings, of
what it means to be truly human. There would seem to be at least two
basic ways in which the evils of the world can be handled in a practical
way. One is to change the world or the nature of reality as hitherto
experienced. The other is to change our attitude and the nature of
human consciousness. In the latter case, the evils may still remain as
external and objective factors but they are assimilated and
transformed in the human experience in such a way that they are not
destructive of an inner sense of a possible ultimate harmony, peace,
and joy of which there may be a foretaste here and now.

As far as the changing of the nature of the world is concerned, there
are obviously severe limits to what can be achieved. It is extremely
doubtful that our finite nature and the fact of death will ever be
eliminated. Modern technology may vastly expand the scope of
human activity and even delay death beyond the present limits. It
seems highly utopian to envisage a situation in this present world in
which finiteness and death are no longer universal features of human
existence as such. It should be noted again that, for the Christian, the
finite nature of human beings and the inevitability of death are not in
themselves simply evil, for it is the divine purpose to preserve finite
creatures after death in eternal fellowship with himself.

Insofar as we are thinking of evil in terms of some basic "flaw" or
"sin," something can be done about this according to the major
religions. We can be delivered from the ignorance which ties us to

karma or from "the sin which doth so easily beset us." The deliverance thus promised may not be complete in this life, but it is possible to have a foretaste even now of the blessedness which such deliverance connotes, whether this is the nibbuta man of Buddhism or the Christian's present experience of eternal life. Whether such an experience can be translated into a social order from which injustice and suffering have been banished is, however, a debatable question. That much can be done, ought to be done, and will be done to lessen the quantity of physical and mental pain in our human societies is a commonly accepted assumption today. Its total elimination, however, appears to be highly problematic.

One is also left with the nagging question raised by Aldous Huxley years ago in *Brave New World* as to whether the total elimination of pain and suffering would not also eliminate the agonies and the ecstasies of love and aspiration which alone give grandeur and meaning to human life. One of the fundamental weaknesses of some liberation theology, as well as of Marxism, is its assumption that radical transformations of the social and economic order can generate faith and hope in the individual. In the short term, enthusiasm and costly self-sacrifice in the name of a just social order can be generated. The more fundamental problems connected with finitude, death, and personal frustration are not resolved. They may be suppressed or ignored, but they will emerge again and again.

How, then, is the death of Jesus related to the human situation thus described? When we survey the history of Christian thought on this matter, and in particular specific doctrines of the significance of the atoning death of Jesus, we note the distinction between objective and subjective theories. On the objective side, his death has brought about a decisive change in the world, sometimes described as its cosmic significance. Prior to the death and resurrection of Jesus, all mankind was in a negative relationship to God our Creator. This is an objective fact about human status, not simply a perspective determined by the psychology of the individual. After these events, this status has been radically changed and the possibility of a right relationship to God opened up for all men and women. The decisive action has been taken by God, prior to any human response to that action. This, however, does not preclude the possibility and the necessity of human response with the consequent radical transformation of human existence and the change of human attitude and awareness of the divine presence.

On the other side are the so-called subjective, moral, or experiential theories. These do not necessarily deny all objective elements but they tend to concentrate on the subjective conditions for the human response. Such would be the powerful effects upon human beings of the costly and suffering love of God demonstrated, not in the abstract but in the actual life, suffering, and death of Jesus, a man of flesh and blood like ourselves. In the language of Chalcedon, he is *homoousios* with us according to the manhood. Such actualized love in Jesus moves us to repentance and trusting faith and love on the basis of which God can and does freely forgive us and restores us to that relationship with himself which is a present source of strength as we seek to submit ourselves to his transforming power that we may be more and more comformed to the image of the Son.

Two things follow from all this, namely the human situation vis-à-vis God is objectively changed and a power to trust and love is released in human lives which brings about a real change in human existence. Men and women are not exactly the same as they were before, despite their imperfection and sin. A new principle of life is at work.

Our concern with religious pluralism compels us to ask a fundamental question. Granted that empirical human existence is not in a right relationship to God or granted that God, if there is a God, will surely do something to deal with such a situation, how important is the death of Jesus? Why did God choose to remedy the human situation through the death of this man Jesus? Furthermore, was this God's only way of dealing with it? Granted that God had to do something which men and women could not do for themselves by a simple act of will, could not God have acted in other ways to achieve the same result? Has he not in fact so acted in and through the different religions and cultures which make up the history of mankind on this planet?

It is difficult, if not impossible, to answer such questions in the abstract. Theoretically, perhaps, God could have acted in other ways. We can answer the question dogmatically, as Barth and many others have done, by saying that God has chosen to act in this way and that's that. Today this answer is not acceptable to those who wish to affirm a universal saving activity of God which is not linked inextricably either to Jesus or to a particular view of incarnation. In the light of this attitude, is it possible to make an experiential appeal? What is the evidence that God has acted in other ways and has the effect of such action been as potent or as transforming of human existence as his action in the life, death, and resurrection of Jesus Christ? Before we examine the nature of salvation in the non-Christian religions, however, we shall continue our exploration of the meaning of Jesus' death. Most Christian believers would be inclined to say that it is not an either-or alternative between the objective and subjective views. Salvation involves both a saving activity initiated by God and a certain kind of response to that activity in faith which produces certain results on the human level. (See Phil. 2:12.) We work out our salvation in fear and trembling in the confidence that God is fulfilling his chosen purpose through us. Each side of this paradox will be considered in turn.

In what sense can the life and death of Jesus be said to have changed the status of men and women in the world, and therefore, in its relation to God? Does it make sense to talk about the cosmic implications of the life, death, and resurrection of Jesus Christ? We have already contended that if the resurrection is taken in the traditional sense of the raising of a transformed physical body to a new sphere of activity, then this could be said to have cosmic implications. It would involve an act whereby God transcends the normal regularities of nature or physical process to make clear his purpose and his vindication of Jesus of Nazareth. If the resurrection is fact in this sense, then something happened in history which constitutes a real dividing-line between B.C. and A.D. Attempts to spell out in more detail the cosmic implications of the death and resurrection run into difficulties created both by modern science and the ambiguity of the word myth.

Aulén's well-known use of the victory theme rests on the assumption that the cosmos reflects a conflict between God on the one side and personal or personified agencies of evil on the other (for example, the Devil and his angels).[1] Is this myth, symbol, or metaphor and to what realities does such language point? The language of victory implies victory over someone or something. The basic question concerns this latter. On the classic theory, this cosmic conflict between God and Satan exists prior to man's involvement in the battle. Human beings, however, benefit from the struggle which results in the tilting of

---

[1] Aulén, *Christus Victor* (London: S.P.C.K., 1961).

the balance permanently on the side of God and his righteousness through the resurrection of Christ.

Our view is that the postulation of personal evil agencies other than men and women is precisely that, only a postulate to account for certain features of the world as we experience and interact with it. It is no theological solution to the problem of theodicy or to the origin of evil. God in the Christian sense cannot create the devil as the devil, that is, as a wholly evil being. If we explain the devil being what he is through the wrong use of freedom by a preexistent angel, then we have only carried the problem a stage further back. In this case, why not trace the origin of moral evil to human freedom without the dubious and ambiguous assumption of some kind of pre-mundane fall?

We, therefore, reject the classic theory if it means the postulate of the devil in the most literal sense as a preexistent personal agency of evil at work in the cosmos prior to the emergence of the human race. On the other hand, if we demythologize the devil and his angels, can we any longer speak of a cosmic conflict or the cosmic implications of the death and resurrection of Jesus? It all depends on the meaning given to the term cosmic. If, for the devil, we substitute the explanation of evil in terms of social accumulations of evil, rooted in human acts of will, then we might metaphorically talk of the demonic as describing a cumulative power of social evil which the will of any particular individual is powerless to change. Insofar as nature and history are not to be radically separated and that man is organic to nature, then it could be argued that evil has affected not only human society but the physical environment in which the human race is set. We might then properly speak of the cosmic implications of evil, but we need to remember that we have now made radical changes in what Aulen calls the classic theory.

We agree that such radical changes have to be made. If such changes are accepted, then how shall we understand the effects of the death and resurrection of Jesus? If, for example, it could be shown that the death and resurrection of Jesus have effected such radical changes in enough persons to break the entail of personal and collective evil, then it could be argued again that the status of mankind in the universe and in relation to God has indeed been changed. Although evil persists on the personal and social level, we might claim that in no mere symbolic sense, a new age has begun. Persons transformed in Christ constitute a new power of creative love in human affairs which has had far-reaching effects both on human society and even on the natural environment insofar as the historical process cannot be artificially separated from the world-context in which the human race finds itself.

Put more simply, the world, social and natural, can never be the same again after the coming of the Christ. As Albert Schweitzer once expressed it in a graphic illustration, the stream of Christian love now flows like the Gulf Stream through a cold world, warming and fertilizing the environment as it passes through. Let us now ask how Jesus dealt concretely with the evil which confronted him and what is the significance of his death in this connection. Jesus of Nazareth, in his earthly existence, had to confront the human situation as we have earlier described it. Finitude, death, the evil will, and the denial of love were just as much realities for him as for us. How did he deal with them?

As Wheeler Robinson said many years ago, the key word here is "transformation."[2] Suffering in itself is not inherently saving or redemptive. More often it seems to be embittering, frustrating, and even destructive. Whether suffering is creative in the sense of yielding positive results in the form of love, forgiveness, and reconciliation depends on the attitude taken toward the suffering. Yet what determines such an attitude? Why do some people transform their suffering into spiritual fruitfulness and some experience it only as a final descent into despair and meaninglessness? What is it about the suffering and death of Jesus which made it the power of God unto salvation for some rather than the basis of cynical hopelessness about the triumph of holy love?

At this point the problem of religious pluralism arises again in a more acute form. After all, cannot we find other examples in history of men and women who have creatively transformed their suffering by their faith, courage, and endurance? What is so unique about the attitude and death of Jesus which marks it off so clearly from these other examples? To this, there are some, and today perhaps they are many, who would say—in principle—nothing. The way Jesus handled the power of sin, evil, and suffering was a striking and vivid illustration of a principle of creative transformation which has permeated all history. Perhaps Jesus is the finest and most powerful illustration to

[2]H. W. Robinson, *Revelation and Redemption* (London: Nisbet, 1942), p. 274ff.

date. To this extent, he is unique, the spiritual pioneer so far ahead of the rest of the race. For Christians, his example is potent to produce in them the courage and faith to deal with evil and suffering as he did.

However, we cannot say that a relationship to Jesus is the only and indispensable basis for such creative transformation. There may be, and indeed are, other persons who may help us just as much. Perhaps an individual may find his or her own way to such creative transformation apart from a relationship to any specific historical figures. This seems to be the implication of John Cobb's book in which he makes a clear distinction between the universal Logos or Christ-principle and its particular manifestation in Jesus of Nazareth.[3]

While this is Christian in the sense that it concedes the uniqueness, finality, and saviorhood of Jesus for Christians, it obviously falls short of any claim for Jesus as universal savior. Most Christians in the past and present have wanted to say more. The question is: Is this "more" a justifiable claim? In turning back to our earlier question as to why Jesus met sin, evil, suffering, and death in the way he did, it is clear that he approached them with certain assumptions which determined his attitude. He did not face them as a secular humanist or even as a Socrates. Nor was he a mystic of the Plotinian type. Still less did he seek a reconciliation of opposites a la Hegel. He had no assumptions about karma, reincarnation, or metempsychosis, however defined. In short, he faced the sin, suffering, and evil of the world at least as a believing Jew, whatever changes he was prepared to make in his inherited Judaism. We shall not repeat our earlier discussion of the issues between Judaism and Christianity but underline certain points of major importance for our understanding of the death.

1. God is the holy, righteous, and compassionate Creator and Judge of all the earth whose purpose for the human race is being worked out through his covenant people Israel and who is now in this present time acting again to offer salvation under the coming rule of God to all who confess their need and turn to him in repentance and faith.
2. Jesus himself was convinced that he was called to a central and determinative role in the realizing of the divine purpose.[4]

---

[3]J. B. Cobb, Jr., *Christ in a Pluralistic Age* (Philadelphia: Westminster, 1967).

[4]A fuller discussion of whether Jesus regarded his own person as integral to his message and proclamation, as against Bultmann, is treated in more detail in R. F. Aldwinckle, *More than Man: A Study in Christology*, p. 51ff.

3. His own unique experience of God as Abba is central, a point rightly emphasized by Schillebeeckx in his recent book, *Jesus*.
4. His acceptance of his death as in line with the Father's will. Whether this was clear to him at the beginning of his public ministry or whether it became clear as that ministry unfolded in increasing conflict and tension, there is no doubt that he accepted its necessity eventually as the Father's will for him.[5]

It would seem impossible, therefore, to ask about the uniqueness and saving significance of Jesus' death while ignoring the assumptions which determined his own attitude. The result would be only an abstraction far removed from the specific decisions, actions, and faith of Jesus of Nazareth. He appears to have been convinced, not only that God had called him to proclaim in prophetic manner the imminent kingdom. God was already through Jesus' ministry releasing the powers of the new age in the casting out of the demons and in his fellowship with publicans and sinners. In his attitude toward the latter, he conveys his conviction that the gracious God desires the restored fellowship of his erring children. Above and beyond all this was his confidence that God would vindicate his total dedication to the divine purpose. It seems incredible that Jesus should have died in total despair of the Father-God whom he had trusted throughout his earthly ministry. Even the dying thief seems to have had enough faith to believe that Jesus could secure him a place in paradise. Could Jesus have had less confidence, in spite of the agony and suffering?

It seems to the present author that a good deal of unfounded speculation has been based on Jesus' quotation of Psalm 22. The motive behind this speculation seems to have been concerned less with the attitude of Jesus than with presenting a Jesus who will be congenial to modern existentialist despair and meaninglessness. The assumption appears to be that Jesus will make a greater appeal to so-called modern men and women if he lost his faith at the end and died in total despair. This pathological fear of anything which smacks of an optimistic faith and a final vindication may suit the modern mood. There is no reason to think that this was basically Jesus' attitude, even in the final agony. If the Maccabean martyrs could die horrible deaths in the confidence of their ultimate vindication by God, can we refuse the same possibility to Jesus?

---

[5]C. H. Dodd, *The Founder of Christianity* (London: Collins, 1971), p. 139.

In the light of all this, the issue of religious pluralism begins to take on a different look. The question now is not whether Jesus is the unique Savior as an isolated historical figure but whether Jesus in his special relationship to God is unique. These two things are not the same. In short, the saving significance and universal scope of his death is bound up with the reality and activity of the God whose special servant he is. One cannot attach a central meaning to his death without being committed to the God whose "unique Son" he believed himself to be.

The question still arises as to whether Jesus saw his death as effecting something decisive in the relationship between God and mankind which would not have been possible without that death. In other words, was there a "dogmatic" element in his own thinking about his death, where dogmatic means that Jesus had his own interpretation of the significance of his death. It seems fairly obvious that if we confine our attention to the Synoptic Gospels, there is little evidence that Jesus interpreted his own death by presenting a detailed theology of atonement worked out in the manner of the later doctrines. This is not to say that Jesus had no view at all of the significance of his impending death.

Some, indeed, have contended that there was no "dogmatic" factor in the sense that his action was guided by any precise belief as to what his dying would accomplish for the reconciliation of God and man. It has also been advanced that Jesus, in the early stages of his ministry, expected a positive response to his proclamation of the imminent kingdom. Only later did he clearly see the necessity of his death. Others believe this to have been very much a last-minute realization and not something which determined the early stages of the ministry. If this were the case, then it would be difficult to argue that Jesus attached any significance to his death other than the fact that it demonstrated his total commitment to the cause of God's kingdom. This would not signify that the death was trivial. Theologically, however, it would not permit us to go beyond the category of tragic martyrdom. No other "dogmatic" or "theological" factor would be involved.

In sharp contrast to this was the well-known claim of Albert Schweitzer that Jesus' action was indeed dogmatically determined and that without this awareness of his motives, his actions do not make sense. By dogma, Schweitzer did not mean the later orthodoxy, whether Catholic or Protestant. He meant certain basic assumptions about God and his purposes which characterized "late Judaism," in particular the eschatological and apocalyptic expectations. Jesus went to his death, therefore, not as an activist, political or otherwise, clashing with the hated and tyrannical establishment. He went to the cross in the conviction that in taking the messianic woes upon himself, he would force God's hand to bring in the kingdom very soon and usher in the new aeon.[6] On this view, Jesus' death in his own eyes had a precise theological significance within the context of the apocalyptic framework and its interpretation of God's action in history. Schweitzer's view differs widely from later developments in the theology of the atonement. However, both have one important point in common, namely the belief that Jesus saw his death as having dogmatic and theological significance. In other words, his death would be a decisive event in bringing about a radical change in the God-man relationship as well as the occasion for prompting the apocalyptic intervention of God in history to inaugurate the kingdom of God.

The question is whether either of these views can appeal for support to anything in Jesus' self-understanding. Of course, for those who claim that the records do not enable us to claim to know what Jesus thought but only what the early church thought he thought, an answer to these questions is precluded from the start. We are forever excluded from any speculation about the actual motives of Jesus, and in particular how he conceived the significance of his death when he realized it was inevitable. We do not accept this view of our inability to penetrate, at least to some degree, the mind of Jesus. Our plumbing of these mysterious depths, however, can never be total and complete.[7] Do we, then, have to choose between a theory of martyrdom only or the apocalyptic prophet forcing the hand of God a la Schweitzer? Is there another view which does more justice to the Synoptic picture of Jesus and his actions? We believe there is and that Jeremias has given us the basic outline of such a view.

---

[6]A. Schweitzer, *The Quest of the Historical Jesus* (New York: Macmillan, 1961).

[7]T. W. Manson, *The Teaching of Jesus* (London: Cambridge University Press, 1963); *The Servant-Messiah* (London: Cambridge University Press, 1961); Joachim Jeremias, *The Proclamation of Jesus*, New Testament Theology, vol. 1 (London: S.C.M., 1967), pp. 276ff.; Oscar Cullmann, *Salvation in History* (London: S.C.M., 1967).

According to the Gospel record, Jesus announced to his disciples three times his suffering and resurrection (see Mark 8:31; 9:31; 10:33). On the whole, New Testament scholarship has tended to regard these predictions as formulations of the early Christian community. They are predictions after the event and, therefore, we cannot be sure that Jesus ever made such a reference to his death and resurrection. If this is the case, then the only grounds for thinking that Jesus attached special significance to his death would be if we could make reasonable deductions from other sources, for example, the parables, such as the parable of the wicked husbandmen. Jeremias, however, advances reasons for thinking that the passion predictions may in fact go back to something Jesus said, even if the form of these in the Gospels has been shaped by the early church. Jeremias, therefore, contends:

1. The external course of the ministry must have compelled Jesus to reckon with the possibility of a violent death.[8] The fate of John the Baptist must have been a powerful reminder to Jesus that he could not expect a different fate.

2. Both the course of Jesus' ministry and his view of himself as the last prophet to proclaim the imminent kingdom tell against the view that he would make no reference at all to his possible suffering and death.

3. The three passion predictions in Mark are only a small excerpt from comprehensive logia material which deal with Jesus' future suffering.[9]

If we accept Jeremias' conclusion that Jesus did refer to his suffering and death, then did he interpret its significance in a special way? Here again Jeremias claims that he did and that he found the answer to the question of the meaning of his death in Isaiah 53 and Zechariah 13:7. But could Jesus have seen his death as in some way representative? "If He believed Himself to be the messenger of God who was to bring God's final message and if He reckoned with the possibility of a violent death, then He must have been concerned with the question of the meaning and the atoning power of His death."[10] But what kind of meaning? The centrality of Isaiah 53 for Jesus' own

---

[8]Jeremias, *Proclamation of Jesus*, p. 278.

[9]Ibid., p. 283.

[10]Ibid., p. 288.

thinking is defended by Jeremias by an analysis of the eucharistic words and concludes that "without Isaiah 53 the eucharistic words remain incomprehensible."[11] This has important implications for the ransom sayings in the Markan predictions of the death. The *lutron* (λύτρον) thus implies a substitutionary offering, an atonement offering, which *asham* ('āšām) suggests in Isaiah 53:10.

Jeremias concludes that "the only answer to the question how it could be possible that Jesus attributed such unlimited atoning power to his death must be that he died as the servant of God, whose suffering and death is described in Isaiah 53. It is innocent (v. 9), voluntary (v. 10), suffering patiently borne (v. 7), willed by God (v. 6, 10), and therefore, atoning for others (vv. 4 ff.). Because it is life with God and from God that is here given over to death, this death has an unlimited power to atone."[12] It is not to be assumed that Jeremias' emphasis on the representative, atoning, and substitutionary character of the death, as understood by Jesus, means that Jesus was thinking in terms of the later Calvinist doctrine of penal substitution. There are important differences, as we shall see later. It does mean, however, that he saw his death as a ransom for many, that is, as a means of deliverance and a way of acceptance for repentant men and women into the kingdom of God, the rule of God already inaugurated in his earthly ministry.

This implies that the meaning of his death, even for Jesus, is not to be found exclusively in psychological, sociological, and political factors. There is a "dogmatic" element in his thought, that is, his action was determined by specific ideas as to what God was doing in and through his ministry and the death which fulfills it. Thus, Jeremias agrees with Schweitzer as to the dogmatic element but gives a different version of the nature of the dogmatic or theological presuppositions involved.

Oscar Cullmann is in agreement with Jeremias' basic thesis, despite differences of exegesis in regard to detail. "We can, therefore, conclude that the concept *ebed Yahweh* characterizes the person and work of the historical Jesus in a way which completely corresponds to the New Testament witness to Christ."[13] Cullmann further observes that the

---

[11] Ibid., p. 291.

[12] Ibid., p. 299.

[13] Oscar Cullmann, *Christology of the New Testament* (London: S.C.M., 1959), p. 80.

extension of the work of the *ebed Yahweh* into the present and future is not developed in the Old Testament, though the idea is present. In Jesus, it is extended to the present and future function of Jesus. Manson also accepts the fundamental importance of the *ebed Yahweh* but links it with the idea of the righteous and saving remnant embodied in the Son of Man concept. While Manson strongly insists on the original collective connotation of the term Son of man, he believes that the term is finally narrowed down to Jesus himself as a result of the events of the ministry and Jesus' conflict with the authorities. "The last part of the way he travels alone; and at the cross he alone is the Son of Man, the incarnation of the Kingdom of God on earth. The Son of Man is rejected and slain."[14]

It seems not unreasonable to say, therefore, that Jesus did anticipate his death and that he saw it, not simply as a martyrdom but as a divinely willed event which was inevitably involved in his own role as the Suffering Servant. If we ask how the death, thus interpreted, could have the universal atoning significance which Jesus believed it would have, the answer can only be found in the way Jesus understood his own role in the history of God's saving activity in Israel, now finally consummated in his own ministry. Jesus' actions were divine actions because of his special and unique relation to the Father. "But because it was an act of God it had in it an infinite power to the radiation of which no limit can be set."[15]

Even if the above conclusions are accepted, there still remain difficult and controversial questions. Jesus may have anticipated his death and interpreted its significance in a certain way, but could he have predicted his own resurrection and what light would this throw upon the suffering and death? The difficulty for many today is with the idea of resurrection as such, whether corporeal, spiritual, or some combination of these in the notion of a spiritual body. The very idea that Jesus could survive death in any form runs counter to the positivist, empirical, and scientific temper of our age. Even if Jesus spoke of his resurrection, which a number of New Testament scholars deny, it still may not have been true, if by true we mean the real existence of Jesus after death, not to mention his power to be seen by

---

[14]T. W. Manson, *The Teaching of Jesus*, p. 235; cf. also pp. 178ff.

[15]A. Farrer, *A Faith of our Own* (New York: World Publishing Co., 1960).

men still living in the present world. Skepticism about the possibility of resurrection at all, in any form, has undoubtedly influenced exegesis negatively against the further possibility of Jesus actually speaking of his resurrection. In any case, some today, even if they admit the role of the *ebed Yahweh* in Jesus' interpretation of his own death, might be tempted to interpret this fact without any essential reference to the resurrection. The death of the *ebed Yahweh*, in this case Jesus, could be interpreted in terms of the tragic hero, vicariously suffering for others, and no more than this. This is well put by F. W. Dillistone where he speaks of the tendency to see Jesus as "the tragic figure, the victim of the disjointed structure who, though relatively innocent himself, is caught in the toils of tangled and ambiguous forces and suffers accordingly. Yet through his patient suffering, social evils are purged, the entail of the past is broken and the healing of the community is made possible."[16]

There is no doubt that this vision of Jesus has a great appeal to many who are otherwise completely secular in their outlook. Even in Christian circles, it is perhaps the dominant image in some exponents of what is called "liberation theology." Against this must be put two other quotations cited by Dillistone. One is by C. S. Lewis: "The whole cosmic story, though full of tragic elements, yet fails of being a tragedy."[17] The other is by Philip Toynbee: "Christianity is not a tragic religion and the crucifixion was not a tragic event. The greatest message of Christianity is redemption and the most execrated Christian sin is the sin of pride."[18] If our previous argument is sound, Jesus is not the tragic hero battling against ineluctable fate with the courage of despair. He is acting in a way which will liberate the redemptive power of God in human affairs and bring about the ultimate reconciliation. He is the agent of the loving Father, not the victim of an impersonal fate.

We began by asking whether Jesus thought of himself as *the* Savior of the world in the sense in which this was understood by the juridical theories of satisfaction and penal substitution. Our answer to this must

---

[16]F. W. Dillistone, *The Christian Understanding of the Atonement* (London: Nisbet, 1968), p. 115.

[17]Ibid., p. 153.

[18]Ibid.

be negative as far as the mind of Jesus can be discerned in the Synoptic Gospels. On the other hand, we have affirmed that Jesus did see his death as having some kind of universal atoning or redeeming significance and that he interpreted his death as more than that of the tragic hero. A final judgment will have to be delayed until we have considered more carefully the question as to whether the Pauline understanding of the death of Jesus was "juridical."

Assuming, then, that there was a "dogmatic" element of some kind in Jesus' thinking about his death, how is this related to later doctrines of the atonement? Here we confront some of the most difficult theological problems. The so-called subjective, moral, or experiential theories (Abelard, Schleiermacher, Bushnell, R. S. Franks, to name only four significant figures) do not deny outright an objective side to God's action in the death of Jesus. After all, the manifestation of the costly love of God in the death of Jesus is an historical actuality, something which happened prior to any response made in penitence and faith by the believer. However, what distinguishes all exponents of the moral theory is their deeply held conviction that whatever the effects of the death of Jesus, its prime purpose is not to change the attitude of God to human beings but the attitude of men and women to him. God is by nature loving and ever ready to forgive. The only obstacle to acceptance by God and the receiving of his forgiveness and restoration to fellowship is the human attitude. Attitudes can only be changed at the deepest personal level by love. This is what the cross has done and can do. We are moved to penitence and then to loving, trusting faith. As a consequence, the will, which is the whole person in action, is redirected Godward. The barrier of human enmity and hostility is removed and reconciliation achieved. Jesus could still be said to be the unique Savior because his total dedication to the will of the Father made possible the release of the Father's love into the world and its transformation of persons.

The appeal here must be to experience. That Jesus saves is shown, not by a theory, but by the impact which his manifestation of costly and vicarious love has had upon men and women throughout the ages. If the unique saviorhood of Jesus is to be defended on these assumptions, it must be on the basis of his influence and the experiential difference he has made. The vicarious, costly, suffering love of God is shown through his life and death in a manner more potent and efficacious than in the lives and deaths of other men and women. Can this be demonstrated beyond cavil by the appeal to experience? Can we not find other examples of vicarious love?

This is an extraordinarily difficult question to answer. One can no doubt find other striking examples of sacrificial and loving action for others. What are such instances? We can hardly appeal to Christian "saints" or even ordinary Christians, for they would attribute their power to love to Jesus. Can we, then, find examples in the non-Christian religions? What about the suffering of the Hebrew prophets (Hosea and Jeremiah) or of Socrates or of Al-Hāllāj or martyrs for what seemed a good cause? What about Maccabean Jews, dedicated Marxists, unselfish sacrifice for others in time of war? Certainly there are other examples to be found of suffering, vicarious love. Is their influence on history comparable with that of Jesus? Was not the decision of Gotama to live and postpone nirvāna an act of profound compassion for men and women in bondage to karma?[19]

If we give a positive answer, and gladly, to these questions, is the difference between them and Jesus only one of degree and is this idea compatible with any claim for the unique saviorhood of Jesus? No doubt many Christians would want to admit the reality of other instances of vicarious, suffering love but claim a radical difference in the case of Jesus. It is a fact, however, that the issue becomes more complicated because of the assumptions which lie behind the actions and death of Jesus. In his case, it is not simply a case of vicarious, suffering love exhibited by one man for other men and women. Rather the key is to be found in his conviction that such love reflects the love of God, the will of the Father. Such love is, therefore, cosmic in scope and intention; it has transcendental implications.

This means that the love manifested in Jesus is not an unintelligible surd in a dark and meaningless world. It is an expression of the nature of the power which made the "heavens and the earth" and who guides the natural and historical process to its ultimate consummation in the kingdom of God. It is, therefore, the character of God which gives the special quality to the vicarious, suffering love of Jesus. Any talk about the unique saviorhood of Jesus must obviously give full weight to this fact, for this does distinguish the death of Jesus from other deaths if

---

[19]See the discussion of this in R. F. Aldwinckle, *More than Man: A Study in Christology.*

Jesus' own assumptions about God and his purpose are valid. Whatever the limitations of the "moral" theories, its appeal to the experiential difference which Jesus made must surely be pronounced valid. It must be taken into account in any appraisal of the development of Christian doctrine. William Temple commented a long time ago in a manner relevant to this concern: "The sin of Arianism is that it shifts the center of interest from the hope of salvation to the hope of explanation. If Arius had triumphed, the church would have become a society of persons holding certain highly disputable opinions. What Athanasius preserved is the ground of the hope of salvation."[20]

We now turn our attention to another strand in Christian thinking about the cross, namely that his death effected a change in the attitude of God, a change which human repentance alone could not have effected. This introduces us to another set of concepts which are related to the meaning of the death of Jesus, namely holiness, law, judgment, acquittal, and justification. This requires a look at the juridical theories of the atonement, especially those of satisfaction and penal substitution. We shall not go over again the all-too-familiar historical material[21] but seek to uncover the basic issues with which such theories are concerned. While defenders of the juridical theories admit that the cross is a manifestation of the costly, vicarious, suffering love of God, they do not think that this goes far enough. The reason given is the inadequate attention paid in the moral theories to the holiness of God, the claims of the divine righteousness upon us, the seriousness of sin, and the related themes of guilt and punishment, the importance of God's vindication of the moral order at the same time as he shows his forgiving love. Or put as a question: How can a holy and righteous God forgive sinful men and women without giving the impression that God does not care for righteousness enough actively to seek its realization in the human community? As we saw in our discussion of Christian anthropology, certain assumptions are made here without which the argument cannot be developed.

---

[20]William Temple, *Christus Veritas* (London: Macmillan, 1934), p. 131.

[21]R. S. Franks, *The Work of Christ* (London: Thomas Nelson & Sons, 1962); F. W. Dillistone, *The Christian Understanding of the Atonement*.

The first assumption, of course, is the reality of God in a specific sense of that term. We simply take for granted here that a valid case can be made for Christian theism.[22] The second assumption is the holiness and righteousness of God. The third is that man is by his creation a social being and that in his life in community, he grows into an apprehension of a moral order which reflects the will of the holy God. On the philosophical level this means the objectivity of moral values.[23] The fourth assumption is the reality of free will. This does not mean that persons are absolutely free to do or be anything they like, which would be nonsense. Nor does it mean the freedom of sheer indeterminacy, which would be meaningless freedom in a vacuum. It is rather the ability and the willingness to be determined by an "apparent good." That is, we freely give our allegiance to what at the time seems to us to be "good," even though bitter experience may later teach us that what we thought was "good" was indeed only an apparent good, not the real good which fulfills our deepest aspirations.[24] The fifth assumption is that this has in fact happened. Human history shows the prevalence of the choice of the apparent good over the real good, the choice of satisfactions for the self which are basically selfish rather than the choice of God and his will which is concerned with the well-being of all. Hence arises the doctrines of sin and of original sin as explanatory of this state of affairs. That more is involved here than a merely intellectual analysis is clear.

The practical problem then becomes: How can God deal with this situation in a manner which does not destroy human freedom and responsibility and which at the same time does not attenuate the holiness and righteousness of God to vanishing point? The above assumptions are behind all the attempts of the juridical theories of atonement to deal with the problem. When we move beyond this point, we enter the hotly disputed areas of biblical exegesis and hermeneutics.

---

[22]H. P. Owen, *The Christian Knowledge of God* (London: University of London, 1969).

[23]For penetrating discussions of the objectivity of values, see C. A. Campbell, *On Selfhood and Godhood* (London: Allen & Unwin, 1957); H. P. Owen, *The Moral Argument for Christian Theism* (London: Allen & Unwin, 1965); I. Trethowan, *Absolute Value* (London: Allen & Unwin, 1970).

[24]W. Temple, *Nature, Man and God.* Lecture IX (London: Macmillan, 1935).

A further set of assumptions made by the juridical theories is as follows:

1. The historical fall which traces man's first disobedience to a free act of the first human beings, Adam and Eve.
2. The transmission of the consequences of such an act biologically as well as socially, an emphasis basic in Augustine but not in the Greek fathers.
3. The further implication that not only the first human pair but also all their descendants are guilty and deserving of punishment, for they are physically born with a corrupt and guilty nature.
4. The assumption that God cannot overlook such deviation but must inflict punishment in the form of suffering upon someone. He cannot simply forgive when penitence is there, however serious the repentance may be. The moral law (that is, the holiness of God) must be vindicated through punishment in the form of suffering.
5. Hence arises the doctrine of penal substitution in its strictest sense. In a manner mysterious to our understanding, the sin of the race is transferred to Christ who bears in our stead the punishment which should have been inflicted on us. On this view, the most important thing about the death of Jesus is that it changes the attitude and action of God. It turns away his wrath and makes it possible for him to forgive.
6. If we ask where the love of God is in all this, the answer is that he has brought about the once-for-all penal and substitutionary death of his Son on the basis of which, through faith, we are acquitted of guilt and eternal punishment, are declared righteous (that is, justified), receive forgiveness, are implanted in Christ, and enabled through the power of the Spirit to be conformed to the image of the Son. We are no longer subject to the fear of the divine wrath, whether in time or eternity.
7. These claims are further complicated by the assumption that sin is sin against the infinite and holy God, therefore its gravity is infinite. All are born into the world shaped by original and actual sin. All are subject to wrath unless they turn and accept in faith the offer of salvation made through the penal substitutionary death of Jesus. To this is added in some traditions (in particular the Augustinian and the Reformed) the further idea of election as

limited and double predestination. Not all will be saved because such universal salvation is not within the eternal will and purpose of God, for experience shows that some respond in faith and others do not. If this offends our sense of justice or of moral values, the reply usually is that these are human criteria and cannot be applied to the actions of God. Who are we to dictate to him how he should act on the basis of merely human judgments of value? Our ideas of justice are no measure of God's.

8. It is true that even on this view, salvation in its fullness is still in the future in the comprehensive sense of salvation earlier defined. However, the most important thing has happened, namely the restoration of a right relationship of elect faithful believers to God their Maker and Redeemer. They may still have to face death and suffering, physical and mental. They may still have to struggle with the "old Adam." No matter: the grace of perseverance will be given to them and they know that in the end all will be well, as Julian of Norwich asserted, at least for the elect.

Many details, of course, have been left out of this account.[25] We hope, however, that enough has been said to justify raising again the issue of religious pluralism against the backdrop of such a view of how we come to be saved. Now if we could be satisfied with the theory of penal substitution in all the features just indicated, it would be a powerful answer to the problem of relativism previously discussed. Jesus would be unique, not only as the paradigm of self-sacrificing love. He would also be the one who by his death brought about such a fundamental change in the attitude of God to mankind. Granted the reality of God, this means a change of objective status. On this view the unique saviorhood of Jesus would stand out in sharp contrast to all other religious figures past and present. For this reason, among others, conservative evangelicals tend to cling to the penal substitutionary theory in its classic Calvinistic form. It seems to offer a firm and unshakable bulwark against all the relativizing tendencies of so much contemporary thought and in particular of much modern theology.

---

[25]For a detailed exposition and critical evaluation of Anselm and the Reformers, cf. L. W. Grensted, *A Short History of the Doctrine of the Atonement* (London: Manchester University Press, 1920), pp. 144ff., also ch. 9.

There are, however, serious problems with this view of the atonement, which we shall note in a moment. The result has been a tendency for Christian thought to polarize. There are those who reject the juridical theories in all and every form. Having done this, they then find it difficult to argue persuasively for the uniqueness of Jesus and in particular of his death. If, as is sometimes the case in the more radical thinkers, they reject also the doctrine of the Incarnation, then the uniqueness of Jesus has to depend on showing that he is the noblest ethical figure in history or the most striking paradigm of selfless love. It is not surprising that at this stage, any claim to uniqueness is often allowed quietly to disappear. Further, what the title Savior means becomes rather ambiguous and obscure. It is not surprising too that the enemies of this watered-down version of the atonement charge that the gospel itself has vanished in the process of reinterpretation.

On the other side are those who dig in their heels and defend the penal substitutionary view in all its Calvinistic detail and rigor. This alienates some who dislike the idea of God this seems to imply and who believe it to be alien to the spirit of Jesus himself. When it comes to defining the attitude of Christians to the non-Christian religions, the defenders of the penal view often assume that the adherents of these religions are "lost" because they lack the knowledge necessary to their salvation and therefore cannot make an act of responsive faith. If they have heard the gospel and do not respond, this shows that they are not of the elect. If they have never heard the gospel and therefore cannot respond, they are "lost" also. This is an inscrutable divine mystery and the human mind must not presume to penetrate it with the categories of merely human thinking.

Furthermore, if they are to be truly converted and saved, they must not only acknowledge Jesus as Lord and Savior but they must also affirm in uncompromising terms this particular view of the atoning death. This alienates those who react against a God who simply writes off all non-Christians to hell and eternal punishment. Of course, the defenders of this view will say that it is not a question of whether we like a doctrine or not but whether it is true. If it is firmly rooted in the inspired Scripture, and they claim that it is, then it is true and binding on our belief, whether we like it or not. The question we wish to consider now is whether these are the only alternatives—either a human Jesus who gives us an example of self-giving love at its highest or the substitutionary victim who turns away the wrath of an infinite and holy God by his penal death.

We shall make our own comments in a moment on these various views. It may be useful, however, to pause for a brief digression into the kind of language which has been used in the traditional doctrines of atonement. The recent concern with language has seen the revival of interest in the role of metaphor. It is obvious that all forms of atonement doctrine depend heavily on the use of metaphor.[26] Not that religious language, including atonement language, is peculiar in this regard. Ordinary language is shot through with metaphor. Perhaps the only difference is that in the area of religious experience, we are concerned with disclosure situations of profound significance for human life. Human language thus becomes unusually strained in the effort to express verbally a fresh apprehension of reality, a transformed vision of what human life is all about.

The dying of Jesus on the cross has been the place where some people have experienced what I. T. Ramsey has called a cosmic disclosure. The word *cosmic* may not be the best choice of language for this. It is intended, however, to emphasize that this disclosure is not simply a deeper apprehension of human existence, true as that may be, but an apprehension, in the human, of a transcendent factor or presence. Whether this transcendent element is to be schematized by personal or impersonal models or perhaps some kind of integration of both, it seems evident that atonement language must again depend heavily upon the personal model, whatever place we give to the impersonal. Ramsey himself seems to agree with this.[27] The cross has been an event potent in changing the human vision of the nature and purpose of God. The effect of this has been the daring use of metaphor as descriptive of what this means. Examples of this are Aulen's use of the metaphor of victory, Anselm's application of feudal analogies to the God-man relationship, the substitutionary theory's use of juridical

---

[26]I. T. Ramsey, *Christian Discourse* (Oxford University Press, 1965); Paul Ricoeur, *Biblical Hermeneutics* (Chico, CA: Scholars Press, 1975); *The Rule of Metaphor* (University of Toronto Press, 1977). Charles Reagan and David Stewart, *The Philosophy of Paul Ricoeur* (Boston: Beacon Press, 1978). Sheldon Sarks, *On Metaphor* (University of Chicago Press, 1979); W. M. Urban, *Language and Reality* (London: Allen & Unwin, 1939).

[27]Ramsey, *Christian Discourse,* ch. 3.

language (law, judge, guilt, punishment, acquittal, justification), the moral theory's use of language taken from interpersonal relationships (love, breach of fellowship, forgiveness, reconciliation, the union of love). In the religious context, the crucial difference is the application of the metaphors to God. We are not talking only about human action.

The problem with the traditional atonement language is the degree to which the metaphors are taken literally and what is the meaning of literal. It may be argued that the very fact that they are metaphor means that they are not to be taken literally. Yet the issue is not so simple. If the atonement metaphors are not literally true, then what are they saying and to what kind of reality do they point? If, for example, the metaphor of victory is not to be taken in a sense quite different from the ordinary use of victory language, then what have we said when it is applied to the death and resurrection of Jesus? If judgment, transgression, and punishment bear quite a different connotation when used in thinking about atonement, then again in what sense are they being used? We are back with the age-old problem of analogy and the precise meaning or meanings which the word symbol can bear. When we reach this point, it may well be that we cannot justify our selection of the key metaphors for our vision of reality except by developing some general theory of meaning.[28] The question then arises as to whether we can have a viable theory of meaning apart from a metaphysic of some kind by which the root metaphors are justified by integration into a coherent and total vision of nature, man, and God. We believe this to be the case.

We now turn to our discussion of and comments upon the points previously mentioned. We accept the view that an appeal to a literal Adam and Eve can no longer be made simply as a dogmatic pronouncement. Yet Tillich is also correct in maintaining that we cannot totally demythologize the concept of the fall because the time-element cannot be eliminated. Sin, alienation, and estrangement came into the world through a temporal act or acts. In this sense, it must be considered historical, even if the details cannot be filled in as the literal interpretations of the Genesis narratives tend to do. The human race had a temporal beginning, and if this is so, sin, however defined, must

---

[28]C. E. Reagan and David Stewart, *Paul Ricoeur: An Anthology* (Boston: Beacon Press, 1978), ch. 10.

have had a temporal beginning too. If sin is defined as a deviation of the will, conceived as the whole person in action, then it cannot be trasmitted biologically. This does not eliminate the idea of the transmission as a psychological and sociological inheritance, but it does compel us to separate this from the idea of guilt as an automatic inheritance of every human being prior to any specific acts.

Original sin may still be used to refer to the cumulative and social consequences of the first sinful act or acts but must not be linked so closely with guilt as in the traditional Augustinian version. It follows from this that we cannot assume that the human race as a whole is guilty and deserving of punishment merely by the fact of being born. This, however, does not inevitably entail the view that the notions of guilt and punishment can be totally eliminated from the theological vocabulary. The question then concerns the precise sense in which such language is to be used.

The crucial issue, then, is whether the holiness of God and its vindication requires the notion of punishment as integral to our understanding of God and his purpose. The problem is easily solved if we identify agape-love and holiness and conclude that God never punishes at all but forgives automatically when there is the appropriate response of penitence. Does this, however, do justice to the biblical understanding of God's holiness and righteousness, our own moral experience, and the conviction that there is a moral order which is not to be explained solely in psychological and emotive terms. This takes us back to the root metaphors for our language about the atoning work of God in Christ.

We shall now concentrate on one particular metaphor, namely that of divine judgment and acquittal, so central to the juridical theories of the atonement. Metaphor is, of course, involved because we are taking analogies from legal systems and processes and applying them to the special relationship which God has toward persons and they to him. The question, then, is: Do legal metaphors apply at all in this realm, and if so, how? Even before we get into any particular atonement model, this juridical approach raises strong emotions.

For some the whole concept of God as Judge is obnoxious, for it seems to take analogies from one area of human activity where hardness of heart, insensitivity to human suffering, and downright injustice sometimes seem to dominate. Often this includes a profound contempt for law as such and for the obviously imperfect systems of jurisprudence which the race has evolved in the course of its long history. For others, law, however inadequate, is a basic requirement of any ordered, civilized, or truly human existence. Human nature being what it is, without law there is only anarchy and violence; and man's life, as Hobbes contended, is nasty, solitary, brutish, and short. The tendency in some quarters today to downgrade the notion of law is one of the saddest and most ominous signs of the fragility of our culture. The reader is referred for a fuller discussion of this question to Whitehead.

Despite Whitehead's insistence that God only works persuasively and never coercively, he does not seem to apply this principle to human society. "Lacking an element of law, there remains a mere welter of details."[29] Although Whitehead is talking here of nature, what he says applies to civil law, a fact which he also recognizes. By his own admission, "As society is now constituted a literal adherence to the moral precepts scattered throughout the gospels could mean sudden death."[30] Law would seem, therefore, to be a necessity for any civilized society, even if the mark of a high civilization, according to Whitehead, is to be judged by its ability to coordinate the various human activities with a minimum recourse to brute force. It is sometimes difficult to distinguish in theological discussion between the pejorative reference to legalism as the abuse of law and contempt for the whole concept of law as such.

The question now becomes whether the concept of law, however limited in the hands of imperfect men and women, can be properly applied in the God-man relationship. Is there any element of truth in the metaphor of the divine Judge? To answer this question fully would require a more detailed and extensive study of several distinct and related topics. The fundamental issues for us, considering the matter from a Christian perspective, are the following:

1. Does the Old Testament and later Judaism think of God as Judge in any way at all?

---

[29]A. N. Whitehead, *Adventures of Ideas* (Cambridge University Press, 1933), pp. 139ff.

[30]Ibid., p. 18.

2. Does Jesus employ juridical concepts to talk about God's relationship to his creatures?

3. While Paul obviously does employ such concepts, are we justified in seeing them as basic and fundamental for his understanding of the God-person relationship? Does he build on Old Testament presuppositions as well as the teaching of Jesus and does he significantly modify both for reasons which seem convincing to him?

4. How far does the later use of juridical metaphors and analogies in the evolution of Christian doctrine build upon the biblical material? Does it correctly interpret that material or does it distort it under the influence of cultural and social factors of a later age?

In view of the complex exegetical and historical issues raised, he would be a bold person who would confidently dogmatize about all these questions. Nevertheless, they cannot be avoided. We shall, therefore, plunge into the discussion, well aware of the hazards which confront us in an area where all the major disciplines overlap. The idea of God and the created order is often discussed on the basis of a naive view of human nature and of the realities of personal, social, and historical existence. If all human beings were spontaneously overflowing with love and good will, then law as imposition would be superfluous, as Tolstoy insisted. As it is obvious that men and women are not spontaneously "good" in this sense, it is clear that law in some sense is necessary to save us from Hobbesian anarchy. Some would blame God for this situation. He should have made us in such a way that unselfish action would flow freely from each one of us. There have been learned and subtle debates as to whether God could have done it this way if he had wanted to do so.[31] Yet there are compelling grounds for thinking that an automatic or robot unselfishness, kindness, love, compassion, and so forth is a contradiction in terms. Some measure, however limited, of freedom and initiative, together with the resultant responsibility, would seem to be involved in the production of authentic moral and spiritual values on the personal level. The Bible

[31]See John Hick, *Evil and the God of Love* (London: Collins, Fontana, 1970); David Griffin, *God, Power and Evil* (Philadelphia: Westminster, 1976).

presents God as creating man/woman with potentialities for such goodness but not as an automatic producer of such goodness.

If this is so, then how could God realize his purpose except by indicating what it is through commands, precepts, rules, and guidelines of some kind. Otherwise, how could we ever learn our authentic destiny and where our true peace lies? Life totally devoid of norms would be a nightmare. What we are suggesting is that the notion of God as law-giver is not inherently an unworthy one, even if we have to be careful about forgetting the inadequacy and imperfection of the human way of practicing law.

This need not mean that God is only Judge and nothing more. Much will depend on how we think of the role of the judge. As man from his earliest beginnings had to grapple with anarchy in human society, it is not surprising that he has had to take this model of the judge from his role in human society. As all legal systems are imperfect and some judges are harsh, corrupt, and unjust, it is again not surprising that the worst examples have sometimes determined human thinking in regard to human society or God. Yet can we abandon the idea of law and justice altogether in our thought of God any more than we can in regard to the structures of human society? Could we endure an unjust, corrupt, or indifferent God? Would we want to live in a universe in which men and women can literally get away with anything with impunity? Could we endure a human society equally indifferent, a question which is again becoming painfully urgent in our modern societies with their endemic violence?

The point of these general remarks is to try and remove the mental block which prevents countless people today from even giving a hearing to any theological doctrine which uses juridical metaphors and models. This is at the root of the suspicion of the Old Testament, not to mention the language of the New Testament and of later Christian doctrine. For the Old Testament and later Judaism, the holiness and righteousness of God are basic assumptions which are never questioned. These, of course, are precisely the assumptions which our modern society does not naturally make.

It follows inevitably from this that to present Jesus as the Savior, in the sense of our deliverer, not only from the psychological sense of guilt but from the painful consequences of the transgression of the law of righteousness, simply does not make sense to many people today. We are prescribing a cure for a disease which modern people do not admit to having. It is obvious that Sartrean man does not need a savior at all, or at least he is never likely to admit that he needs one, for he only transgresses a law of his own making. As long as his philosophical assumptions are what they are, this is inevitable. Likewise an emotivist theory of ethics or a resolute denial of the "objectivity" of values must dispense with any unconditional holiness or righteousness. The same is true of the Freudian reduction of ethics in his postulate of the superego.[32] Presumably, even for a Freudian, one can "sin" against society and experience overwhelming guilt as a consequence. Yet for the "enlightened," society's demands can never have the same unconditional and binding authority as when the sacred reflects a cosmic order or righteousness as the will of the sovereign God.

It is clear, therefore, that to present Jesus as the Savior from the consequences of the holy will of God depends on certain assumptions about the reality, nature, character, and purpose of God as well as something about the nature of man/woman as made in his image. Where these assumptions are not made, the question of salvation takes on a different character. For example, how can the doctrine of justification by faith be made intelligible to a Buddhist unless the latter is prepared to adopt radically different premises for his thinking about human life and destiny? We are fully sensitive to the importance of these questions and even to the indignant question as to why the Buddhist should be asked to change his basic presupposition about the self, karma, and nirvāna. It is also true that in the later mahayana, there are some remarkable structural similarities between the Savior Buddha and Christ the Savior. Nevertheless, we believe our point is a valid one.

For the moment, however, we shall confine our attention to the juridical theories of the atonement which, of course, do rest on certain assumptions about the nature of God and man. Here again our concern is not with details but with the underlying issues and their relation to any claim advanced that Jesus is the Savior in a special sense. It is common ground to both Jews and Christians that God is

---

[32]We have no intention here of pursuing the intricate philosophical issues which such modern views entail. The interested reader may be referred to such works as: Brand Blanshard, *Reason and Goodness* (Allen & Unwin, 1961), chs. 5 and 8; and John Bowker, *The Sense of God* (New York: Oxford University Press, 1973), ch. 6.

both holy and righteous. We have already discussed in some detail the concept of salvation in the Old Testament and later Judaism. Note has also been taken of E. P. Sanders' criticism of those Christian thinkers who accuse Rabbinic Judaism of being a legalistic religion of works-righteousness. He insists that "covenantal nomism" includes as a basic premise the power and grace of Yahweh. Although the Jew is expected to obey the commandments if he is to remain an accepted member of the covenant community, the salvation which such membership implies is not in the last analysis earned or granted on the basis of merit but is due to the free mercy of Yahweh. In other words, obedience and ethical fruits are expected of the faithful Jew, but they are not the ultimate ground of his salvation. Christianity also expects faith to produce works, even though works are not the ground or condition of forgiveness and acceptance by God. If this is the case, then Judaism and Christianity are at one in the belief that salvation is of God's free mercy and not the result of earned merit treated as the ground of salvation. This, however, is a reminder to us that the model of God as Judge needs to be supplemented by other models, but it does not eliminate the model altogether. We return, therefore, to our original question. If we take the holiness of God seriously, then can we eliminate entirely the penal element from human experience and, therefore, from the suffering of Jesus? Nevertheless, it is extremely important how we conceive this to operate.

It is tempting to reduce it to a law of consequences, conceived in an impersonal way, in order to avoid language about the wrath or anger of God as well as to free God from direct responsibility for the painful consequences of the transgression of his holy will. C. H. Dodd seems inclined to take this view in his well-known commentary.[33] Whiteley also maintains that in Paul, the wrath of God is an *effectus*, that is, the inevitable result of the transgression of law, rather than an *affectus*, that is, a personal emotion or feeling of anger on the part of God toward mankind.[34] Yet if we wish to stress the legitimacy and necessity of personal analogies in our God-talk, it seems difficult to eliminate

---

[33]C. H. Dodd, *The Epistle of Paul to the Romans* (London: Collins, Fontana, 1959), pp. 45ff.

[34]D. E. H. Whiteley, *The Theology of St. Paul* (Oxford: Basil Blackwell, 1964), pp. 44ff.

entirely the idea of a feeling-reaction by God. We may wish to qualify and purify the notion of anger from a too-close resemblance to our human "righteous anger" which is often more anger than righteous.

Yet can we get rid of anthropopathic language without losing the reality of the personal God? Of course, it would be fatal to the Christian view of God to insist that his attitude is one of steady and unchanging anger toward the human race. This would not make sense either of the Old Testament or the New. Provided we retain the truth that God's reactions of anger are rooted in a deeper and unalterable loving concern for his children, then the language of divine anger may still be properly used of specific divine reactions to specific human actions. "The truth of retribution is not denied if God himself shares in the suffering which it entails."[35]

Again, although the law of consequences, the sowing and the reaping, may be understood as effectus rather than affectus, a mode of working rather than a feeling which God has, it still remains that insofar as God is the author of the moral law, then he is responsible for the law of consequences which is built into the created order by the Creator. God has willed that certain consequences follow in the moral realm as well as in the physical realm if that order is transgressed. If, of course, there is no God and moral values are not referred to him as their source, these arguments would not hold. We have already rejected such a view and drawn attention to the arguments advanced by H. P. Owen. The law of consequences could, of course, be retained as a cosmic law such as karma in the Hindu tradition without it being related to the further notion of a loving and redemptive activity of a compassionate God.

Even on the Christian view, however, it is not necessary to hold that all human suffering and pain is due to sin or the human transgression of the divine will. All that we need to say is that some suffering is to be accounted for in this way and to this degree it is penal. The word *punishment* is also loosely used and this causes theological difficulties. We talk of a boxer receiving punishment when it means simply receiving hard blows. Or we equate punishment with vindictiveness, vengeance, or sheer sadism. Obviously, no Christian theology can work with such ideas. We still contend that this does not

[35]H. W. Robinson, *Revelation and Redemption* (London: Nisbet, 1942), p. 274.

compel us to abandon altogether the related ideas of guilt, judgment, and punishment in the divine-human relationship, even if we insist that these are not the only factors at work and perhaps not the most important when seen in the light of God's ultimate purpose.

As far as this bears on the death of Jesus, the question concerns whether in his suffering there was a penal element. Does his suffering reveal, not only God's vicarious, costly love but also Jesus' submission as our representative to a judgment of God upon sin? Christian faith and experience has always declared this to be so. If it is a fact, then the uniqueness of his death takes on a depth and dimension which it would not otherwise have. There are also problems which arise from the side of Christology. If the suffering of Jesus is exclusively a suffering of the man and in no way the suffering of God to whose will he was related in total union and dedication, then God is left out of the picture at the crucial point. This is why the classical view of divine impassibility has to be modified.[36]

Again this is not to say that no form of impassibility can be defended or that the ancient view was not trying to express some truths about God which a serious theology has to take into account. At the deepest level, it may be necessary to modify our language and use it more carefully than does the traditional penal, substitutionary view of the Reformers. The New Testament nowhere says in so many words that God punished Jesus. It would be theologically more accurate to say that God in Christ himself bears the painful consequences of his own judgment. This, however, presupposes a "high Christology" which many today will not accept. Being left only with the suffering of the man Jesus, they find it difficult to see this suffering other than a judgment inflicted on him by a remote God who stands aloof from his suffering. A more profound understanding of the Father-Son union can alone resolve this issue. In which case some doctrine of Incarnation has to return.

If the above is true, then it is obviously improper to talk in simplistic terms of the death of Jesus changing the attitudes of God. This would seem to imply that God does not wish the saving of the sinner and that he has to be compelled by some fact extrinsic to himself to show forth his mercy and forgiveness. If, on the other hand, the

---

[36]H. W. Robinson, *Suffering Human and Divine* (London: S. C. M., 1940).

suffering of Jesus is not only the suffering of the Son but of the Father and if the judgment of sin is borne by Jesus, not in a manhood isolated from the Father but in the deepest union with the Father, then our understanding of what the costly love of God meant to the Father as well as to the Son will take on another dimension.

Nevertheless, there is a proper sense in which we can talk about a change of God's attitude as well as of man's. If the alienation of men and women from God is conceived of in personal terms, then the breach of fellowship has results on both the divine and the human side. Reconciliation equally involves a change on both sides. However much God loves and desires our fellowship, this cannot become a reality for him as long as we are totally unrepentant and spurn the proffered grace. This is true on both the human and the divine level. The weakness of the language of penal substitituion in its classic form is its implication that God, conceived in remote transcendence and wrath, has to be forced to love by so much penal suffering inflicted on another than Himself. The unity of Jesus' will with the will of the Father is somehow lost. God, therefore, must be thought of as taking the initiative through the Son in bearing the penal suffering which rightly falls on us.

If we are to use the language of punishment, then we would have to say that God punishes by attaching various kinds of suffering to transgression of his will but actively bears or participates in that punishment through the assumption of the real humanity of Jesus. In a sense, the cross is God's inflicted self-punishment out of love and Jesus knows this to be the case in his acceptance of the cross as the Father's will. H. Wheeler Robinson has put this point finely in his own words and those of Denney. "As God's self-limited circle expands to take in that sin of the world which He cannot ignore, the sin becomes so much suffering for the holy God—in no other way can it enter the circle of His holiness. James Denney seems drawn to such a view when he writes: 'I have often wondered whether we might not say that the Christian doctrine of the Atonement just meant that in Christ God took the responsibility of evil upon Himself, and somehow subsumed evil under good'."[37] When we see the cross in this light, we can never treat sin lightly or regard our reconciliation as simply a matter of divine forgive and forget.

---

[37]H. W. Robinson, *The Cross in the Old Testament* (London: S. C. M., 1960).

Finally, what does this mean for the issue of religious pluralism with which we started? It means that the unique saviorhood of Jesus, and the central role of his death in this saving activity, cannot in the end be divorced from an interpretation of the total fact of his life, death, and resurrection. Furthermore, a Christology "from below," which remains that and no more, cannot do justice to this event. We are forced back to the doctrine of the Incarnation and the Godward side both of the life and the death. The critic will no doubt object that we have come full circle to the exclusivist and dogmatic claims of the Christian past. These, however, are emotive terms. In a sense, we admit the charge. We do not admit that the claims made are exclusive in the bad sense which would make them inconsistent with the universal, saving love of God toward all mankind and his intention to bring all who deeply desire it to eternal fellowship and communion with himself. We shall try to show in what follows that this can be justified and defended in the light of the position which we have just outlined.

The view of the cross we have just outlined does not depend on the biological transmission of sin and the notions of inherited guilt and sin inextricably linked to the traditional doctrine of eternal punishment. It is possible to retain the view of God as judge and to insist on a penal element in human suffering as well as in the suffering of Jesus through God's total identification with us through Jesus. However, this model of God as judge is only one model. It is not the only model. Taken alone, in a strictly legal sense, it would seriously distort the full activity of the God and Father of our Lord Jesus Christ. Nevertheless, it is a model which cannot safely be completely ignored or eliminated without encouraging a superficial view of sin and responsibility and without depriving the cross of that disclosure of the depth of the costly divine love which is the power of God unto salvation.

Chapter Six

*Salvation and Saviors**

We have examined various ways of dealing with the challenge of religious pluralism and have found many of them wanting. This judgment has been made from a Christian perspective and in the light of the almost universal Christian conviction that Christ is the Savior in a sense which is not true for any other person. By taking this stand, the importance of personal mediation for salvation has been stressed. Here again, however, it is a case not merely of many forms of personal mediation but of one particular form, namely Jesus of Nazareth.

How, then, can we understand the relationship of Jesus Christ to the universal history of the race? How can the atoning and reconciling work of Christ be brought into effective relationship to all men and women at whatever point in the time-process they happen to be? This is the inevitable question for all Christians who are not ready to adopt an ultimate pluralism and a thoroughgoing relativism in regard to all religious claims. As we shall see, there are some religions which would not accept our principle of personal mediation except in a secondary sense, that is, as a practical but not indispensable means of salvation. This will be looked at in due course.

*Note: In view of the technical difficulty of achieving consistency in the diacritical marks for the Sanskrit and Pali terms which occur below, those marks deliberately have been omitted.

There are two ways, however, in which this issue of personal mediation can be considered. The first is to say that what saves is not the person as such but the truth which he or she is instrumental in bringing to the rest of mankind. The other view is to claim the centrality of the person as not only the mediator of truth but also as the living truth. Christianity, of course, belongs to this second category. The truth cannot be detached and separated from the Mediator, however much importance is given to the latter as exemplar and spiritual helper. In other words, Christ is not a guru or teacher who can be dispensed with when the pupil has reached a certain level of spiritual attainment. This involves a view of truth which transcends the conceptual, propositional, or logical forms with which in our Western tradition we associate the nature of truth. This does not mean that all verbalizing and conceptualizing is useless but only that it is transcended in the living person. The category of life is more comprehensive than that of intellect alone.[1]

Needless to say, it also involves a view of truth which transcends what we usually mean by scientific truth. Therefore, to find in a specific person the source of the living truth in this sense involves some kind of appeal both to history and experience. "Merely knowing a doctrine has a certain conceptual content and merely holding correct doctrines are not enough: there remains the actual undergoing of the experience to which the doctrine points."[2] The undergoing of such an experience involves for us a relationship to Jesus Christ.

The word *experience* is itself ambiguous and calls for further analysis. It is important, however, to make one further distinction. Hindus and Buddhists, to mention only two, would agree that "truth" transcends the merely intellectual understanding without excluding the latter. They would not, however, hold to the unique mediation of the living Truth through one particular person alone. This is the real divide between Christian incarnational doctrine and other religions. Christianity is distinctive in the sense that it not only claims that God is a Savior (as, for example, in Judaism) but also that God has acted in Jesus of Nazareth in a unique way and that the person of Jesus has become an integral factor in the saving relationship between God and individual men and women.

---

[1] H. W. Robinson, *Revelation and Redemption*, p. 27.
[2] John E. Smith, *The Analogy of Experience*, pp. 25ff.

For the Christian, there is no way by which he or she can kick away the ladder (that is, Jesus Christ) by which one has climbed to the saving knowledge of God. This distinguishes it from all those forms of mysticism which treat all personal mediators as only helpful stages on the ascent to a self-evidencing communion with the divine apart from any mediator. There is really no parallel to this in the Hindu conception of many avatars or in Buddhism (Hinayana or Mahayana) or in Plato and Plotinus or even in the Old Testament. The Old Testament prophets from Moses onwards do not themselves claim to be saviors in their own right. Yahweh alone is the Savior and they are mouthpieces and agents of the saving God through the proclamation of his Word.

We have tried to defend the uniqueness of Jesus as the Savior on this basis. This is not to deny that God is the Savior but that God in his action in Jesus is the definitive and final saving act. This means that no other saving action is as complete and fundamental as this one because it puts us in a relationship to God in the truest and profoundest sense of the word God. An appeal has also been made to experience in the sense that God in Jesus has dealt with the problems of sin, suffering, and death in a way which effects the transition in human existence from life *en sarki* to life *en pneumati.* To be "in Christ" is to be saved at the deepest levels of human existence in such a way that an unshakable bond has been established between God and the believer. Whether the "in Christ" should be described as mystical or not is perhaps a matter of language. In view of the ambiguity of the many meanings which can be attached to mysticism,[3] it might be better to find other language.

In starting from this point, we have created special difficulties for ourselves and in particular for our treatment of the issue of religious pluralism. Does our definition of salvation in the Christian sense arbitrarily exclude millions of people from the possibility of salvation? What of those who lived before Christ and could not have known the incarnate Lord? What of those belonging to the non-Christian religions, whether before or after Christ? Or what of those who are not "religious" or who have deliberately rejected the Christ in favor of a different diagnosis of the human predicament and have chosen another solution to the problem diagnosed?

---

[3]See the long list of definitions of mysticism in W. R. Inge, *Christian Mysticism* (London, 1899).

Some consideration has been given to this latter point in our previous discussion. of Christian anthropology and Don Cupitt's charge that its diagnosis of the human situation is only one among many and not necessarily the normative one. We tried to rebut his arguments, although fully aware that the strength of the Christian diagnosis can hardly be convincing in isolation from the Christian faith as a whole, which includes both the diagnosis and the answer to it. A thoroughgoing pluralism accepts as given this diversity of diagnoses of the human situation and of the remedies offered. Salvation must, then, by its very nature, be pluralistic. No one form of salvation can be universally normative.

How can the Christian, who denies this assumption, meet this challenge and particularly the charge of arrogant exclusivism and religious imperialism of the worst kind? Some, of course, will deny that it is possible and suggest that the Christian should accept this with as much grace as he can muster. After all, he or she can still have Christ as the Christian way to salvation. The Christian finds it difficult to accept this solution because he is not convinced that the concept of God which emerges from a thoroughgoing relativism is in fact the true God. He does not necessarily have to say that God in the Christian sense has left himself without witness outside the Judeo-Christian tradition. Nevertheless, he does believe that something occurred in Jesus which transcends all other religions, including the Judaism out of which Christianity emerged. What is new is not a fresh set of theological or philosophical ideas, even if these are the consequences. What is new is the fact of Jesus Christ himself. He can never be reduced to a concept or a set of religious ideas. The problem, for the Christian, therefore, is to defend the universal significance of a specific fact, namely Jesus Christ. It is the old problem of the scandal of particularity. From the Enlightenment onwards, Christian thinkers have sometimes attempted to alleviate this problem by searching for a universal essence of religion. The major difficulty here is that religious experience, taken as a whole, does not speak with one voice as to the nature of the saving reality (that is, God) or the nature of that from which we need to be saved. Furthermore, it is difficult on this view to avoid a relativism in regard to the types of salvation offered on the basis of such a study.

Another way of handling the same theme is to seek for the essence of Christianity and define it in such a way as to make it possible to relate the Christian understanding of salvation to the totality of human history, including all the manifestations of the religious spirit. Troeltsch's classic discussion of this issue can hardly be bettered as a starting-point.[4] The reading of his essay, which dates back to 1903 and 1913, is of special interest in the light of the recent debate, already alluded to, about *The Myth of God Incarnate*. It is clear that Troeltsch, despite the charge of historical relativism, wishes to defend in some meaningful sense the self-identity of the Christian religion and even its normative superiority to all other manifestations of the religious spirit. Yet he believes this can be done only if essence is defined as no longer determined by the dogmatic view of incarnation held throughout the Christian centuries until it was seriously challenged from the eighteenth century onwards. He admits that the distinctiveness of Christianity is its relationship to the person of Jesus but not if this means setting Christianity in absolute opposition to the rest of humanity.[5]

We cannot absolutize the Christian community which emerged from Jesus' life and action as if it were "the eternal, absolute center of salvation for the whole span of humanity."[6] Rather, Christianity only "fulfills in its own particular way what is a general law of man's spiritual life."[7] Furthermore, he insists that we cannot define the essence of Christianity on the basis of the original Jesus discovered by historical research. "The recognition of the essence cannot be exclusively based on the original time and on the preaching of Jesus."[8] We cannot select elements from the teaching and experience of Jesus, such as God the Father, and define essence on that basis. If the concept of essence is to be retained at all, it must be in regard to the character of Christianity in its totality as a developing historical phenomenon and the values which emerge in that development.

Still less can we define it in terms of an exclusivist doctrine of Incarnation. He sharply contrasts his view of Christianity and the traditional dogma. "And we had best abandon altogether reading this

---

[4]Ernst Troeltsch, *Writings on Theology and Religion* (Atlanta: John Knox Press, 1977), ch. 3.

[5]Ibid., p. 188.

[6]Ibid., p. 189.

[7]Ibid., p. 202.

[8]Ibid., p. 151.

meaning into the christological dogmas of Nicaea and Chalcedon, however elastic they may be."⁹ He admits, of course, that the historical existence of the person of Christ is absolutely necessary given a certain view of redemption and salvation. If salvation involves a redemptive act whereby creation, trapped in suffering and death because of sin, is liberated, then, of course, Jesus is absolutely necessary. If Jesus is given a superhuman divine dignity, guaranteed by the infallibility of the church and/or Scripture, then again there is no dispensing with Jesus. Again, if Jesus is the primal and indispensable miracle, then again we cannot do without him.¹⁰ It is clear, however, that Troelsch does not assent to these conditions. If there is an "absoluteness" about Jesus or Christianity in all its multi-faceted development, then it must be found in the creative ideas and values which Jesus historically set in motion and which shaped the life of the Christian community and through it the whole of humanity ever since. How modern this all sounds in the context of the recent debate about Jesus without the dogma of the Incarnation.

It should, however, in fairness to Troeltsch, be said that he does not let the classic view of the person of Christ go without a pang. He is fully conscious of the break he is making with the tradition, nor does he exult over this in a mood of satisfied complacency. He is clearly exercised at a level deeper than historical research with the preservation of certain moral and spiritual values which have come into the world through Christianity, and which he does not wish to see destroyed. This he calls critical idealism. Furthermore, he wishes to preserve continuity between the old and the new versions of Christianity. He is not an iconoclast intent on dismantling Christianity from top to bottom. Yet the more he sees Christianity assimilated to the universal, ongoing historical process, the less easy does he find it to give that central position to Jesus which characterized traditional dogmatic interpretations of his person.

Troeltsch is also well aware of the significance of cult and community activity in any living religion and that "lectures on religious philosophy will never produce or replace a real religion."¹¹ As

---

⁹Ibid., p. 206.

¹⁰Ibid., p. 191.

¹¹Ibid., p. 197.

long as Christianity survives as a distinct religion, it will have Christ at the center of the cult. On the other hand, it is not the absolute uniqueness of the redeemer which matters,[12] but that around him cluster the effects of the Christian and prophetic type of belief and the moral and spiritual values which emerge therefrom. The tension in Troeltsch's thought is evident. It is equally clear that if we remain where Troeltsch left us, we cannot talk of Jesus as the Savior except in the limited sense which Troeltsch can give to this. Any reply to Troeltsch must grapple once again with the concept of a unique redemptive act accomplished in the life, death, and resurrection of Jesus. Nor will we be able to discard so quickly the dogmas in which the church first expressed its conviction that in Jesus Christ, God acted in a saving way which has no exact parallel. We shall first turn our attention to the concept of salvation and saviors in the non-Christian religions to see if there is any substance in this Christian claim. Then it will be time to turn again to the atoning work of God in Christ and to ask whether this stands only as an illustration of a general principle or whether it involves the centrality of Christ both in time and eternity for our salvation. Is it, in fact, the case that no parallel can be found elsewhere to the idea of a personal mediator of salvation?

We shall concentrate on Buddhism because Gotama has come to occupy a central position in both forms of Buddhism in a way which is hardly true of the avatars of Hinduism. We shall also follow the guidance of Dr. Conze at this point because of the clarity with which he expounds the essential features of Buddhism and his sober and realistic appraisal of the similarities and differences between Christianity and Buddhism. He warns us at the start that there is no exact equivalent in Buddhist terminology to the Christian conception of a "Savior."[13] He also warns us of the need to listen to how Buddhists talk about "Saviors" in their own terms. Loaded terms like worship, prayer, sin, love, eternal, or supernatural should be avoided. More neutral terms are required, for example, revere (that is, regard with extreme respect), vow, evil, devotion, deathless, supernormal. Care must also be taken in ascribing to Buddhist saviors such words as grace, mercy, and forgiveness.

---

[12]Ibid., p. 203.

[13]Edward Conze, *Buddhist Saviours;* cf. ch. 5 of E. O. James, *The Saviour God* (Manchester University Press, 1963).

It seems to be generally agreed that original Buddhism did not have savior figures and that Gautama himself stressed, not his own person, but the doctrine which he taught. The concept of savior, therefore, is found only in the later development of what is known as the Mahayana. The Lotus of the Good Law belongs to this literature. Here we find such language as that all beings "who experience sufferings will, on hearing the name of Avalokiteśvara, the Bodhisattva, the great being, be set free from their ills."[14] The devotee is told to learn his name, bear it in mind, invoke and implore him, pay homage, revere him, and so forth. As a consequence "in death, disaster and calamity, He is the savior, refuge and resort (savior here = saranam). He has great might, miraculous, psychic, and magical powers. He is their savior (trataru) and "destroys all sorrow, fear and ill."[15] Avalokiteśvara is not, however, unique. He only does what all Bodhisattvas can do. "Comforted we shall comfort those beings who are yet as without comfort! Gone to Nirvana, we shall lead to Nirvana those beings who have not yet got there."[16]

We have already noted how in the Old Testament Yahweh is presented as a deliverer from specific ills and misfortunes. The idea of Yahweh as savior in the course of Israel's history, under prophetic influence, becomes also the liberator from sin, judgment, and from moral and spiritual ills. It is necessary to ask, therefore, what precise meaning is to be attached to the idea of saviorhood when applied to a Bodhisattva. From earliest times, Buddhists have conceived of salvation as a process of crossing over. Later, Tara, who ferries across, became the savior par excellence and was closely connected with Avalokiteśvara, a kind of female counterpart who in China evolves into Kwan Yin. Tara's merciful intent is to free all beings from birth and death. What is needed is to "correctly repeat her names."[17]

In Buddhist mythology, Avalokiteśvara and Tara, two Bodhisattvas, are dependent on a perfectly enlightened Buddha, Amitabha. The latter, when he was the monk Darmakara, made forty-eight vows of which the eighteenth is considered the most important

---

[14]Ibid., p. 68.

[15]Ibid.

[16]Ibid., p. 69.

[17]Ibid., p. 70.

and involved the promise that when he became a Buddha, he would not enter into enlightenment "unless all beings who believe in me and love me with all their hearts are able to win rebirth in my kingdom if they should wish to do so."[18] Avalokiteśvara, Tara, and Amitabha are three saviors who belong to one family (Kula). They are connected with the Paradise or Buddha-field situated in the West. They are not alone, however, for the Scriptures mention thousands of Buddhas and Bodhisattvas.

Hinayana continued on the whole to ignore this idea of a multiplicity of Buddhas, with the exception of Maitreya, the coming Buddha. In other words, the older Buddhism claimed the historical Buddha was not a "Savior" and that everyone must save himself by obedience to the Buddha's teaching. This aspect of early Buddhism has led to the use of the epithets "rationalistic" and "humanistic" to describe its basic character. Conze cites the comment of the Ven. Walpola Rahula: "A man has the power to liberate himself from all bondage through his own personal effort and intelligence. . . . If the Buddha is to be called a 'Savior' at all, it is only in the sense that he discovered and showed the Path to liberation. But we must tread the path ourselves."[19] Before proceeding to a further look at the Mahayana, we pause to consider the bearings of what has been said about the Hinayana in regard to the questions we have raised about religious pluralism and the saviorhood of Jesus Christ. While Hinayana Buddhism and Christianity both claim to be "saving" in some sense, it seems evident that it is not the same sense. Wherein lie the differences?

There is no concept in the Hinayana of a transcendent Creator, Holy, Righteous, and Compassionate. "The most distinctive feature of Buddhist ethics is its freedom from theism which leaves room for rationalism and rules out submission to some superhuman power controlling the world-process."[20] This judgment is accepted by Ling, and also by Conze who says: "If indifference to a personal Creator of the universe is atheism, then Buddhism is indeed atheistic."[21] It is also

[18]Ibid.

[19]Ibid., p. 72.

[20]Trevor Ling, *The Buddha* (London: Penguin, Pelican, 1976), p. 54.

[21]E. Conze, *Buddhism: Its Essence and Development* (New York: Harper & Row, 1955); cf. also R. F. Aldwinckle, *More than Man: A Study in Christology.*

confirmed by such Buddhist scholars as Prof. Thittila: "In Buddhism there is no such thing as belief in a body of dogmas which have to be taken on faith, such as belief in a supreme being, a creator of the universe, the reality of an immortal soul, a personal savior or archangels who are supposed to carry out the will of the supreme deity."[22] Since there seems to be widespread agreement on this issue, at least in regard to the Hinayana, it does not seem necessary to belabor the point. There is lacking in the Hinayana both the idea of a transcendent creator and sustainer of the universe as well as of the concept of "saviorhood" applied to a historical figure. We may, therefore, accept Ling's summing-up: "What is certain, on the other hand, is that the Buddha was not regarded by the earliest generation of Buddhists as a superhuman figure of any kind . . . or in any sense a superhuman Savior."[23]

It is clear from our previous discussion of Judaism and Christianity that the idea of a transcendent and personal Creator-God is at the heart of both. Salvation is held to depend upon a certain relationship to this God, whether conceived of in terms of Exodus-Sinai and obedience to the Torah in the covenant community or in terms of this God becoming man or incarnate in the person of Jesus as the Christ, the crucified and risen Lord. The issue of religious pluralism seems to take on an acute form at this point. It appears that we are concerned, not only with variations on a single theme, but also with two completely different world-views and two quite different concepts of what it means to be saved.

The Buddha in the Hinayana does not claim the kind of role which Jesus occupies for the Christian, nor does he appeal to the will of a transcendent God, active in history, as does Judaism. Any kind of synthesis between Hinayana Buddhism, Judaism, and Christianity would seem to be impossible except on certain conditions. Either we must try to show that Hinayana is implicitly theistic, a position which the historical evidence forbids us to take, or that the idea of God is not central to Judaism and Christianity. It is true that in recent times, some attempts have been made to show the plausibility of the latter. Apart

---

[22]K. W. Morgan, ed., *The Path of the Buddha* (New York: Ronald Press, 1956), p. 71.

[23]Ling, *The Buddha*, p. 142.

from the so-called "God is dead" theology of a few years ago, it could be argued that some forms of process theology have so radically modified the traditional theistic idea of a transcendent and sovereign Creator-God to the point where some reapproachment with the Hinayana might be possible. Some modern biblical scholars, notably Bultmann (but he is not alone in this), have questioned whether Jesus put his own person in any sense at the center of his proclamation of the coming kingdom. On this view, neither Gotama nor Jesus claimed the central role which later followers were to ascribe to them.

If all these points could be established, although they are still a matter of vigorous debate, then some of the tensions and disagreements between the Hinayana and the Judeo-Christian tradition might be ironed out in a synthesis which includes but transcends the basic elements in these different religious traditions. The crucial question is whether the adherents of either religion could recognize themselves in such a synthesis. Is not the Buddhist under pressure to make fundamental revisions of his total world-view? Is the Judaism or Christianity which emerges from such reductionist attempts anything like the actual religion by which Jews and Christians have lived and continue to live? The answer would appear to be no.

It could, of course, be argued that the proposed synthesis is in fact a new religion, a fresh and creative religious advance and that Buddhism in its Hinayanist form and Judaism and Christianity need to be superseded and that this is in fact what is happening in the global village of which we are now a part. If this is what is being claimed, then it should be frankly admitted and also realized that the new synthesis now takes the place of the historic religions.[24] In this case, the question can properly be asked why we should accept the new synthesis as a more profound and valid interpretation of the nature and meaning of human existence than any of the specific religions we have considered. The conflict of world-views would still be with us, except that we have added a new one.

It seems evident that Hinayana Buddhism is without some of the key elements in Judaism and Christianity, such as the holiness of God

---

[24]We use here our Western vocabulary which, at least in recent times, permits the description of Buddhism as a religion. In so doing, it is assumed that religion is not equated with any form of theism. This, however, is a semantic matter, not a theological or philosophical judgment.

conceived as moral righteousness, sin as the transgression of the holy will of such a God, the reality of such transgression and the consequent alienation of the human race from God, the need for forgiveness, reconciliation, and the restoration to trusting fellowship with a personal God, the present experience of the grace and love of God through the activity of God's Holy Spirit, faith in the power of such a God to act in history with a view to the ultimate consummation of his kingdom, eternal life as not only a quality of life here and now but also as a foretaste of a blessed existence after death in a transformed personal and individual existence. Judaism and Christianity would agree on these basic points but the latter would add the decisive experience of being "in Christ" as the condition of the fullest possible realization of the divine purpose for his creatures.

To ask the Hinayanist to think in these terms is rather absurd, for it would require such a fundamental change in his outlook as to make him wonder whether in fact he is not being asked to surrender his Buddhism. If we are expecting this of the Buddhist, we should be frank and open about it. According to the Hinayana, the Buddha exhorts his followers to depend upon themselves for deliverance, for the Tathagatas are only teachers (Dhammapade V. 276).[25] In this case, perhaps we should think of early Buddhism as the new wisdom rather than as a religion. If "salvation" for the Hinayana is not the establishing of a right relationship with a Creator and Redeemer God, then what is it? It is at least a theory of existence, that is, human existence as seen in a cosmic setting. It is a diagnosis of the human malaise and an offered cure. The malaise, however, is not alienation from a personal God rooted in willful disobedience. Rather it is the consequence of the human involvement in karma and the inevitable law of cause and effect which gives to all living existence, human and non-human, the character of suffering.[26] The cure, however, is not only a theory but a technique which can help to break the entail of action through karma and liberate the individual into nirvana.

In asking for the meaning of salvation in this context, therefore, we need to know what is involved in the kind of deliverance offered. A quick answer would be into nirvana as the sacred. For the person who

[25]Ling, *The Buddha*, p. 142.
[26]Ibid., pp. 134ff.

is still influenced by Jewish and Christian ideas, it is almost impossible to separate the notion of the sacred from the holiness of God's will. It is clear that Buddhism has some idea of the sacred but completely divorced from the idea of God in the above sense. Nibbana or nirvana is sacred as the source of Buddhist values. Whatever is venerated as sacred has some relationship to nibbana, whether it be the Dhamma or doctrine, the bhikkus who are bearers of the Dhamma, or the stupa or image which symbolically represents it. Buddhism may be secular and humanistic as defined over against theism. In its own terms, however, there is no basic conflict between its humanism and its sense of the sacred as nibbana.[27]

The same problem arises in regard to transcendence. This term is not often used by Jews—or Christians, for that matter. Its use tends to depend on a certain level of theological and philosophical sophistication. However, when it is used, it is invariably applied to the sovereign Creator-God. In philosophers like Kant, for example, it has quite a different significance. Again we find Ling claiming that early Buddhism had an awareness of a transcendental dimension, a sense of the absolute sacred though not expressed in terms of a belief in God.[28] But what exactly is this sacred, this transcendental dimension, this "not-born, not-become, not-made, and not-conditioned"? Taken out of context and at first glance, we might take this as pointing to the God of Judaism and Christianity who is likewise "not-born" (that is, eternal), who is Being rather than becoming (with due respect to the process thinkers), who is "not-made" but exists *a se*, who is not conditioned, that is, not affected by any powers or influences outside his own nature. This, however, as we have seen, would be a complete misreading of the Hinayanist position. What, then, is the sacred of Buddhism if it is not the holiness of God? Perhaps it is impossible for a Westerner to get more than a distorted glimpse of what this means. It is clear that nibbana is not a transcendent and holy Creator and Redeemer of the world. Entry into the state of nibbana, either partially in this life or after death, is not the salvation of the immortal soul or the total person in some kind of resurrected or embodied existence. This is made impossible by the basic Buddhist repudiation of the notion of the individual soul.[29]

---

[27]Ibid., p. 147.

[28]Ibid.

[29]Ibid., p. 149.

One of the interesting things in Ling's treatment of this question is the way in which he has shown the significance of the Sangha and the social and political implications of this for the Buddhist concept of community and even of the Buddhist state. "For the Buddhist, it (that is, the search for salvation) meant a life in the community,"[30] in the first place in the Sangha and later in the wider community permeated by the Buddhist values preserved by the Sangha. Here at first sight there seems again to be some kind of significant affinity between this emphasis and the Jewish and Christian concepts of the kingdom, or of the church in later Christian developments. This, however, we are warned against. The Sangha is not a group of monks nor is it a fellowship of believers under the rule of God, for the latter concept is missing. Nor is entry into nibbana deliverance from sin, for if the latter is defined as transgression of the holy will of God, this idea too is lacking. Nor is it union by faith with a personal savior, for the Hinayanist is not dependent upon a relationship to any historical figure, not in the sense which this language might have in a Christian context. Certainly Gotama may be highly revered as the source of the Dhamma or the doctrine, but he is not the Savior.

The thoroughgoing pluralist, who wishes to see all religions as expressions of a common goal or understanding of human existence, must be in great difficulties at this point. One can appreciate a Buddhist claiming that Buddhism is the most satisfactory diagnosis and cure of the ills to which human flesh is heir. It is difficult to take seriously the claims of those who insist that Hinayana Buddhism, Judaism, and Christianity are basically saying the same things and offering the same kind of salvation. Against this, it may be argued that the Hinayana is not to be equated with Buddhism per se. The later development of the Mahayana finally led to what looks like a theistic religion in the sense of a theism not wholly different from that found in Judaism or Christianity. It is these which should be compared before making any final appraisal of Buddhism. We shall now try and see how far this is the case, taking Conze as our guide. We shall list the basic points in Conze's work which are relevant to our question about religious pluralism in relation to the Christian claim that Jesus is the Savior.

---

[30]Ibid.

1. Buddhism and Christianity.—Faith is a word used by Conze and seems to mean a relationship of trust which calls forth a certain kind of devotion. In this broad sense, one can talk about faith in the Buddha, but this does not mean that he is a savior except "in the strictly limited sense that he had discovered the doctrine (dharma) which faithfully followed would lead to salvation as deliverance from karma and samsara."[31]

2. The Bodhisattva as Savior.—Is there a richer and more comprehensive idea of salvation involved in the idea of the celestial Bodhisattva? The latter is one who resolved to win enlightenment by following the way of the Buddha. As he progresses along this way, he reaches a stage when he is completely disinterested. His personal problems are resolved and he has acquired more than enough merit for himself. The introduction of the idea of merit may repel certain Christians, but it has to be remembered that it has played a not inconsiderable role in Jewish, Catholic, and even Protestant Christianity, despite the latter's formal repudiation of it. In any case, the Bodhisattva operates within the context of the karmic doctrine with its attendant ideas of reward and punishment, merit and rebirth, in a kind of existence which has been earned by previous conduct. "Killers will be short-lived, jealous people will be of little account, the stingy will be poor."[32] A gluttonous person could become a hog; a rapacious one a tiger.

To return to the Bodhisattva: at the seventh stage he becomes the celestial and disinterested one and acts only out of concern for others. His motive is pure compassion. He chooses to remain here rather than enter immediately into nirvana. At the ninth stage, he takes a second vow which is a completely disinterested intention. As a purely spiritual act, this second vow has marvellous effects and releases wonder-working powers. He now has the "dharmic body" of the sages and is able to bring about magical transformations which open the minds of people to his message.

There is no doubt some resemblance here between Buddhist and Christian ideas, but the total absence of the God-concept in the Judeo-Christian sense makes it precarious to stress the similarities. The idea of merit, accumulated by the Bodhisattva in the context of karmic

---

[31]Conze, *Buddhism*, p. 74.

[32]Ibid.

doctrine, is very different from the idea of merit as developed by Anselm in his "satisfaction" doctrine of the atonement. Ideas of God's honor, holiness, righteousness, and so forth, are completely absent from the work of the Bodhisattva. Jesus, like the Bodhisattva, is a worker of miracles and the doer of extraordinary deeds but there the comparison ends. Certainly one shared characteristic is that of compassion. The Bodhisattva renounces immediate release and chooses to remain within the karmic cycle out of compassion. Jesus voluntarily renounces life and submits to the suffering and death of the cross in order that God's kingdom may come and the divine purpose be fulfilled. His motive, too, is love and compassion, but the context in which these operate and the ultimate goal envisaged for individuals and society is different from that of the Buddhist.

We are not concerned at the moment to argue for the truth of one rather than the other. It is simply a case of seeing clearly that the differences are deep, and that neither religion nor historical honesty are served by using the word *savior* of the Bodhisattva and Jesus on the assumption that the word has the same, identical meaning in each case.

3. Other-Power and Self-Power.—Christians, with their emphasis on the unique saviorhood of Jesus, are sometimes heard to criticize Buddhism as a religion of self-salvation. Man saves himself without any dependence on a higher power. Hence the absence of divine grace in Buddhist faith and practice. Conze shows how this antithesis of Other-Power (*Tariki*) and Self-Power (*Jitiki*) has played a notable role in the historical developments of Buddhism. The idea of dependence on the grace of another, higher Being seems present in Mahayana and its idea of Amida Buddha or Amitabha represented most notably by the Pure Land School. This concept is absent from the Hinayana which seems—on the surface, at any rate—to fit neatly in the Self-Power concept. The representatives of the Hinayana admit frankly that man/woman must save himself/herself by his/her own efforts, as Gautama told them, remembering again that "save" here means deliverance from karma and samsara into nirvana.

However, Conze is sceptical of this antithesis between Self-Power and Other-Power on the grounds that all duality is falsely imagined.[33]

---

[33]Ibid., p. 76.

Such a way of expressing things must obviously be provisional in a system of thought in which there is no "self" in the Western sense and in which the very distinction of "self" and "other" is itself provisional and the result of the limited perspective from which we now view things.

We note here again a profound difference between Buddhism, Judaism, and Christianity in regard to the nature, separateness, and distinctiveness of selves, both here and after death. It is enough to emphasize that whatever salvation may mean in Buddhism, it cannot mean the preservation, transformation, or continued existence of separate and distinct selves.[34] Conze agrees with this and also insists that in accordance with the basic presuppositions of Buddhist thought, "no dogmatic statement about the agent of salvation can be expected."[35] While he agrees that salvation or emancipation for Buddhists and Christians must involve the cooperation of the individual with some spiritual force, the precise character of this spiritual force is another matter.

For Christianity, God is the supreme Agent and man is an agent dependent upon him but, within limits, free to act on his own responsibility. Hence the long and never-ending debates in the Christian tradition about divine grace and human freedom. For the Buddhist, this is a non-question. The God-man relationship in the Judeo-Christian sense is simply not a basic presupposition of this way of thought. Whether the term grace (love or compassion) can be ascribed to a spiritual force which is in no way a personal agency is doubtful. Nirvana seems to transcend any such possible communion of divine and human wills in a love relationship. Thus the compassion of a Bodhisattva is only a stage toward a reality which transcends such a relationship.

Conze, whose sympathies are with the Mahayana, regards the statements for and against "self-activity" in Buddhism as pedagogic devices, not statements of universal validity. He then goes on to make a series of comments which show the gulf between Christian and Buddhist ideas of salvation. Moksa (salvation) is the fading away of

[34]R. F. Aldwinckle, *Death in the Secular City* (Grand Rapids: Eerdmans, 1974).
[35]Conze, *Buddhism*, p. 77.

the bonds which imprison persons in the conditioned and defiled world of samsara and the restoration of absolute freedom of the unconditioned and undefiled reality of Nirvana. This negative view of our present existence and of the world we know is in sharp contrast to the Christian view of the world as a divine creation which is "good," even though corrupted, defiled, and alienated as the result of sin.

At first sight, it might be thought that Buddhism is much more realistic and nearer the mark than the apparently more positive and optimistic view of Jewish and Christian doctrines of the "good" creation. Is not the empirical evidence of history strongly on the side of Buddhism, not to mention the ruthlessness of natural forces to which man is in the last resort in bondage? Nor can it be forgotten that Christianity has often been accused of having a very pessimistic and negative view of the world, of the body, and of sex, despite its formal doctrine of creation. It is true, of course, that for Christianity, too, this present world is not the final reality. "For the form of this world is passing away" (1 Cor. 7:31). Albert Schweitzer argued that Christianity itself involves an ironic detachment from this present order. This, however, seems to be an exaggeration. It would not appear to be true of Judaism or of Jesus with his obvious delight in nature and people, despite all sin and distortion.

Once again, however, despite superficial resemblances, there is a vast difference between the depreciation of this world in view of its consummation and fulfillment in the kingdom of God which transcends history and the depreciation of it in view of nirvana. The former is characterized by very positive views both of the reality of God and the preservation of transformed selves in the kingdom. While Judaism and Christianity, therefore, did not put their absolute trust in the eternity of this present world-order or process, this has not prevented their acknowledgement of the worth of our present existence both for the legitimate enjoyment of the earth's fullness and as the sphere for the doing of the divine will here and now.

Conze expresses the opinion that while Buddhists would be willing to accept Jesus as one of many Bodhisattvas, they are repelled by any claim for his uniqueness as the Son of God.[36] Buddhists, he says, desire

---

[36]Ibid., p. 79.

to multiply saviors, not to restrict them. He further charges that such a claim leads to intolerance, persecution, and bloodshed. It is difficult for Christians to reply to this kind of charge because of the ambiguities of Christian history. One can hardly deny that violence and persecution have marked the course of Christian history at certain times, although it would be unfair to take this as the whole of Christian history and refuse to acknowledge the outpouring of sacrifical love which Jesus' activity through his disciples has liberated. Also it must be said that Buddhist history is not free from the same blemishes, despite the argument in recent years that Buddhist culture produces a more peaceful society than the Christian. In actual fact, the history of both religions has been marred by violence and injustice. Whether this is directly traceable to these religions as such or to the imperfectly transformed existences of their devotees is again a difficult question. Certainly in reply to this charge, Christians are obliged to make some distinction between Jesus Christ and the imperfect reflection of his way in the lives of his followers. There is in the teaching and practice of Jesus himself no hint of the legitimacy of a holy war against the enemies of the faith. This idea finds expression at certain stages of Jewish history, in later Christian developments after Constantine, and in the teaching of Mohammad and the Koran. It would be very difficult to get it from Jesus himself. It is also not unfair, as we have said, to point out that other religions are open to the charge of violent conduct, even among Buddhist states and rulers. Another classic instance is the conversation between Krishna and Arjuna in the Gita about the legitimacy of engaging in battle. These remarks are not made with a view to unfair denigration of these other religions. Our point simply is that all religions are open to the charge of serious discrepancies between their professed ideals and their actual practice. Another aspect of the Christian claim to uniqueness centers upon the cross. Dr. Conze goes on to make the somewhat surprising statement that the stress on the "blood of Jesus" and on the crucifixion is distinctly distasteful to Buddhists.[37] What is the root of this distaste? It is not easy to say. Is it a kind of aesthetic revulsion in the face of the unpleasant reality of suffering and bloodshed? It is true that some

---

[37]Ibid.

Christian preaching and devotion have put undue stress on the blood as such, often with revolting detail. Nevertheless, one would wish that Conze had at least conceded that the blood of Jesus in the New Testament is closely connected with the idea of the perfect and costly self-offering of Jesus. No doubt the thought of bloodshed is unpleasant, to put it mildly, and no attempt should be made to present the crucifixion of Jesus as other than horrible and revolting. It is, however, unfair to detach the idea of the blood from all other considerations which led Jesus to turn his face steadfastly to go to Jerusalem. At a deeper level, the fundamental difference is to be found in the sharp contrast in regard to the nature of salvation.

For Conze, the whole idea of sin as rebellion against a holy God is obviously unacceptable. In the Hindu and Buddhist sense of avidya, salvation is primarily deliverance from ignorance. It is not the reconciliation of the divine and human wills in a new and transformed existence which releases the power of agape-love into the world. There is no forgiveness of sin, for karma must take its course. It is clear that we are dealing here with such vastly different basic assumptions about the nature of the world-process and the human role within it that no superficial attempts to combine them can be satisfactory. Nevertheless, the question can be asked about the experiential backing for the Buddhist diagnosis of the human situation and the Christian understanding of what John E. Smith has called the circular predicament [38] Hinduism, Buddhism, and Christianity all agree that there is some basic flaw in human existence as we now know it, "That existence is in some sense separated from its true nature and being."[39] The difference lies in the way this separation is understood and what is required to overcome it. This estrangement concerns not only human doing, specific deeds and actions, but human-being. How, then, do we escape from this circular predicament? How does man find the power or the resources to lift himself or herself out of this situation? This again depends in part on the diagnosis. The basic flaw for Buddhism is ignorance, the failure to understand that the only way to escape from karmic law and its endless consequences in suffering is to wear away

---

[38]John E. Smith, *The Analogy of Experience* (New York: Harper, 1973), ch. 4.
[39]Ibid., p. 63.

and eventually destroy the craving or desire which is at the root of the problem. This escape, however, is possible by resolute human action. Gotama the Buddha, or the Bodhisattvas, can bring the enlightenment needed, but its application rests fairly and squarely on the individual. The Buddha exhorted his monks to work out their own salvation.

For the Christian, the basic flaw is the self-assertion which puts man and not God at the center of things with the consequent deification of man, a role which denies the true nature of reality. This flaw, however, develops, not as the result of a deterministic karmic law with its exact proportioning of punishment and reward. Its root is in the freedom or power of self-determination whereby the person is allowed under God to shape his or her own destiny. The flaw, as separation from God, is not built into human existence by a law which nothing can change. It is internal to the self, and only external in the sense that society, reflecting this flaw on the collective level, stands over against the individual. By contrast, for Buddhism, the flaw is external, and not only internal, in a more radical sense. Suffering and desire are brute facts of existence as such, which hold the person in their ineluctable grip. Smith also cites Marxism as another striking example of a philosophy which refuses to acknowledge a flaw in man himself. Rather, the flaw originates in the way in which material and economic forces operate in the "real" world.

Here again it can be argued that both Buddhism and Marxism are nearer to "reality" than the Christian diagnosis. Is it plausible to try and trace all the suffering and disjointedness of the world to man's willful choice of himself as the center rather than God? What about natural disasters, disease, innocent suffering, and so forth? If we no longer assume a historic Adam and a historical fall which dislocated both nature and man as part of nature, must we not go along with the Buddhist and the Marxist in finding the flaw, not in man but in reality as a whole external to man? In this case, salvation would have to mean deliverance in some sense from this reality. Buddhism acknowledges this and seeks nirvana as completely transcendent to a universe dominated by samsara. Marxism puts its final hope in some future transformation of present reality into the perfectly just and classless world-society as a historical goal in the future.

There is, however, a curious ambivalence in Marxist thought at this point. While according to the strict letter of its theory, history moves by irresistible law to this historical future utopia, men are encouraged to align themselves with this process and even help it on. Freedom seems to enter again by the back door, whatever the Marxist theory says. If this is so, then the inevitability of the classless community itself becomes ambiguous. How can we be sure that Marxist man's freedom will not disrupt the smooth transition to the Marxist goal, that he will not put himself and his love of power at the center rather than justice, freedom, and equality for all? Contemporary history has impressive evidence to this effect in all the communist experiments so far.

It is true, as we have seen, that the New Testament, like Buddhism, sees the world as transient and subject to decay and perishing. Apart from sin and dislocation introduced by sin as the misuse of freedom, the present world-order is not for the Christian eternal. Suffering and death are an inevitable concomitant of this present order. However, this does not drain it of all value because the Christian sees it as an arena for the working out of a divine purpose, even though the complete fulfillment of that purpose ultimately takes us beyond the spatio-temporal order altogether. Thus, in spite of apparent similarities, there is a great difference of attitude in Buddhism and Christianity toward a world process which both acknowledge to be ruled in the present by suffering and death. For the Buddhist, the key concept is nirvana, with no suggestion that the achievements of history are taken up into, preserved, and transformed in an eternal realm. For the Christian, the present world will pass, but the work of God in history, and most notably human selves or persons, will be transformed in Christ and preserved in a new and creative existence in the eternal kingdom beyond space and time.

It may be contended that the contrast we have drawn between Buddhism and Christianity is only valid if the Hinayana is taken as the normative Buddhism. For someone like Conze, who does not accept this sharp distinction between the Hinayana and the Mahayana and who favors the latter as a legitimate development from the former, it might be answered that concepts of savior (*Amitabha*), grace, and even a positive understanding of nirvana bring such Buddhism much nearer to similar affirmations in Christianity. Is this, however, really so? Conze, it must be admitted, is not anxious to stress the resemblances but rather the differences.

For example, Conze roundly declares that Buddhists have no historical sense and do not worry about the exact time and place of actions and deeds ascribed to Amitabha and the Bodhisattvas.[40] He defends this Buddhist indifference to history by hinting at the destructive analysis of modern biblical criticism upon the biblical narratives and upon such important sources as the Gospels and the accounts of the resurrection. The implication is that history is a shaky foundation for any faith and that Buddhism is much to be preferred because such problems of historicity are irrelevant to it. This is a profound difference between Buddhism and Christianity. It is not the moment here to argue in detail for the biblical understanding of history or the historical evidence for specific events deemed important for Christian faith.[41] It suffices to insist that the difference is there, that it is of crucial importance and that no ingenious argumentation can pretend that it is not there. There arises on this issue a real parting of the ways. Again he chides Christians for having been so affected by centuries of theological argument about grace and good works that they are no longer capable of seeing that grace can be based on good works or merit.[42] We shall not repeat here our previous discussion of this issue in our earlier treatment of Judaism and Christianity.

Yet again Conze explains how easy it is for the Buddhist to subordinate the personal to the suprapersonal, that is, the Buddha to the Dharma (that is, the doctrine) or Amitabha to the dharmadhatu (that is, the Absolute which transcends personal categories, the world of cosmic law, suchness, the indescribable source of truth). This, he says, goes against the grain of Christian thought and he is correct in this. It is important, however, to understand clearly the nature of the contrast. It is not sufficient to place the Buddhist suprapersonal over against the most crudely anthropomorphic conception of divine personhood.

First, the word *suprapersonal* is itself ambiguous and could be interpreted in two ways. It could mean either the total denial of the meaningfulness of personal analogies in relation to the Godhead or it could signify that which transcends human personality as found in our

---

[40]Conze, *Buddhism*, p. 79.

[41]See R. F. Aldwinckle, *More than Man: A Study in Christology* for a fuller discussion of these matters.

[42]Conze, *Buddhism*, p. 79.

present experience. The long discussion in the history of Christian theology about the relationship of the negative theology to positive statements about God shows that Christian theology has not been committed to the idea of God as simply man writ large. Whatever the defects of popular piety at this point, and we have to admit them, we are justified in asking that the critic of Christianity attack it in its most thoughtful expression as this is found in its most self-aware representatives.

Nevertheless, it has to be conceded by the Christian that when all qualifications have been made, when we have said of God—not this, not that— the truest thought of God must accept as its basic model personal agency and the personal reality of the divine selfhood at the transcendent level. Two quotations are in order at this point. "We conceive his (that is, God's) active existence as an infinitely higher analogon to our own."[43] And that, says Farrer, means that we do not conceive it in its proper form at all. This statement, however, must not be understood in Conze's sense of the subordination of the personal to the suprapersonal. Farrer is simply reminding us of the obvious truth that finite man cannot conceive God if this means that the finite can, as it were, get inside the Godhead and understand with that perfect understanding which belongs to God alone. It is hoped that no theologian in his senses has ever believed this to be possible, for it would mean that he was claiming to be God. This may be one of the hazards of the theological vocation, but we may still hope that most have been sane enough to avoid such a preposterous claim. However, to say that we cannot conceive God in the above sense is not to say that nothing can be said about God at all and that we have no clues at all to help out our finite understanding. To quote Farrer once more: "Man is, in truth, taken as the clue to the whole, and it is probably stupid to suppose that we can escape from this and still think theologically."[44]

The basic cleavage between Buddhism and Christianity is at the level of our understanding of what it means to be a person. The Buddhist does not, in Farrer's sense, take man as the clue to the whole, and, therefore, it must be suspicious of all personal analogies for God except as ephemeral human personifications which need to be

---

[43]A. Farrer, *Reflective Faith* (London: S.P.C.K., 1972), p. 137.

[44]Ibid., p. 138.

transcended and left behind in our path to the suprapersonal.[45]

On the above view, God's intention can express itself in many different ways, nor can we rule out the possibility of unique personal acts which are a fuller disclosure of that intention than others. The historic doctrine of the Incarnation would make such a claim for Jesus Christ. Bearing in mind what we have already said about history, it is clear that Christians find it incomprehensible, as Conze asserts, to accept the Mahayana assertion that "all saviors, Buddhas and Bodhisattvas alike, are mere fictions and images in a dream that have issued from the void and are the projections of man's inner consciousness."[46] It is clear once more that we have come to the parting of the ways. We agree with Conze's judgment that although Buddhism and Christianity seem often to come very close to each other, "in fact they never actually do meet."[47] That this has important implications for our discussion of religious pluralism is evident, but we delay such discussion until later. Two fundamental issues will have to be tackled first.

We have concentrated so much on Buddhism because in our judgment, it is the most universal religion among the major non-Christian religions. One can conceive of "conversions" from Buddhism to Christianity and vice versa on a considerable scale precisely because of the sharply contrasting world views which they represent. The only other faith which has this kind of universal claim and appeal is Islam. In the case of the latter, however, despite the central and dominating role of Muhammad, Islam does not offer a personal savior but rather a divine truth, infallibly dictated and communicated and preserved in the Koran. Islam, like Judaism, does not stress timeless truths in the manner of a philosophy but emphasizes the dynamic and powerful will of the one God. The supreme sin is "shirk," the associating of any other being with the single, unique divine being.[48] It follows from this that no human being can be put on the same level as the one supreme God. Muhammad never claimed

---

[45]A further acute discussion of the personal agency model in relation to God is to be found in R. H. King, *The Meaning of God* (Philadelphia: Fortress, 1973).

[46]Conze, *Buddhism*, p. 79.

[47]Ibid., p. 80.

[48]Trevor Ling, *A History of Religion East and West* (London: Macmillan, 1968), pp. 224ff.

such a status for himself.

One may observe in passing, therefore, that the opposition to any kind of claim for the unique saviorhood of Jesus can take one of two forms. From the side of Buddhism, it can be denied in the interest of a multiplicity of saviors, none of whom is theologically decisive in the sense of being the one and only way to salvation. From the side of Islam and, of course, of Judaism, it is challenged in the name of a rigorous monotheism. The only way in which Christianity could be reconciled with these positions would be if it were willing to classify Jesus as one of many possible Bodhisattvas or strip Jesus of any claim to divinity and see him as only the greatest prophet of the one true and sovereign God. Some Christian theologians today appear to be moving in one or other of these two directions, but whether the Christian faith could survive as recognizably Christian in either of these two forms is the issue with which we shall be concerned in the rest of this book.

Our discussion so far has underlined the fact that it is possible to have a belief in a Savior-God without this necessarily implying one specific and normative manifestation of that God's presence and activity. This is not to deny that any form of divine activity must involve media for that activity. Apart from a mysticism which claims union with a transcendent reality which can dispense with all media whatsoever, all religions see the divine reality as manifesting itself in and through some media, whether physical or psychological, whether through nature or the human person. The question we are concerned with is the precise role, status, and importance of these media.

Another factor involved is the wide variety in the types of savior-gods to which the history of religions has drawn attention. Furthermore, does the word *God* or its equivalent have any common or shared meaning in all these instances. For example, what is the common element, if any, in Yahweh, the God and Father of our Lord Jesus Christ (the triune God), Allah, the Hindu Brahma or Brahman-Atman, the Chinese T'ien or Shang-Ti, the supreme Being, Olorun or Olodumare of the Yorubas, Japanese Shinto and its Kami or superior beings?[49] Another crucial question is the degree to which the "gods"

[49]E. O. James, *The Saviour God,* pp. 117ff. See also Trevor Ling, *A History of Religion East and West.*

are truly transcendent and what does transcendent mean in this connection? Yet another complicating factor is the degree to which the above gods, in addition to their active role in connection with rite, ceremony, and sacrament, have been conceptualized at the philosophical level. When this point has been reached, the further question arises as to whether we are dealing with theism, pantheism, or panentheism and how these terms are to be defined. Or should we ignore the philosophical developments and concentrate on the practical and existential meaning of God for the practicing devotee who may be almost totally free of theological and philosophical sophistication?

One of the major difficulties in the discussion of religious pluralism is whether we really know what we are trying to compare. Our question about the unique saviorhood of Jesus might be taken to imply that there are many saviors, all of whom are doing their best, but that Jesus is the most successful or the most effective savior. This again implies some common and shared notion of what constitutes salvation and that the fundamental question is which savior most powerfully embodies this common notion of salvation. Yet all these assumptions are, as we have seen, very problematic. It could be that some of the saviors do not even claim to be doing what Jesus is supposed to have done or is still doing. The fundamental questions and answers are different. For example, as we have noted, Buddhism and Christianity ask similar questions about death and suffering, but give radically different solutions based on their differing views of the nature of reality and their diagnosis of the human predicament.

The other solution is to try to show that despite apparent radical differences in the idea of God and the salvation offered, at bottom the questions and the answers are the same and so is the salvation, despite the diversity of symbolic forms which have been used to express the nature and the meaning of the salvation. Our ever-increasing knowledge of the diversity of the human race's religious life makes such a thesis more and more difficult to sustain. Are we, then, left only with a limited number of options—either agreement to differ, at best peaceful coexistence of all the religions, or the final abandonment of any attempt to assess the truth-claims of any of the many offers of salvation? We shall try to discuss and evaluate these all-important issues in the remaining chapters.

Chapter Seven

Grace and Salvation in Non-Christian Perspective

We have seen how difficult it is to discuss salvation as if it had one univocal meaning in all the contexts in which it is employed. When the question of Jesus' unique saviorhood is raised, we find that we are driven to compare world views, that is, to evaluate basically different apprehensions of the nature and character of Transcendent Reality. It has been our contention that in relation to Jesus, words such as *God, grace, forgiveness, death, resurrection,* and *eternal life* have specific meanings which cannot be detached from a particular understanding of the divine action in Jesus of Nazareth. We have also expressed our agreement with the view that Christology is not a mistake, as Maurice Wiles has suggested, but a necessary conceptualizing of the meaning of the said divine action.

Without committing ourselves to every detail of the Chalcedonian dogma, we agree with Grillmeier[1] that the Fathers were trying to express the basic intention of the New Testament and that they succeeded insofar as the thought categories of their day permitted. He is also correct in his contention that the Greek vocabulary did not

---

[1]A. Grillmeier, *Christ in Christian Tradition* (Atlanta: John Knox Press, 1964).

commit them to a specific metaphysic, whether Platonic or Aristotelian. "Moreover their grasp of the content of their expressions is more intuitive than speculative."[2] Against the objection that Chalcedon only expressed the choice among the various Christologies and heretical versions, this is, of course, true. If we ask why the church did not follow up and give its blessing to all those other forms, the only answer can be that "they (that is, the Fathers) meant to express the full reality of the Incarnation."[3] If they were mistaken in their basic value-judgments about this, then, of course, Christianity is a mistake. Chalcedon, however, is not offering a faith other than that of the New Testament nor is it offering Bradley's ballet of bloodless categories for the one Lord Jesus Christ of the New Testament witness.

In view of this, Grillmeier's judgment must be accepted that "we cannot say that the Chalcedonian Definition marks a great turning-point in the christological belief of the early church."[4] They were expressing in substance what the early Christians of the New Testament believed about their Lord and they did it in a formula corresponding to the needs of the hour. If this, then, is our chosen starting-point, and it seems right to let the reader completely into our confidence at this point, then further questions concerning religious pluralism can be pursued. What can an incarnational Christology and a trinitarian view of God say about the relationship of the unique saviorhood of Jesus to the claims made by other religious faiths? Using the word *grace* to indicate the action of the divine love in the atoning and reconciling activity of God in the life, death, and resurrection of Jesus of Nazareth, how can we deal with Rahner's question as to whether there are grace-filled elements in the non-Christian religions? If we say yes to this question, then how does this relate to the Christian answer as to what it means to be saved? An attempt will be made to deal with this in separate stages.

Rather than rely on vague generalizations which try to cover the whole variegated pattern of religion past and present, we shall consider Rudolph Otto's analysis of India's religion of grace to see where the differences and the similarities are to be precisely located. We have

---

[2]Ibid., p. 545.

[3]Ibid.

[4]Ibid., p. 550.

chosen this question of grace and Otto's treatment of it because there appear to be remarkable similarities in the basic apprehension of the nature of the Transcendent. It would have been possible, of course, to have chosen as our model a religious world-view such as Hinayana Buddhism where the differences would appear to be more evident and striking than the similarities. In so doing it might seem as if we were weighting the scales in our favor from the start. It seemed better, therefore, to consider India's religion of grace where it might appear more than permissible to give a positive answer to Rahner's question about grace-filled elements. This will enable us to see more clearly where the differences are and precisely what they are in a situation which, at first sight, seems to tell against the uniqueness of the Christian faith in regard to such a fundamental theme as the grace of God.

No one can accuse Otto of being unsympathetic to or ignorant of the Indian religion of grace of which he made a special study. What makes him interesting and stimulating is his willingness to depart from a "neutral" phenomenology and frankly express value-judgments which seem to him to come inevitably from his faith as a Christian. It is with this side of Otto that we are concerned. The fundamental question for us is the nature of salvation as understood and experienced in India's religion of grace and the resemblances and differences between that and the Christian way of salvation. Especially are we interested in the value-judgments which he makes in the presence of such resemblances and differences. Before we go any further, it should be emphasized that Otto departed from a view, widely held in his time, that non-dualist Vedanta was the classic and most profound expression of Hinduism. He was concerned to draw attention to another important and enduring strand in the Hindu religious tradition—namely, what he calls India's religion of grace. In this latter, we find a prolonged and consistent battle against the monistic mysticism of an impersonal Absolute.[5] Neither non-dualist Vedanta nor Buddhism could ever become truly theistic, that is, acknowledge the personal God above the world as the creator of it.[6] In the Indian

---

[5]R. Otto, *India's Religion of Grace and Christianity Compared and Contrasted* (London: S.C.M., 1930).

[6]Ibid., p. 20.

bhakti religion, however, we do find Isvara as personal God in this sense. Here we have a transcendent, personal Creator-God with whom communion is possible and whose saving grace can be experienced. Ramanuja (ca. 110 A.D.) is not the only but the key figure in this connection and in the Hindu tradition which stems from him. In such bhakti religion, Otto sees the real competitor to Christianity among the non-Christian faiths. We shall now take a look at the resemblances and differences as he sees them.

The Creator God as Personal

The living God of Jewish and Christian faith is transcendent, Creator, and personal. God is sovereign and active will. He is not personal only in a secondary sense as a concession to finite minds on the level of popular devotion. He is in himself properly designated as personal. Thus an I-Thou relationship is possible because he is the eternal Thou. There is no mysterious Godhead above and beyond the personal God who has manifested his nature as such in specific acts in history and in and through persons. Jewish and Christian faith has on the whole resolutely refused to qualify the personal symbols and the anthropomorphic language in such a radical way as to destroy the personal character of God. We are well aware of the many discussions which have taken place in Jewish, Christian, and Islamic philosophers about the precise meaning to be attached to the personal symbols and analogies applied to the transcendent God. Philo, Maimonides, and Aquinas could be cited as three examples of the way in which the "Semitic" religions have tried to grapple with this issue on the philosophical level. Also the prolonged and continuing discussion in recent years about the nature of religious language reinforces the same point.

However, whatever the philosophical and linguistic difficulties and complexities, neither Judaism nor Christianity nor Islam have been content with the monism of an impersonal Absolute. Individual thinkers here and there may have moved beyond the personal symbols which makes them "atypical" in the religious traditions in which they were nurtured and for the most part continued to live. On the level of worship and devotion, the three Semitic faiths as "living faiths" continue to emphasize the character of the transcendent God as personal will and activity. Austin Farrer speaks correctly for Christian faith on the existential and theological level when he says: "It remains that if we talk theology at all, we are committed to 'personality' language."[7]

On this issue, Ramanuja is in agreement, as Otto points out. "Brahman is the eternal, personal Isvara, that is, the Lord or God, with divine self-consciousness, with the knowledge of himself, with the conscious will to create the world and to bestow salvation upon his creatures."[8] We shall not dwell longer on this issue because the question of salvation does not arise at this level. Neither Jewish, Christian, nor Islamic thinkers nor Ramanuja would have seen saving power in the mere "idea" that God is personal, important as this is. Salvation becomes a matter of more than theoretical interest only when the personal God chooses to act. We are not suggesting that the personal category only appears in bhakti Hinduism. It is the ontological or metaphysical status of the personal symbols which is the crucial issue. As Professor Rarma states, the impersonal Absolute Brahman becomes a personal manifestation in various ways, as in the Hindu triad of Vishnu, Krishna and Shiva. However, as he is careful to point out, the ultimate reality is the one, eternal, universal spirit in which there are no distinctions—no cause and effect, no time and space, no good and evil, no pairs of opposites and no categories of thought.[9] The theological ideal in all its purity has to be adjusted to average human nature and the laborer needs a different kind of religion from the scholar.[10]

The Relation of God to the World

In the Semitic faiths, the most important initial divine activity was the bringing of this world into existence, including the human race. This was an act of sovereign, creative will, not an emanation from some kind of transcendental "substance." The analogy of a spider spinning his web is an impossible one for the Semitic faiths and would have been also, we suggest, for Ramanuja. There are subtle points here which it would be proper to discuss at some length if this were a book on theism in all its forms and developments. As is well-known, the Christian

---

[7]B. Mitchell, *Faith and Logic* (Allen & Unwin, 1957), p. 96.

[8]Otto, *India's Religion*, p. 37.

[9]Morgan, *The Path of the Buddha*, p. 3.,

[10]Ibid., p..5.

doctrine of creation took the form of the *ex nihilo* doctrine. This safe-guarded the faith in a truly transcendent God, not only an artificer or celestial workman shaping pre-existent material. It secured what Farrer has called "the prior actuality of God"[11] and ruled out any form of pantheism which identified God and the world. On this point again Ramanuja is very near to a Christian theism. Brahman is eternal and infinite. Before and above all worlds (Farrer's prior actuality) and as in Judaism and Islam, He is advitiya, without any rival.[12]

Again there is agreement on the point that the world and multiplicity are real and that the individual ego is not illusory. It is clear that Ramanuja holds this view, not only on the basis of a philosophical understanding of the world, even though he advances such arguments.[13] His view of salvation is also a determining factor. "If a man who longed for salvation were made to understand: as a redeemed soul I myself shall no more exist as this identical self, he would decline such a redemption and be off and away".[14] There is, however, an ambiguity as to the relation between the personal Lord and a Creator in the *ex nihilo* sense. Ninian Smart, in defining the concept of Lord in the Indian tradition, observes, "Here it should be noted that I mean a personal God but not necessarily a Creator."[15] In other words, the two may go together but not necessarily. Where does Ramanuja stand on this issue?

On this point, Otto was of the opinion that when he calls the world the "body" of the Lord, he is really making the same point as the Christian exponents of the *ex nihilo* doctrine. The world is not fashioned by the Lord out of some alien and pre-existent material but produces it out of Himself.[16] Ramanuja is really concerned to maintain the absolute dependence of the world on God in a manner similarly conceived by Schleiermacher. "For this is the significant thing in the

---

[11]A. Farrer, *Reflective Faith.*

[12]Otto, *India's Religion*, p. 37.

[13]S. Radhakrishnan and C. A. Moore, *Source Book in Indian Philosophy* (Princeton University Press, 1957).

[14]Otto, *India's Religion*, p. 37.

[15]Ninian Smart, *Doctrine and Argument in Indian Philosophy* (London: Allen & Unwin, 1964), pp. 127-128.

[16]Otto, *India's Religion*, p. 38-39.

relation of the body to the soul, that the body is absolutely dependent on the soul."[17] Ramanuja, of course, does not know the Christian doctrine of creation out of nothing. The creature for him is not merely through God but also out of him. This, however, is not to be taken as a strict monistic pantheism. Nor is it a reason for giving self-existence or divinity to the world. There is never identity of Creator and creature.[18] Some process theologians have recently adopted the body-soul analogy in working out their panentheism. However, it would seem that Ramanuja, despite his use of this analogy, is in fact nearer to classical Christian theism than to the process philosophers and theologians who wish to be rid of a pre-existent Creator. It is also true that Ramanuja's emphasis on the idea of the immanence of one real being in another replaces the idea of identity[19] but allows a warm mysticism which finds little place in the Protestant reformers, although an exception might have to be made for Luther.

The Diagnosis of the Human Situation

Having said this, we move nearer to our central concern about salvation when we ask what view of human existence springs from the above assumptions. Certainly, the idea of a personal God, met with in prayer, emphasizes adoration and worship and a warm relationship of dependence, love, and trust in the personal Lord. Indian bhakti (what Smart calls devotionalism) closely resembles what we may loosely call the evangelical emphasis in Christianity. While the term evangelical is often limited almost exclusively to certain forms of Protestantism, it would be unfair to suggest that it is absent from Catholic piety. As we have already noted, all religions have claimed in some sense to be offering a way of salvation. What distinguishes one religious form from another concerns that from which deliverance is to be sought. In comparing and contrasting Christian faith and India's religion of grace in the bhakti tradition, the question we must ask is whether the Indian view conceives the saving deliverance in an identical or at least similar manner to the Christian faith. The reader is reminded again that we are trying to discern in the Indian tradition in one of its forms those grace-

---

[17]Ibid., p. 39.
[18]Ibid., p. 40.
[19]Ibid.

filled elements of which Rahner speaks. While all the great religions diagnose the human situation as involving a flaw which prevents men and women from fulfilling their true goal and reaching true blessedness, how is this flaw conceived? It is this which determines the way in which salvation is conceived.

Holiness, Guilt, Sin, Repentance

As we have seen in our previous discussion, the meaning of these terms will depend upon the idea of God involved, upon the way the "flaw" is conceived, whether the flaw is external or internal to man himself or both, or whether any initiative from beyond man is taken to achieve human deliverance. We have also talked of the appeal to experience, not to exclude reflection, understanding, or even metaphysical construction but to stress the point that lived religion and authentic worship transcends, while it may include, the understanding and reflective judgment. John E. Smith is right to say that while "religion has never lived from proof, it cannot, however, afford to dispense with understanding."[20] He also criticizes Kierkegaard's critique of the Socratic method. Neither Socrates nor the Socratic method is the Savior but "then no interpreter of the Christian view is the Savior either."[21] In other words, Kierkegaard, in rejecting Socrates, is still left with the problem as to how we select and defend a particular interpretation of the Christian faith. This, of course, is the problem with Karl Barth's distinction between the one authentic revelation and Christianity as a religion, an empirical historical phenomenon. The decision as to what is the authentic revelation depends upon somebody's interpretation, whether it be that of the New Testament witness or later Christian thinking or Karl Barth himself. However, it is not our intention to try and work out here a complete Christian theism which could then be offered as a reasonable, if not logically demonstrative, defense of the interpretation we favor. Rather, we want to make clear the experiential elements to which an appeal could be made in such an undertaking.

Now it is clear that India's bhakti piety and Ramanuja in particular exhibit real and not fancied similarities between its interpretation and

---

[20]Smith, *The Analogy of Experience*, p. 19.

[21]Ibid., p. 18.

Christianity's emphasis on grace. Yet, as Otto points out, similarity of language and ideas does not constitute necessarily identity of meaning. Furthermore, on the existential level of worship, devotion, and action, there may be profound differences which cannot easily, if at all, be conceptualized and intellectually categorized but which result in types of piety which are marked by real and significant differences. This is evident in the holiness-sin contrast which, as we have seen, is so vital to both Judaism and Christianity. Holiness for the latter is a quality of an active, personal, sovereign will of the Creator and covenant-making God. Nor is such holiness, as Otto himself points out, only the numinous, the *mysterium tremendum et fascinans*. The holy has also the aspect of moral righteousness. Otto has often been accused of reducing the holy to the weird and the uncanny but this view does not result from a careful reading of *The Idea of the Holy*. In Otto's language, the greatness of biblical religion is the way in which the numinous holy has been schematized in terms of ethical values.[22] To recognize the numinous form is not of itself to recognize the "worth" of the holy which appears only "when the numinous-irrational form is filled out with rational matter, which is given by autonomous moral valuation."[23]

The question we wish to raise now is whether the gracious God of bhakti, of Vaishnavism and of Ramanuja is a "holy" God in the above sense. Obviously, the way sin, guilt, repentance, and grace are understood will depend upon the answer to this question. The following points may be made.

1. While Otto rejects the idea that religion in India has been devoid of the sense of sin, he does insist that it never had the weight or depth it had in the West.
2. There are great difficulties in translating such words as sin, repentance, and confession into Sanskrit. Deliverance in the Indian tradition as a whole tends to take the form of deliverance from Klesa, the trouble caused by the bondage of the atman in the enchainment of samsara.[24] It is not

---

[22]R. Otto, *The Idea of the Holy* (New York: Oxford University Press, 1957).
[23]Otto, *India's Religion*, p. 82.
[24]Ibid., p. 94.

primarily deliverance from sin as disobedience to the will of a righteous God.

3. Isvara is undefiled, not in the sense of the ethical holy, but because he is not absolutely bound by the pleasure and pain which bondage to samsara entails.[25]

4. Atman-Brahman is "the most serene rather than the most holy."[26]

5. Where repentance is a strongly emotional experience of a "sinful conscience," this is not considered as good or a sign of superiority, as in, for example, Judaism and Christianity. The goal of deliverance is to transcend such signs of bondage as "terrors of conscience, the tortures of remorse, or a broken and a contrite heart."[27]

6. The Gita knows nothing of redemption from sin in the biblical sense. The word papa, often translated as sin (that is, Gita 13, 66) does not really mean sin as a Jew or a Christian would understand it. The Indian deliverance from sin is not also the deliverance from the burden of guilt of the Christian conscience.[28]

7. The God of the Christian gospel is not one who rescues from "the wheel of becoming" but the one who seeks the sinner.[29]

Otto sums it up this way. "Isvara is a Savior of those who suffer the torments of samsara, and are strangers to their true home. The Father of our Lord Jesus Christ is the Savior of the hearts who are broken by guilt and of the conscience stricken by God's holiness."[30] Again, "Christianity is the religion of the conscience per substantiam, bhakti religion that religion per accidens."[31] Otto then goes on to explain that the difference between Christ and Krishna and Rama is not that Christ is a mediator because they are all in some sense mediators. Nor is the

---

[25]Ibid., p. 95.

[26]Ibid.

[27]Ibid., p. 96.

[28]Ibid., p. 98.

[29]Ibid., p. 103.

[30]Ibid.

[31]Ibid., p. 194.

uniqueness to be found in the idea of incarnation, for India had this idea too, and long before Christianity appeared on the scene. We have put great stress on the uniqueness of Christ in terms of the historic doctrine of Incarnation but it is clear that the word incarnation is in itself ambiguous. Otto sees the essential difference in the claim that Christ is the propitiator or the expiator of sin and that Christianity is the religion of the 'expiated or reconciled conscience.'[32] We have already briefly discussed in a previous chapter the juridical theories of the atonement. Otto, we believe, would have accepted the results of that investigation. I do not find in Otto any adherence to satisfaction and penal theories in the sense earlier discussed. On the other hand, he obviously wishes to preserve the centrality of the cross as expiatory, that is, a divine act by which sin is covered over or blotted out, forgiveness made real, and reconciliation brought about between God and the creature through "sheer grace."

It is also clear that for Otto, the subjective side of this is manifest in an experience which goes far beyond logical concepts and theological propositions. The element of feeling enters powerfully into this because expiatory grace makes no sense apart from a profound recognition of the burden of guilt when smitten by the holiness of God. This experience, however, can never be reduced to or adequately expressed by concepts or logical categories. It is true that Isvara forgives, but this forgiveness is an overlooking of the fault which the person acknowledges as the suffering entailed in the bondage of samsara. But such compassion (karuna) is not expiating grace to the sinner.[33] "For India has no expiator, no Golgotha and no Cross."[34] In Indian terms, these are only Judaistic remnants, rajas (passion) and tamas (darkness).

One final point needs to be made. In talking of the essential difference between Christ, Krishna and Rama, the problem of historical actuality needs to be stressed. Krishna, for example, does not have to be a historical reality to perform the function which bhakti piety assigns to him. There may well have been an historical Krishna whose life history is narrated, with legendary accretions, in the

---

[32]Ibid., p. 105.

[33]Ibid., p. 106.

[34]Ibid.

Mahabharata, especially the Harivamsa and the Bhagavata Parana.[35] Many of these stories of the child god's exploits are the themes of popular devotion and the temple images. Yet how important is it that Krishna, as an incarnation (avatar) of Vishnu, should be a historical figure? The answer seems to be that it is not necessary and that devotion to Krishna is quite compatible with regarding him as a legendary figure or the hero of an allegorical romance.[36] Krishna's human origins may have been sufficiently strong in the tradition to make it necessary for him to be regarded as a god in human form, as Trevor Ling suggests.[37] Yet this historical actuality of his humanity does not appear to be stressed or to be a necessary element in the "saving" role of Krishna as avatar of Vishnu.

Here again the difference with Christianity is profound. The latter has never been able to dispense with the historical actuality of Jesus of Nazareth. Whatever one thinks of the classical Christian dogma of the Incarnation, or whether one wishes to dispense with the dogma altogether as some of the contributors to *The Myth of God Incarnate* wish to do, it seems to be common ground that the fact of Jesus in the actuality of history cannot be dispensed with in any adequate interpretation of the New Testament. It was this which led H. H. Farmer years ago to suggest that it might be a good idea if Christians dropped the language of incarnation and talked of "inhistorization" instead.[38] Whatever the merits of this suggestion, it seems as if the "inhistorization" of Krishna is not necessary in the same way that it is for Jesus of Nazareth in relation to the Christian faith. For the latter, the holiness of God and such related terms as faith and repentance, the assurance of the reality of saving grace, and the blessedness of deliverance from guilt and from the power of sin and the assurance of ultimate victory over death—all this is dependent upon the historical act of God in the life, death, and resurrection of Jesus of Nazareth.

India's religion of grace can in the last resort be detached from historical actuality. Certainly many Hindus of all schools would regard this as a decided advantage and a sign of Hinduism's superiority

[35]Morgan, *The Path of the Buddha,* p. 58.

[36]Ibid., p. 41.

[37]Trevor Ling, *A History of Religion East and West,* p. 147.

[38]H. H. Farmer, *Revelation and Religion* (London: Nisbet, 1954), p. 195.

over Christianity. It must also be admitted that some modern Christians are becoming crypto-Hindus in this regard. Yet in our view this is a cul de sac, a dead-end. A Jesus who is primarily like Krishna, an allegorical or a mythical figure, is not the Jesus from whom the Christian faith originally developed and there is no reason to believe that Christianity could survive such a radical sea-change.

The Necessity for Grace

Now to return to our original question: Can we regard the Krishna cult as containing what Rahner calls grace-filled elements? Is the bhakti devotee an anonymous Christian? Insofar as the bhakti experience has arrived at the idea of divine initiative as gracious, loving, and in some sense forgiving, it is difficult for the Christian to deny to this experience anticipations of what is fundamental to the Christian understanding of God. It is difficult to think that Jesus would have totally rejected such an experience and might very well have said, "thou art not far from the kingdom of God." Nevertheless, as we have seen, it is difficult for the Christian to see in the devotion to Krishna a path to the fullest salvation offered to men and women. We have to remember again that we are not simply comparing two sets of ideas. There are obviously differences at the existential level in the basic meanings of such terms as holiness, repentance, faith, and grace. Above all, there is the profound difference between experiences interpreted in allegorical or symbolic terms and the Christian belief, right or wrong, that God's action of free grace is rooted in the actuality of the historical existence of a God who has participated to the full in the reality of sin, alienation, and the finiteness of human existence.

It is not proper for the Christian to consign the bhakti devotee to eternal punishment and to exclude him or her from the grace of God as he or she understands it. It is not, however, improper for the Christian to believe and hope that the devotee of Krishna might be brought to the feet of Christ and find in him that fullness of salvation and divine grace of which he has had true and meaningful anticipatory experiences in his devotion to Krishna. Beyond this it is not possible to go, and perhaps we should not wish to go further. We must leave some issues in the hands of the God and Father of our Lord Jesus Christ and the sheer grace which became historical actuality in him. After all, the basic issue is not our relationship to the idea of grace but to the actuality of grace. For the Christian, the actuality of that grace cannot be separated from the "inhistorization" of the incarnate Lord.

What we have said does not imply that because there are grace-filled elements in the experience recorded in the Gita, there is, therefore, no need to present the Christ to the bhakti devotee. It would be difficult to read into the Gita the God of agape-love of Christian faith and experience. There are serious ethical deficiencies in Arjuna's final acceptance of the principle of indifference and detachment from the consequences of his actions, in this case warfare and the subsequent slaughter. Nor is his intuition of Krishna's friendliness to him comparable to the actualizing of the love of God in the historical figure of Jesus of Nazareth. Nor is there in the Gita the suggestion that response to Krishna's love includes and demands a love of neighbor without restriction. Nor does the principle of detachment from the fruits of action agree very well with a profound sense of responsibility for others in the spirit of love. Nor is there more than a superficial sense of sin if sin is defined, not merely as transgression of external code and command, but as churlish ingratitude in the face of the divine love. Nor is there any sense of the need for a radical remaking of human nature and how this can be effected without a more powerful manifestation of divine love and forgiveness in action.

All this being so, we have no option but to pronounce the inadequacy of "anonymous Christianity," if this is really present in the Gita. A more radical divine action would seem to be necessary than is involved in the Gita in its present form. Before we leave this aspect of our discussion and turn specifically to Rahner's concept of anonymous Christianity, we turn briefly to the work of Raimundo Panikkar for another approach to our problem of religious pluralism. No attempt will be made here to try and expound in detail the rich and complex nature of Panikkar's thought as contained in all the works listed below.[39] Rather, we shall concentrate on myth, faith and hermeneutics, and on certain elements which bear upon our fundamental question concerning the finality and uniqueness of Jesus Christ in relation to the nature and possibility of salvation.

---

[39]R. Panikkar, *The Unknown Christ of Hinduism*, 1964; *Worship and Secular Man*, 1973; *The Intrareligious Dialogue*, 1978; *The Trinity and the Religious Experience of Man*, 1974; *Myth, Faith and Hermeneutics*, 1979.

Panikkar, both for family reasons and because of his life on the boundary between diverse cultures and traditions, is obviously concerned to situate the Christian claim in the broadest possible context of the world's religions. He writes as a Roman Catholic but also as one who returned to India to "search out his cultural roots and study Indian philosophy and religion."[40] It is clear that he is concerned to establish certain basic points as a prerequisite for understanding the meaning of the Christian faith in relation to other faiths. These are as follows:

1. To encourage creative dialogue between representatives of diverse religions and cultures. This, he believes, will result in posing ancient questions in new and more fruitful ways.
2. This involves the possibility of a Christian assimilation of the insights embodied in the mythical forms of the universal religious experience of the race.
3. He disclaims the intention of seeking a "least-common-denominator" and ending up with a superficial syncretism.
4. He is also suspicious of all attempts to work out a closed theological system.
5. The basic question is whether we can live by a faith which is both incarnational and transcendent.[41]
6. In the light of this, how can the faith of the individual combine the stress upon the specific and the particular with the universal experience of faith throughout human history?
7. It is important to see clearly the way in which Panikkar understands faith. It is not itself a specific religion but the experienced reality which underlies all religion.[42] Truth as apprehended by faith is not propositional. Faith-statements, when verbalized and conceptualized, are translations of an experience which transcends all language.[43] It follows from this that faith cannot be identified with any particular dogmatic, propositional, and conceptual expression of it.

---

[40]Ewert Cousins, *"Introduction" The Panikkar Symposium at Santa Barbara Cross Currents*, 29 (Summer 1979): 131-32.

[41]Panikkar, *The Intrareligious Dialogue*, pp. 7-8.

[42]Panikkar, *Myth, Faith and Hermeneutics*, p. 69.

[43]Panikkar, *The Intrareligious Dialogue*, p. 7.

8. The question of pluralism must not be prematurely resolved in the interest of a dogmatic solution which begs the question of truth and validity.
9. On the other hand, he wishes to take seriously the Christian claim that Jesus is the way, the truth, and the life. Precisely for this reason, "I cannot reduce his (that is. Jesus') significance to historical Christianity."[44] It is not altogether clear what this involves, but we shall return to this point later.
10. One deduction, however, from the previous point is clear. An exclusivist position must be rejected if it means the repudiation of all other claims to truth, that is, the possibility of saving faith in traditions distinct from historical Christianity. If Christians, when they talk of the "scandal of particularity" in relation to Jesus mean it in this exclusivist sense, it must be rejected.
11. One cannot, however, rest satisfied with a move from exclusivism in the bad sense to a comprehensive inclusivism which claims to include the truth found in all the other traditions. There may be a subtle arrogance in the claim of a specific faith that it is large enough to include all other truth. Furthermore, it evades the real challenge of pluralism by ignoring the unique truth-claims which all religions make for themselves in one way or another.[45]
12. Panikkar, therefore, opts for what he calls parallelism, that is, the view that traditions may run parallel and only perhaps meet at the eschaton. This involves the patience and the modesty to hope that the traditions may converge and to explore that possibility actively and not simply wait in blind faith that somehow all will finally converge.
13. If we ask how this is to be achieved, the answer is to be found in Panikkar's sometimes obscure use of the word *myth* and the law of tolerance which he formulates.
14. His use of the word *myth* is one of the most acute problems which Panikkar sets for us. The breadth of meaning and

---

[44]Ibid., p. 54.

[45]Ibid., pp. xvii-xviii.

application which he gives to it is, to say the least, remarkable. This will require a more extended treatment of this point than we have given to the others. We shall try to make clear to ourselves what he means by myth and hope that we have interpreted him correctly.

The basic issue concerns the relationship between myth, logos, and ideology in his thinking. The essential points seem to be as follows. "Myth is not an object of discourse but the expression of a *sui generis* form of consciousness."[46] It is an apprehension of reality prior to the analytic and discursive dissection of that apprehension in terms of the subject-object dichotomy. It means that man cannot be reduced to logos, that is, to the reflexive consciousness. It would not, therefore, be correct to think of myth as an interpretation of reality because this would imply that reflection (that is, the logos) is already at work. Once we attempt an hermeneutic, an interpretation of myth, it is no longer myth but logos.[47] As long as myth is living as myth, it does not need interpretation nor an intermediary through which to convey its truth. The myth as such is not the object of thought but rather a purification of thought by virtue of its unthought communion with reality. It is transparent like the light. It is the horizon within which man experiences an ever-growing awareness of his "ontic solidarity" with the whole of reality.[48] "When the thinking has not yet landed on the thought so that it cannot yet know what is being thought in the thinking, we are still in the domain of myth."[49] This brings us back to faith which is that dimension in man which corresponds to myth.[50] It is the basic human response, therefore, to reality prior to the work of the reflective consciousness.

At this point, one is tempted to raise all the difficulties associated with the attempt to get back to the pre-cognitive, pre-linguistic, pre-

---

[46]Panikkar, *Myth, Faith and Hermeneutics*, p. 4.

[47]Ibid., pp. 6-8.

[48]Ibid., p. 4.

[49]Ibid., p. 4-5.

[50]Ibid., p. 5.

reflective level of experience. How could one possibly know or talk about that kind of experience? Perhaps Panikkar could reply that we cannot know it in the sense which "knowledge" has in the highly intellectual and analytic Western tradition. We can, however, in some way directly experience it. However, he assures us that we must not despise thought or ignore the inviolable rights of the logos.

Where, then, do we go from this point? The first task is that of *mythos-legein*, to bring the myth to speech and verbal expression without turning the myth into a form of objective knowledge which destroys our awareness of reality as inexhaustible mystery. The problem is to regain and retain the spontaneous vision of faith in the sense defined before it is reduced to logos. Once this happens, the myth as living myth is destroyed. Once myth is knowledge, it is no longer myth. Mythology, as the word indicates, is already destructive of myth for it is a logos of myth, a reflective interpretation of myth. In seeking *mythos-legein* rather than mythology, there must be some intermediary between myth and logos. The crucial role is here played by the symbol and the latter must be clearly distinguished from the reflexive use of symbol by the logos. "Symbol does not mean an epistemic sign but an ontomythical reality that is precisely in the symbolizing."[51] By ontomythical is presumably meant that immediate vision of reality which is conveyed in and through the symbol before the latter is worked up into a theory of symbols which claims to be knowledge. Is Panikkar saying the same as Tillich when the latter talks of the symbol conveying that which it symbolizes?[52] Or the same as Kaufman when he says that theology cannot talk directly of God but only of the symbols which emerge from the faith-consciousness?[53]

There are, however, other complications for we must not, according to Panikkar, identify the symbol with the symbolized.[54] To do this is precisely avidya, ignorance, confusing the appearance with the reality.[55] Yet again, as soon as a symbol requires interpretation, it is

[51]Ibid., p. 6.

[52]F. E. Johnson, *Religious Symbolism* (New York and London: Harper & Bros., 1955), ch. 6.

[53]G. Kaufman, *An Essay on Theological Method* (AAR Studies in Religion, Scholar's Press, 1975), pp. xiff.

[54]Panikkar, *Myth, Faith and Hermeneutics*, p. 6.

[55]Ibid., p. 7.

no longer a symbol but a mere sign. However, he also says, "Man does not live by symbols alone."[56] Many things demand interpretation. Hence the logos must enter into the picture at this point. What, then, is the task of hermeneutics? Not to turn the myth and its symbols into "knowledge" for this is to destroy the living myth and its original "vision" of reality. The aim of hermeneutics must be to lead us back to a "narrative innocence" that allows myth to function as myth. "A demythicized myth is a cadaver."[57] Yet how can a hermeneutic be developed which does not have this result, seeing that all interpretation must by the nature of the case be the work of the logos?

The first thing is to keep steadily in mind that myth is not an "object" but an instrument of knowing, a fundamental human attitude, if you like, beside, not in front of, the logos. The answer to this seems to be given in his discussion of the third moment of any hermeneutical process, what he calls "diatopical hermeneutics."[58] The method here is a dialogical dialogue, that is, piercing the logos (dia-logos) in order to reach the translogical realms of the heart.[59] This allows the original myth to emerge in a manner which permits us to have real communion with the original vision and thus permits us to understand it (not in the sense of the kind of knowledge which the logos gives) but to appreciate it under the same horizon of intelligibility.

Here again, the latter must not be taken to mean logos-knowledge. Obviously such a hermeneutics, which enables us to recover myth as myth, is not dealing with objective knowledge as this is understood in a tradition dominated by the logos. Yet this leads to his law of toleration, that is, the willingness to be open to other mythical visions of reality which have been rendered opaque to us because embedded in intellectual and dogmatic constructions (the work of logos) which hide the real meaning from us. "Mythical tolerance represents a non-objectifiable vision of the world and implies the conviction that every human act has a value that is not purely objective."[60] This makes

---

[56]Ibid., p. 8.

[57]Ibid., p. 40.

[58]Ibid., p. 9.

[59]Ibid., p. 91.

[60]Ibid., p. 23.

possible, therefore, transcultural and trans-religious dialogue in a meaningful sense and enables us to have mutual communion and understanding, even when the intellectual constructions or the objectified world-views seem to be in absolute contradiction and conflict.

This brings us to the next key term, ideology. This latter is defined as the "demythicized part of the view you have of the world."[61] "An ideology is a system of ideas formulated by a logos incapable of transcending its own temporality. The problem of ideology arises once the human logos is assumed to have lost its trans- and/or in-temporal character."[62] This has a crucial bearing on tolerance. "The tolerance you have is directly proportional to the myth you live and inversely proportional to the ideology you follow."[63] If we start from such presuppositions, what conclusions would we arrive at concerning the person of Jesus? Faith is not belief if by that we mean an interpretation or a dogmatic construction in which the logos has been at work. Faith always needs belief, but it is not to be identified with it. Since the "function of faith is to connect one with transcendence,"[64] its role must be a kind of discernment of the original vision of Jesus in regard to the nature of transcendence. This cannot be the work of the logos but of some kind of intuitive and empathetic communion with the original vision. Once the vision of Jesus is identified with belief, that is, ideas or theological constructions, then these appear to be sometimes in direct contradiction of other visions. The vision of the Buddha and the vision of Jesus seem totally different when they are compared and contrasted on the level of belief. There seems no obvious way in which we can reconcile a world-view operating with such key concepts as samsara, karma, and nirvana and the Judeo-Christian view of God as transcendent Creator and Personal Agent working out a purpose in and through history. On this level, we have a conflict of orthodoxies, whether Christian, Buddhist, or some other correct belief is pitted against another correct belief. Two different ways of understanding (in the logos sense of understanding) are in conflict.

---

[61]Ibid., p. 21.

[62]Ibid.

[63]Ibid., p. 20.

[64]Panikkar, *Intrareligious Dialogue*, p. 18.

There is no way out of this dilemma except by a dialogue in which we seek to penetrate through the beliefs, concepts, and dogmatic constructions of a particular religion to the original vision which lies behind all belief and all intellectual constructions. Obviously, on this view, such penetration of any specific orthodoxy to the original vision cannot be the work of the logos. It can only be some kind of non-intellectual apprehension of transcendence given in some form of immediate awareness. The problem is compounded by the fact that an orthodoxy, of whatever kind, only makes sense in a homogeneous culture, that is, a culture in which certain assumptions and certain conceptual articulations of experience are taken for granted. When we move into a different culture where this is not so, the orthodoxy in question loses its self-evidence because its basic assumptions are no longer taken for granted. The result is to stress difference, tension, and contradiction. Often this degenerates into intolerance and religious imperialism of the worst kind.

The first necessity, therefore, is to move from orthodoxy to orthopraxis via orthopoesis which focuses on ethics and practical conduct. However, since faith is more than ethics, it cannot remain at the level of ethics alone. One must turn to orthopraxis as a dynamic movement toward fullness of being on the basis of the vision of, and communion with, the Transcendent. "The quintessence of faith, then, reflects this aspect of Man that moves him towards fullness, this dimension by which Man is not closed up in his present state but open to perfection, to his goal or destiny, according to the scheme one adopts. Faith is not fundamentally the adhesion to a doctrine or an ethic. Rather, it is manifest as an act that opens to us the possibility of perfection, permitting us to attain to what we are not yet."[65]

It seems clear that on this view, no normative claim could be made for Jesus' vision or indeed for any other vision. Apart from any special claims that one might want to make for some specific "vision," there is the difficulty of how one compares what appear to be ineffable visions stripped of all conceptual and dogmatic constructions of the meaning of the symbols. If all logos constructions, by the very nature of the case, are distortions of the original vision, then no comparisons or evaluations can be made on the logos level. Yet Panikkar seems to be

[65]Panikkar, *Myth, Faith and Hermeneutics*, p. 201.

the victim here of a basic contradiction. He insists that myth and faith need interpretation (a hermeneutic). Yet he gives us no guidance as to what we should do when confronted with what Paul Ricoeur has called "the conflict of interpretations."[66] "Diatopical hermeneutics stands for the thematic consideration of understanding the other without assuming that the other has the same basic self-understanding and understanding as I have."[67]

Does this mean that we must rest content with an ineradicable plurality of self-understandings? This would appear to be the case. What, then, is the status of Jesus' vision of God? Why should we go on calling ourselves Christians or Buddhists for that matter? Panikkar's answer to this is the advocacy of a "Christian Hermeneutic." If it is asked what this means, the reply is a hermeneutic of freedom. This is both puzzling and ambiguous. If there is no strict need of any religion, let alone Christianity, for the fundamental act of faith, then the person of Jesus Christ is obviously dispensable.[68] He only becomes a useful medium through which we attain to a non-symbolic and non-conceptualized act of freedom in relation to a transcendent which cannot be more precisely characterized. This is apophatic (that is, negative) religion carried to the nth degree. It is clear to this reader at least that the Hindu side of Panikkar has finally triumphed over the Christian, even if this was not his intention. A friend of the author, after reading Panikkar's book, made the observation: "I still want faith in something other than the concept of freedom." I believe this to be fair comment on Panikkar's book.

This is reinforced by such statements as, "It is not Christianity as a religion but Christ as Symbol that becomes central."[69] Now there is no doubt that there is a proper sense in which we can speak of the Christian faith as a religion of true or authentic freedom. Yet can we go so far as to say that "Every truly free act is a religious act that relates us with the Ultimate, in whatever sense we may interpret it."[70] It is this

[66]Paul Ricoeur, *The Conflict of Interpretations* (Evanston: Northwestern University Press, 1974).

[67]Panikkar, *Myth, Faith and Hermeneutics*, p. 9.

[68]Ibid., p. 454.

[69]Ibid., p. 453.

[70]Ibid., p. 454.

latter qualifying clause which causes difficulty for many Christians. If Christ is Symbol, is he only one among many possible symbols? In what sense is the symbol necessary to the experience of true freedom? In appealing to Paul, Panikkar takes no notice of his language about being a "slave of Christ." Nor is it very clear as to the relation between Christ the symbol of the liberator and Jesus of Nazareth in his historical actuality. We only have such elusive language as "only an interior Christ (which does not deny a historical Christ identified with him) can make possible the realization of an act that is truly free, spontaneous and fully human."[71]

What does such a phrase as "the historical Christ" mean to Panikkar? This question is not answered by his hermeneutic of freedom. Insofar as he is attacking dehumanizing legalism, servile and craven obedience, the merely external imposition of doctrinal concepts, and so forth, there is no reason to quarrel with what he is saying. Nor does Panikkar appear to do justice to the fact that true freedom of the Christian person is expressed in a community of faith and that this involves obvious limitations upon my freedom in the loose popular sense of the word. No doubt he is reacting against the highly dogmatic and institutionalized forms of the Christian faith in the Catholic tradition to which he belongs, although he wishes to claim the support of Vatican II for his view of "the primacy of the freedom of the person over against any other value whatsoever."[72]

Our own view is that in trying to pierce through all myths to an original vision which leads to authentic freedom, he is able to achieve some kind of integration of myths through narrative innocence at the cost of surrendering the centrality of Jesus Christ as the Lord and Savior in a sense more far-reaching than the use of the term *symbol* would seem to allow. A more serious criticism of Panikkar's work as a whole must be directed against his understanding of the role and function of logos in relation to original vision and the symbols which emerge. Certainly logos in the sense of human reflection cannot be identified with conceptuality alone, divorced from experience and what he calls orthopraxis. On the other hand, unless we are to be left only with ineffable visions or a multitude of symbols whose reality-

---

[71]Ibid., p. 453.

[72]Ibid.

reference is left obscure, the assessing and evaluating functions of the logos must be given a more positive role than Panikkar seems willing to concede. He has resolved the problem of religious pluralism by finding an essential resemblance in the act of freedom which constitutes all truly spiritual acts. He has not given us much help as to which symbols should be chosen as the most valuable aids to such acts.

Finally and most important, he has so obscured the living Lord and Savior of Christian faith that we are left only with an open-ended freedom which seems to be identified with salvation itself. This seems a harsh criticism but is not meant to be so in any personal sense. The problem arises not concerning his own personal faith in and devotion to Christ but whether his hermeneutic as such makes adequate provision for the centrality of that devotion. It is, of course, possible that the way in which we have interpreted his thesis was not his real intention, but it is certainly possible to read this remarkable work in this way.

Perhaps the real root of the trouble is the assumption that all forms of religion and human spirituality are basically saying the same thing and referring to the same reality. This, however, as we have had occasion to note before, is by no means self-evident. Grateful as we sincerely are to Panikkar for the insights and illumination of his work, we believe that the problem of religious pluralism has been resolved, if it really has, at the cost of what makes the Christian faith Christian— namely, the centrality, uniqueness, and indispensable character of Jesus Christ as the mediator of our salvation.

We have now considered the specific case of Hindu bhakti to see if we can discern there those grace-filled elements to which Rahner refers. Another approach to the issue of religious pluralism has been examined in the work of Raimundo Panikkar. We found this to be rich in insights but not satisfactory in the role which it is able to give to the person of Christ. The tension has been noted in all this discussion between the claim for the unique saviorhood of Jesus and the status of those both B.C. and A.D. who have not known the Word made flesh. We now turn specifically to the question of "anonymous Christianity." As Karl Rahner has been particularly associated with this theme, we shall follow his exposition of it and make our own comments.

Chapter Eight

Anonymous Christianity

It must be admitted that the very phrase *anonymous Christianity* is in itself ambiguous and liable to be misunderstood. Those Christians who stress the importance of personal faith, which implies a conscious awareness of what it means to be committed in total trust to Jesus Christ, are apt to interpret the phrase to mean that one can be a Christian without knowledge of Jesus Christ or faith in him. This in turn would imply that salvation, however defined, is in no way dependent upon a conscious relationship to Jesus Christ. Is this not, in effect, to deny the unique saviorhood of Jesus?

This, however, does not do justice to Rahner nor does it mean a full understanding of the issue with which he is trying to deal. There are many possible citations which could be taken from Rahner which stress the unique character of Christian salvation and the indispensable relationship to Jesus Christ. One will suffice: "The Christian is convinced that in order to achieve salvation man must believe in God, and not merely in God but in Christ . . . this faith is, in itself, necessary and therefore, demanded absolutely."[1] It seems clear

---

[1]Karl Rahner, *Theological Investigations*, vol. 6 (New York: Seabury, 1974), pp. 390-91. See also Gerald A. McCool, ed., *A Rahner Reader* (London: Darton, Longman & Todd, 1975), pp. 211ff.

that Rahner in no way wishes to deny or obscure the unique saviorhood of Jesus. Why, then, develop this concept of "anonymous Christianity"?

As we have already observed, there are two basic questions which arise. (1) How is the Christian understanding of salvation related to those who, through no fault of their own, have not heard the gospel of Jesus Christ and cannot, therefore, respond to or reject what they have never known? (2) Is it also a fact that those who know about Jesus Christ but have rejected the gospel as presented to them, are necessarily excluded from salvation in the Christian sense? This would include those who adhere to non-Christian faiths as well as orthodox Jews who are not unaware of Christian claims but feel compelled to reject them for reasons which we discussed in an earlier chapter. It raises the question of atheism, one which is pardonable and does not exclude the person in question from "salvation": the other which is culpable and blameworthy and must, if persisted in, result in final separation from God. For most Christians, the second is a much more difficult question than the first, but we will deal first with the latter.

Admitting that there are millions of people both before and after Christ who have not been confronted with the gospel, where do they fit into the divine saving purpose concretely expressed in sheer grace manifested in Jesus Christ? Rahner answers this question by appealing to what he calls the "supernatural existential."[2] By this, he wishes to indicate that all men and women, by the very fact of being creatures of God, are in their deepest nature oriented to the supernatural, that is, God.[3] Sin may have distorted this or rendered it difficult of fulfillment, but it has not destroyed it. There is no such thing as a pure or mere human nature cut off entirely from its roots in the transcendent and the supernatural. Such a "nature" is an abstraction. All persons have been created for fellowship with the eternal God. This remains a fact in spite of sin and its consequences.

Further, God's purpose for all persons is a gracious one, concerned for their salvation. His salvific purpose is universal both in time and space. This means that God's grace has been active and present from

---

[2]Karl Rahner, *Foundations of Christian Faith* (New York: Seabury, 1978), pp. 126ff.

[3]Ibid., p. 127.

the beginning of human history even when the terms *God* and *grace* are neither known nor understood in the full Christian sense. The reality of the "supernatural existential," plus the reality of divine grace in human affairs, even before the incarnation, means that God has always been seeking to draw men and women to himself, even through their ignorance, immaturity, and superstition and also through the "higher" religions of the world. Does this mean that all men and women have the same opportunity to be saved at whatever point in space and time they happen to be? Here again care must be taken to understand the subtleties of Rahner's thought. He does not wish to say that "every man, whether he accepts the grace or not, is an anonymous Christian."[4] The "supernatural existential" is a universal potentiality for responding to divine grace, but it does not guarantee such a response by mechanical necessity.

It does mean, however, that "it is a priori quite possible to suppose that there are supernatural, grace-filled elements in the non-Christian religions."[5] The question now becomes how we discern these grace-filled elements and how do we distinguish the authentic from the inauthentic in the religious pluralism which is a global fact? It is obvious that in seeking an answer to this question, we shall not look for an explicit understanding of God in the Christian sense, still less for a conceptualized Christian theism. Nor, by the definition of the issue, shall we look for a knowledge of Jesus Christ. In the absence of any conscious awareness of all these elements, how, then, shall we discover in the non-Christian religions those grace-filled elements of which Rahner has previously spoken?

Rahner himself explains that an individual man or woman of a non-Christian religion, despite the error, depravity, intellectual inadequacy, and moral and spiritual perversity which it may as a whole exhibit, may in fact respond to the gracious approach of God. This is made possible both by the "supernatural existential" of which we have already spoken, and the fact that God in his grace is seeking him or her in and through the religion and faith which he or she professes. "It follows, therefore, that if the human subject's free response to his world includes in its intentionality an act of loving surrender to the

---

[4]McCool, *A Rahner Reader*, p. 213.

[5]Ibid., p. 215.

world's Absolute Horizon, the human subject has made an implicit act of salutary Christian faith. Ontologically, and not just metaphorically, he has become an anonymous Christian."[6] Further, "And hence we have every right to suppose that grace has not only been offered even outside the Christian church (to deny this would be the error of Jansenism) but also that, in a great many cases at least, grace gains the victory in man's free acceptance of it, this being again the result of grace."[7]

It is obvious that Rahner, on these premises, is obliged to reject the sharp Barthian dichotomy between religion as only a human searching for God and revelation as sheer grace in the true sense which can only be known in an actual and conscious response to Jesus Christ. Says Rahner again, "We must, therefore, rid ourselves of the prejudice that we can face a non-Christian religion with the dilemma that it must either come from God in everything it contains and thus correspond to God's will and positive providence, or be simply a purely human construction."[8] Again, "It would be wrong to regard the pagan as someone who has not yet been touched in any way by God's grace and truth."[9] We have quoted so extensively because we are anxious not to misrepresent his position.

However, we now have to return to our former questions. Are we ever in a position to say that a particular non-Christian is an "anonymous Christian," that is, one who, in his basic intentionality, has in fact freely responded to the approach of the divine grace? If he or she has so responded, does this mean that he or she is "saved" and does not need to be brought into a conscious confession of Jesus as Lord and Savior? It is not altogether clear what Rahner's answer would be. We shall, therefore, permit ourselves to speculate, we hope responsibly. It could, of course, be argued that we could never be in a position to give a confident answer to the first question as far as any particular individual is concerned. In this case, we would have to say that although there are "anonymous Christians" in the non-Christian religions, we can never know precisely who they are.

6Ibid., pp. 211-12.

7Ibid., p. 217.

8Ibid., p. 219.

9Ibid.

It is enough to affirm that the potentiality for salvation is there in the non-Christian religions because God's grace is there and that we must leave the knowledge of those who have responded or not to the omniscience of the wise and compassionate and gracious God whom Christians worship in and through Jesus Christ. The importance of this view is that if taken seriously, it will mean an important change of attitude on the part of Christians to members of the non-Christian religions. We shall approach them not as automatically lost (that is, condemned to judgment, the wrath of God, and perhaps eternal punishment because they are Hindus, Buddhists, Muslims, and so forth). We shall approach them in the spirit of hope and the belief that God's grace may have touched them and they may have responded, despite the errors and inadequacies of the empirical and historical religion of which they are a part. It should be further noted that when Rahner talks of the grace of God in the non-Christian religions, he does not mean the grace of an "unknown God" but the grace of the triune God of the Christian faith, even though the non-Christian in question does not know it to be such or interpret it in that way.

In regard to the second question, Rahner's position is still not quite clear. He obviously does not wish to give "anonymous Christianity" a status which would render the explicit preaching of Christianity superfluous.[10] This, on Rahner's premises, is understandable, especially where the non-Christian religion in question is in direct contact with the Christian church and is open to receive the full gospel message of salvation through the proclamation of Jesus Christ and the sacramental channels of grace. Where such a situation obtains, it is not enough to remain an "anonymous Christian," for the fullness of salvation is now being offered. Does this mean that anonymous Christianity can be appealed to only in the absence of a Christian presence? Presumably, only those who have lived and died in a non-Christian religion without benefit of Christ can properly be called "anonymous Christians." Yet this does not seem to be exactly what Rahner is saying. This comes out clearly in his discussion of atheism. Are there anonymous Christians among contemporary atheists?

Here again Rahner appears to have in mind atheists who have encountered Christianity in some institutional form but for various

---

[10]Ibid.

reasons are unable to accept the church's formulated doctrines. What exactly is their position? There are, according to Rahner, two kinds of atheists. There are those who have acted in accordance with conscience[11] and responded to those grace-filled elements in their experience by virtue of the supernatural existential, which is as much a fact for atheists as for members of the non-Christian religions. There are other atheists, however, who have not only repudiated the doctrines of the Christian faith, but have not fulfilled their "supernatural existential" potentiality by obedience to conscience and those grace-filled elements in their experience through which God has approached them with saving intent, even though they did not know that this was what was happening to them.

Here again, the same problem arises as in regard to the non-Christian religions. Are we ever in a position to say to which particular class of atheists any specific atheist belongs? Where, for example, would one place a Bertrand Russell? The only way out of this impasse, and this seems to be the way Rahner takes, is to argue that the human person's orientation to the transcendent and the supernatural is not in the first place a matter of conceptualization and categorization. It is an unthematized awareness of the supernatural goal of human existence. An atheist, for example, may reject a conceptualized theism for philosophical reasons or as traditional formulations of the doctrine of God. As we are dealing with a Roman Catholic in the case of Rahner, we could say that a man might reject the Thomist arguments for the existence of God and thereby believe he is compelled to take an atheist stance. Yet he may not be an atheist in the deeper sense of disregarding conscience, the moral obligation to pursue the truth, or the awareness of the claims of love beyond mere selfish interest. In this case, he may be a Christian in his heart, despite the denial of God with his head. This may be what Rahner calls an "innocent atheism."[12]

There is obviously some affinity here with the position taken by the Protestant John Baillie some years ago when he suggested that there are no real atheists and that it is possible to be a real believer in the depth of the heart where the claim of absolute values is acknowledged, whatever the denials of the head. Belief here obviously does not mean

---

[11]Ibid., p. 221.
[12]Ibid., p. 223.

theological propositions which the unbeliever denies but the awareness of certain absolute values and the recognition of our moral obligation to try to live by and embody such values. "My affirmation at this point is only, if you like, that in the course of human evolution the ideas of absolute honesty, utter unselfishness and pure disinterestedness have appeared in men's minds and that their appearance represents the highest values that have so far emerged."[13] Putting aside for the moment any claims made for Christ in this connection, no specific individual has ever perfectly embodied these ideals. Yet Baillie, I think, would want to say that in acknowledging these values and their absolute claim upon us, men and women are both acknowledging the presence and the reality of God, whatever the head may say in intellectual denial of any formal doctrine of God. As these values come from God and existentially bespeak his presence in some sense, they resemble those grace-filled elements which Rahner recognizes in some members of the non-Christian religions and in certain contemporary atheists. Both men appear to be committed to an unthematic or non-conceptualized awareness of the presence of God, a claim which again has interesting parallels with the well-known position of Schleiermacher.

We may sum up this somewhat involved discussion by saying that we must accept, according to Rahner, the possibility and the reality of salvation for some who have lived and died as non-Christians. This brings us back full circle to our initial question: In what sense, therefore, can claims be made for the unique saviorhood of Jesus and can we any longer claim him to be the sole mediator of our salvation?

There would seem to be no way of maintaining the universal scope of the divine saving activity and the unique saviorhood and mediatorship of Jesus Christ without getting into the area of eschatology. In other words, being an "anonymous Christian" in Rahner's sense does not mean full and complete salvation, for this is only possible through Jesus Christ. This means that anyone who has lived and died as an anonymous Christian must at some point be confronted by the fullness of truth in the living and eternal Christ. This can only take place after death or at the end and the final

---

[13]John Baillie, *The Sense of the Presence of God* (London: Oxford University Press, 1962), pp. 31-32.

consummation of history. If this is so, then why do we need the concept of anonymous Christianity at all? The answer must be to avoid the conclusion that historical and geographical accident permanently excludes all non-Christians from the possibility of salvation. We have to avoid this conclusion because the kind of God in whom Christians believe could not consistently with his just and loving nature permanently reject people on the grounds of an ignorance for which they are not fully responsible. Rahner's speculation, therefore, about anonymous Christianity would seem to require the denial of the idea of final judgment as occurring at the moment of physical death, a view which we share.

We ourselves, however, would like to put more stress than either Rahner or Baillie seem to do upon the necessity for all men and women to have the opportunity for a saving relationship to Jesus Christ eschatologically, that is, after the consummation of history as a temporal process. Rahner has written extensively on eschatology, but it is still not clear to the present author how he would answer the question we have just raised. He rejects our suggestion that the moment of physical death does not have absolute decisiveness for final judgment which much traditional eschatology has ascribed to it. Rahner insists that "death is the breaking in of finality upon the mere transience."[14] It is also the moment when he or she realizes his or her total impotence. At this crucial point, a decision is called for: Either a person willingly accepts his utter impotence and gives himself in faith and hope into the hands of the nameless mystery we call God, or he rebels against such surrender and presumably puts himself outside the divine grace and is forever separated from God. Death can be either an act of faith or a mortal sin.[15] What is not clear is whether, at the moment of death, when the individual commits himself to the nameless mystery we call God, he at the same time is brought into the presence of Jesus Christ, the God-man. In this case, God is not a nameless mystery but the God and Father of our Lord Jesus Christ. In the terms of our basic question, is the individual's anonymous Christianity, if such it be, transformed into a full knowledge of Jesus Christ, the eternal Word, once made flesh?

---

[14]McCool, *A Rahner Reader*, p. 354.
[15]Ibid., p. 355.

In this case, the final decision to commit oneself into the hands of God at death will be conscious committal to Jesus Christ as the author and perfecter of our salvation. If it is possible for the anonymous Christian to give himself to God without at the same time giving himself consciously to Jesus Christ, then it would seem as if he could be saved by God apart from any conscious awareness of the offering of salvation in Christ. If this is thought through consistently, would it not in effect be a denial of the Christian view of salvation? Rahner might reply that we are illegitimately dividing the persons of the trinity. To know God truly is to know the triune God, and therefore, to know Jesus Christ as the eternal mediator of our salvation. If this is what Rahner means, we agree; but it is not crystal clear. Because this is so, it leaves the concept of anonymous Christianity ambiguous and opens up, whether this is Rahner's intent or not, the possibility of salvation apart from Christ. Rahner is also willing to postulate an intermediate state between death and bodily fulfillment at the final resurrection.[16] A person may reach personal maturity in this intermediate state, but there is no suggestion that this is a possibility for all. When the individual's death is a mortal sin because of a rebellious refusal to acknowledge one's impotence and commit oneself wholly to God, it is not suggested that any further possibility of salvation is open. Presumably, however, all "anonymous Christians" will enter the intermediate state and have this opportunity of personal maturity in full salvation on the basis of their full response in this life to those salvific and saving initiatives of God to which he has responded in the absence of a full knowledge of the offer of salvation in Christ.

The difficulty of finding a consistent eschatology in the work of Rahner is confirmed for the present writer by John Hick's discussion of Rahner in his recent book.[17] Hick's judgment is that the "environment of which a departed spirit is conscious and in relation to which it lives is still this world, so that no idea of the next world or of 'another' world or worlds is required."[18] On the other hand, as we ourselves have noted, there are passages in Rahner which seem to insist on the continued individual and personal identity of each soul after

---

[16]Ibid., p. 358.

[17]J. Hick, *Death and Eternal Life*, pp. 228ff.

[18]Ibid., p. 231.

death. Is this consistent with his pancosmic consciousness? This latter would appear to involve the obliteration of personal identity in the sense of a continued finite consciousness after death, continuous in some way with our consciousness in this life. Hick is also unhappy with Rahner's retention of traditional Catholic doctrine about the finality of death as the end of all future growth and decision making. "The fundamental moral decision made by man in the mundane temporality of his bodily existence, is rendered definite and final by death."[19] If this is Rahner's final and considered view, then the "anonymous Christian" who dies without a knowledge of Christ will never have an opportunity to come to a full knowledge of what God intended for the race and the measure of the costly love to which he was prepared to go. It may also, of course, be the case that Rahner's own thinking has not been fully clarified and that certain elements in his thought remain in tension and perhaps in inconsistency.

What conclusions, then, can be drawn from this discussion? We agree with Hick that physical death is not the end of our moral and spiritual development nor of significant decision making. We agree with Rahner that in the universal religious experiences of the race, there are grace-filled elements. By grace here is meant a loving initiative and approach of God to which men and women may respond, even in the absence of a conscious knowledge of Jesus Christ as the Word made flesh. We disagree with Hick, on the other hand, in our belief that all men and women, past, present, and future, will stand before the judgment seat of Christ. The use of the word *judgment* here is not meant to imply that God in Christ will meet us only as punishing judge in the narrowest legal sense. It is the God and Father of our Lord Jesus Christ whom we shall meet. Nor can we ever forget the criteria for judgment listed in Matthew 25. Nor do we rule out the possibility of a final individual repudiation of the claims of the holy God. Final here means that at this point, repudiation may mean a separation from God against which there is no appeal. This deprivation of eternal fellowship with God can quite properly be called a punishment, despite the dangerous ambiguity of this word. Hick's assumption that because God is love, he must give us everlasting time is neither self-evident nor clearly implied by Scripture. Also the time we have is limited by the

---

[19]Karl Rahner, *On the Theology of Death* (New York: Seabury, 1961), p. 27.

parousia or the manifestation of the Christ at the end, even though we have no means of dating this in terms of precise chronology. In other words, one basic weakness in Hick's thesis seems to be his refusal to consider an end at all. Spiritual growth and decision making will go on or may go on forever without God demanding some kind of accounting for what we do with our freedom. Yet such an eternal and open-ended freedom might very well drive us to despair.

Furthermore, if, as Hick admits, God does not coerce us and the fact of creation in his image forbids such coercion,[20] then we have to admit that the "divine therapist," to use Hick's language, may in fact fail to win all free creatures. If this turns out to be the case, then our personal view is that God will permit the dissolution and cessation of such persons, not because God is vindictive but because freedom has opted out of the love of God and thus rendered fellowship impossible both with God and with our fellow human beings. That God would keep persons alive forever solely for the purpose of subjecting them to everlasting retributive punishment in the form of endless suffering is not as clearly spelled out in the New Testament as to make this a necessary dogma of Christian faith. On the other hand, to keep us alive through endless time, with no assurance that the divinely set goal for our lives would ever be accomplished, could itself be an eternal frustration. It is all very well to say that it is better to travel hopefully than to arrive. In the matter of salvation, however, this is in effect to surrender hope. Can one continue to hope forever for an unattainable goal or a goal continually deferred?

We desire, therefore, to offer a middle course between Rahner and Hick in relation to this problem of "anonymous Christianity." Rahner is right in contending that the triune God of Christian faith implies a universal salvific activity of God throughout the whole creative and historical process. God is concerned to bring all men and women, B.C. and A.D., Christian and non-Christian, into eternal fellowship with himself. Against Rahner, however, we question the attachment of finality to physical death which appears to be Rahner's position. On this point, we share Hick's conviction that God's saving purpose is not confined only to this life and that God may very well take more time to reach his goal than traditional eschatology has been willing to give him.

---

[20]Hick, *Death and Eternal Life*, p. 252.

On the other hand, the absence of any concept of the end in Hick is a weakness. Again, neither Rahner nor Hick seem to retain a firm conviction that all believers and unbelievers, anonymous Christians or adherents of other faiths, may one day come face to face with the eternal and risen Christ, the mediator of our salvation. Unlike Christian in Bunyan's famous allegory, we have no certainty as to our arrival in the Heavenly City which, if it exists at all, seems to recede into an ever more distant future.

The fundamental difficulty with Hick's latest position relates to the doctrine of God. If salvation is not defined in terms of a doctrine of God rooted in the finality and uniqueness of Jesus as the most reliable clue to the nature of God, then how is God to be understood? We cannot make our definition of God depend upon some intrinsic or normative finality of Jesus, for this would be to fall back into the former "bad" exclusivism. In that case, we can only fall back either upon a philosophical theology not dependent upon Jesus or try to defend some view of a universal form or essence of religion underlying its various manifestations. Despite his own notable contribution in regard to the former, it is very doubtful whether Hick believes that a philosophical theology, divorced from a specific religion, could in fact provide us with a satisfactory logos about theos. On the other hand, he is too well informed about the history and phenomenology of religion to believe that the search for an "essence" of religion has much prospect of success.

In the case of Rahner, the situation is more complex. As we have seen, he insists that salvation in the fullest sense demands not only belief in God but also faith in Christ. Yet unless all men and women are to be brought at some time into the presence of Christ to decide for or against him, then we cannot define salvation in these exclusively Christocentric terms. The other alternative is to affirm that salvation implies a relationship to God, the absolute or the transcendent which can by-pass the mediation of any specific human expression or expressions of the nature of that transcendent reality. This brings us back to the problem of the universal essence and all its problems. The use of the concept of "anonymous Christianity" does not resolve this issue.

If we insist that the grace of God, which the anonymous Christian receives, is indeed the grace of the Christian God, then we have covertly re-introduced a concept of God which cannot be given intelligible meaning apart from Christ and the special Christian view as to his significance. The doctrine of the Trinity, in the specifically Christian sense, cannot be separated from a specific history of God's activity and in particular the fact of Jesus Christ in that history. We agree with Wainwright: "For my own part I should find it difficult to allow Christian character to a theology which did not attribute to Jesus Christ at least the criteriological uniqueness for which I argued in Chapter II."[21] We also believe that he is correct in discerning a drift in the thinking of Maurice Wiles which would result in the abandoning of the worship of Christ and the elimination of his role as the unique Mediator.[22] This emphasis does not require us to talk of God as "intervening" from outside unless we have already banished God from action in and presence to the entire created order which derives from him. This we are not compelled to do either by the biblical witness itself or by the central role given to Jesus in the New Testament. "I myself judge that a 'high' doctrine of Incarnation, kenotically conceived, is in fact the best safeguard against anthropological or ecclesiological triumphalism: God gives himself in order to bring us to self-giving."[23]

We suspect that the hesitation about making salvation depend upon our relationship to God in Christ springs from the fear that the eternal Christ's attitude to all non-Christians on the day of judgment will be one simply of condemnation and complete lack of sympathetic understanding of the truth already glimpsed on earth through the many forms of religion. To this fear is added the further concern that all non-Christians will be condemned to eternal punishment, whatever the cultural, historical, and personal circumstances which have shaped them and made them what they are. There is also the additional factor that on earth the cause of Christ has been so closely bound up with imperfect institutions and religious societies which have used force and other pressures to compel conformity to certain creeds and ecclesiastical practices. If to appear before the judgment seat of Christ meant that our final relationship to God was going to depend upon the judgment of sinful and imperfect men and women like ourselves, then indeed there would be justification enough to express angry and

---

[21]G. Wainwright, *Doxology* (New York: Oxford University Press, 1980), p. 387.

[22]Ibid., p. 59.

[23]Ibid., p. 72.

fearful repudiation of the Christian claim. It must be insisted, therefore, that it is the God and Father of our Lord Jesus Christ with whom the whole race will finally have to deal. To respond to the eternal and risen Christ as the mediator of our salvation will not, therefore, be a humiliation. Racial and religious pride will make no sense in this context. The Buddhist, the Hindu, the Muslim, and countless others will not need to fear rejection because of the faith they have held in sincerity and tried to live. The only thing any of us will need to fear is not the limitations of our knowledge or our theological understanding or lack of it but the failure to do those acts of mercy and loving succor which Matthew 25 so graphically describes.

If the non-Christian asks, *Then why all this fuss about the centrality of Jesus for salvation?* the Christian can only answer that fullness of life and fellowship with God is not an abstraction but the deepest form of a personal relationship. To be saved is not to have a better "idea" of God but to have God himself in all his grace and truth, in what Karl Barth has called his "unconditional grace." The Christian believes, rightly or wrongly, that the eternal Word has been enfleshed and historicized in our humanity in a way which binds God to our humanity forever in an unbroken covenant of fellowship. When Jesus rose again by the power of God and ascended to the Father, he did not leave our humanity behind but took it transformed into the divine presence forever. Thus men and women of all faiths will not find their true humanity denied in their confession of Christ as Lord and Savior. Nor will they confront a God who despises those other revelations of his love which he himself has inspired. The vision of a redeemed humanity with Christ as its head will not be the triumph of a religious imperialism as this is currently understood. Nor will it be an ecclesiastical victory as men and women often understand this. Rather, it will be the triumph of the grace of God in a community where diversity and individuality will be preserved and not annihilated.

Yet the bond which unites this community or body will not be a principle, not even the Christ-principle, still less a principle of concretion (pace Whitehead). It will be the living Christ himself. A Christian can surely say no less than this. A Christianity without Christ is surely a contradiction in terms. Our failure to convince non-Christians because of our prejudice, complacency, and self-righteousness can only be a call to penitence. It cannot, however, mean the repudiation of the Christ through whom we have experienced our victory over sin, suffering, error, and death, partially and proleptically in the present but with the firm confidence in its ultimate consummation. At this point, all pluralism, but not all individuality and distinctiveness, will be transcended in the Christ in whom all things hold together or find their coherence.

It is along these lines, then, that we would seek to answer the points made by J. C. Robertson in his review of Rahner's book[24] and in his reply to Lonergan's paper.[25] Robertson rightly sees that the rock of offense in the traditional Christian claim has been its insistence that Christ and the Christian revelation have been regarded as "constitutive of salvation."[26] He repeats this in the reply to Lonergan: "The absoluteness of Jesus Christ means that Jesus Christ is constitutive of salvation: apart from an explicit relationship to Him, salvation is impossible."[27] We agree that such is the Christian claim and that Christians cannot avoid making such a claim. The basic reason for this is that Jesus Christ for the Christian cannot be reduced only to a principle or a vivid illustration or paradigm of a relationship to God which is possible quite apart from such a relationship to Christ. Robertson's solution to the problem of the particular and the universal is to see Christ as representative rather than constitutive for salvation. "The claim then would be that the proclamation of Christ represents, rather than constitutes, humankind's authentic possibility."[28] It follows that other voices may represent this possibility too.

Yet does this really solve our problem? Does such a view inevitably minimize the importance of Christ? Not necessarily, says Robertson. Christians may still continue to find in Christ a normative, if not an exhaustive, representation.[29] Again, in a footnote in the Rahner review, "Explicit knowledge of Jesus Christ is not in all cases essential

---

[24]Rahner, *Foundations of Christian Faith.*

[25]B. J. F. Lonergan, "Prolegomena to the Study of the Emerging Religious Consciousness of Our Time," *Studies Religion/Sciences Religieuses* 9:1 (1980).

[26]J. C. Robertson, *Religious Studies Review* 5:3 (July 1979): 190ff.

[27]J. C. Robertson, "A Religion as Particular and Universal: Response to Lonergan's 'Prolegomena'," *Studies in Religion/Sciences Religieuses* 9:1 (1980): 17ff.

[28]Ibid., p. 18.

[29]Ibid.

to salvation: but an authentic response to what Jesus Christ represents is essential."[30] We have admitted the partial truth in this view in our previous discussion insofar as we have conceded that there may be grace-filled elements in non-Christian religious experience. Nevertheless, the identification of such elements presupposes that we have some knowledge of what grace is and the Christian believes he derives such knowledge from the person and work of Christ. Again, if we acknowledge that there are authentic grace-filled elements in religious experience apart from a conscious knowledge of Jesus Christ, then the question arises as to the source of those elements. An orthodox trinitarian Christian could claim that the eternal Word or Son is the source of those grace-filled elements. This in turn presupposes the doctrine of the Incarnation and the pre-existence of Christ the Word as well as the post-existence of the risen Christ who retains his divine-human reality in his risen existence. We could then say that the grace-filled elements in the non-Christian religious experience derive from God through the eternal Christ, even though the Word made flesh is not known in the "inhistorization" of the Word in Jesus of Nazareth.

As we have criticized the radical attempts to deal with the "decisiveness" of Jesus apart from the doctrine of the Incarnation, we believe it legitimate to speak in these terms. If, however, the implications of the orthodox doctrine are not accepted, then in strict logic it would be necessary to affirm that salvation, defined as authentic human existence, is possible quite apart from any doctrine of the Word which links it with the incarnate Lord as Jesus of Nazareth. The phrase "authentic human existence" is itself rather vague and ambiguous. It can mean different things for a Heidegger and an orthodox Christian. If the phrase is used of the "experience" of nirvana in Hinayana Buddhism, which has no concept of a personal Creator and Redeemer God, then the ambiguity becomes more pronounced. We have also found it necessary, not only to trace the grace-filled elements in the non-Christian experience to the eternal Christ or Word, but to insist on the importance of the eschatological dimension and the Christian conviction that all men and women will eventually stand before the judgment seat of Christ and have the opportunity to

---

[30]Ibid.

say yea or nay to him. We believe that this is another way of resolving the problem of the particular and the universal and is more in line with basic Christian faith than the attempt to see Christ as only representative rather than constitutive of salvation. This springs from the conviction that salvation is not the accepting of a new set of ideas nor a new world-view, though this may be involved.

Salvation is a truly personal relationship to God mediated through the person of Christ who is the indispensable mediator of that relationship. To adopt J. A. T. Robinson's phrase, the Christian believes he has a relationship to God "with a human face," where this latter implies the fullness of God, dwelling bodily in the divine-human Christ. In this sense, Christ is not only a temporary or merely temporal spiritual help. He remains the indispensable medium of the saving relationship as such, both now and in the eternal realm. We believe it is possible to say this without denying to non-Christians some authentic awareness of the divine grace and without consigning them to an eternal punishment for not knowing what, by the nature of the case, they could not know if they lived before Christ. If they live in the Christian era and have come into contact with the proclamation of the gospel, they may still have an experience of those grace-filled elements which derive from the eternal Word or Christ, even if they do not formally become converted to the Christian faith.

We are aware of the possible criticism that if this is the case, then does it matter whether a person ever comes to a conscious awareness and knowledge of the eternal Word who became flesh and assumed our full humanity? Should the church abandon entirely its missionary effort and be content to leave the non-Christian with those real and authentic, if limited, grace-filled elements of which we have spoken? Our reply to this has been to affirm that to have the divine-human Christ in the fullness of his personal reality is a richer and more satisfying relationship than to experience those grace-filled elements which, though genuine, must fall short of the divine intention that we should know him, that is, God, not only in limited and always to some extent ambiguous experiences of grace, but know him as the one who became truly man in an act which has eternal significance for all generations. This again implies that God's saving purpose cannot be regarded as consummated in a negative or positive sense only at the moment of physical death.

On the other hand, it does not presuppose a period of endless development after death after the manner of Hick's thesis. There will be an end when we shall be accountable before the God and Father of our Lord Jesus Christ. What this means in precise chronological terms we can never know in detail. The Christian can only work and witness in the faith that God will not permit the end in terms of grace and judgment until all have had the opportunity to behold the Christ free from those personal and ecclesiastical distortions which so often hinder in this world the acknowledgment of him as the one Lord and Savior of humankind.

We have contended in this discussion of "anonymous Christianity" that the ability to discern the grace-filled elements in the other faiths depends upon our knowledge of the free and unconditioned grace manifested in Jesus of Nazareth as the Word made flesh. Grace, love, charity, whatever word we use, is the sign of the presence of the saving God. Yet it is not love in the abstract but a specific kind of love which has been embodied and enfleshed in the actual person of Jesus. Lonergan has emphasized particularly Romans 5:5 and its reference to the love of God which floods our heart through the Holy Spirit. He has further expressed this in his assertions that being in love with God is the fulfillment of our conscious intentionality and that "being in love with God, as experienced, is being in love in an unrestricted fashion."[31] While there is little doubt that this emphasis is for Lonergan derived from his faith in Christ as the incarnate Lord, this is not spelled out in detail in either *Insight* or *Method in Theology*. This has led another Catholic commentator on Lonergan to point out that such a phrase as "the overpowering of the Holy Spirit in the heart," taken by itself, does not really do full justice to or explain the Christian faith as such.

Ecstatic and mystical experience of love, while authentic as far as it goes, does not always clearly express the unique character of, and the ethical implications of, the love to which Christians refer when they say, "We love because he first loved us" (1 John 4:19). "The true charity of Christians," says Christine Allen, "is to be willing to give one's life for another" (John 15:12-13).[32] This has been demonstrated in historical actuality by Christ in his life and death. "Christian charity

---

[31]B. Lonergan, *Method and Theology*, p. 115.

[32]Christine Allen, *Studies in Religion/Sciences Religieuses*, 9:1 (1980): 21.

then cannot be explained fully by the flooding of the heart with love. It needs further development through emptying and consecration to God and to our neighbor."[33] This is an important point which is further summed up by the above author when she says: "Charity does not act by creating a universalist ideology; it acts through the gift of self to our neighbor."[34] This is why the Christian can never remain satisfied with talk about the unrestricted act of loving divorced from the concrete giving of self in the actual life and death of Jesus. The Christian life is a response to the call of Jesus to follow him and reproduce by the power of the Spirit the pattern of the Servant-Messiah. We are to take up the cross and follow him. We do not adopt Christianity as a momentary convention and then proceed to a universal ideology which finds unrestricted love in the religious experience of all times and places. "I suspect that the desire to achieve a unity through a shared ideology leads Lonergan to conceive of a new emerging religious ideology which is above and beyond Christianity."[35]

We too have been critical of attempts to abstract the principle of unrestricted love from the relationship to Jesus Christ in whom the principle has been actualized. While, therefore, as we have admitted, it is possible on the basis of our knowledge of Jesus to discern the reality of love and its ethical implementation in experiences which owe nothing to a conscious knowledge of the Word made flesh, it is not possible to obtain a clear knowledge of the whole dimension of that love in universal human experience apart from Christ, who not only lived it but died for it and gives us for all time a normative actualized manifestation of that unrestricted consecration both to God and neighbor.

Obviously there are many questions which arise here about the nature of agape-love and we shall not enter into the continuing debate about agape and eros provoked by Nygren's classic treatment of the theme.[36] The issue concerns us primarily in relation to the person of

---

[33]Ibid.

[34]Ibid., p. 22.

[35]Ibid., p. 23.

[36]A. Nygren, *Agape and Eros*, trans. P. S. Watson (London: S.P.C.K., 1975). For a full and penetrating discussion of this same theme, see Gene Outka, *Agape: An Ethical Analysis* (New Haven: Yale University Press, 1972).

Christ and the issue of religious pluralism. Certainly, when a Christian uses a phrase like "unrestricted love," he or she thinks, not only of love for neighbor but of God's love towards us. If we believe that our love should be universal and unrestricted, it is because we believe that divine love has shown itself to be of this character in what Jesus Christ was and what he did. Without necessarily subscribing to every aspect of Barth's incisive handling of this issue, we agree again that neighbor-love does not exhaust the meaning of God's love toward us or our love to him. Love for God is not simply identifiable with love for neighbor, although it includes this latter as an integral and indispensable part of it. "The love of God always takes precedence. It always has the character of grace, and that of man the character of gratitude."[37] It was one of the basic weaknesses, practical and theological, of the preoccupation some years ago with sensitivity and encounter groups that it tended to forget this all-important point. The result was to identify encounter and interpersonal relationships on the human level with the love of God. On this point, we believe Barth to have been entirely correct and the point is summarized by Outka in the comment: "Affirmations about grace as enabling power cannot then be converted into anthropological statements."[38]

Again, we do not wish to suggest that where love is spoken of in the non-Christian religions, it is always identified with the love-relationship on the human level. It is clear in some cases that the belief is deeply held that love is a gift "from above" and does not simply arise out of human nature as we know it. To this extent, we are justified, as we have admitted, in talking about grace-filled elements. There is, however, a vast difference between the experience of the divine love in different forms of mystical experience and that further Christian belief that the love of God has come all the way to meet us in the actuality of a genuine human existence and in the actual life, death, and resurrection of Jesus of Nazareth. This latter adds a dimension to our understanding and experience of the divine love which is immeasurably weakened if the main thrust of the doctrine of the Incarnation is abandoned.

Nearly fifty years ago, Edwyn Bevan wrote perceptively to this issue, but his words might very well have been uttered yesterday about

---

[37]K. Barth, *Church Dogmatics IV/2*, p. 752

[38]Outka, *Agape*, p. 238.

our present theological confusion. "We see today a tendency widely at work, both within the Protestant churches and outside the churches altogether, the tendency to imagine a form of religion which, it is thought, would still be distinctively Christian and at the same time be "acceptable to modern man." Such a religion would throw off all traditional belief about a descent and humiliation of God, in the coming and dying of Jesus Christ, and hold up simply the figure of Jesus or the 'values' enunciated by Jesus, extracted from the gospel record."[39] The reader is encouraged to go back and read the whole of this very penetrating chapter by Bevan. He showed a kind of prophetic foresight in anticipating the possibility that Unitarianism in a broad sense, a monotheistic religion not tied to the figure of Jesus, might well become the predominant religion of Europe.[40] It almost seems that this prediction is coming true in our own day.

Today Bevan's comments about tendencies in Protestantism would have to be extended to the Roman Catholic church also. We end on this note because our discussion about grace-filled elements is not taken as the substitution of a universalist ideology of love in a new religious consciousness for the uniqueness of Jesus Christ. "Again, sayings about God which must seem so childishly naif, if they were said about a God who did not 'so love the world', may be simple truth if they were said about a God who came down to win the hearts of men in the Person of the Divine Being one with Himself."[41]

Our conclusion, then, is that any handling of the problem of religious pluralism or of "anonymous Christianity" which destroys this essential point has, in fact, overturned the Christian faith and is offering us a new religion. Some today would claim that this is what we need, but the religious confusion of our time does not show any clear and coherent signs of what such a new religion would be. We prefer, therefore, to explore the problem of religious pluralism on the assumption that a new religion will not emerge capable of attracting and holding the loyalties of modern men and women. If the West retains any real convictions about God, it will be in a form of the Christian faith for which the doctrine of the Incarnation is central. We

---

[39]E. Bevan, *Christianity* (London: Thornton, Butterworth Ltd., 1932), p. 236.

[40]Ibid., p. 242.

[41]Ibid., p. 241.

believe it is still possible to start from this point and do real justice to the universal saving activity of God in the totality of our human history.

Chapter Nine

None Other Name

In the light of our previous discussion, we turn again to the theme of none other name. Is Jesus necessary to salvation? The traditional Christian will obviously say yes to this, but can the claim be substantiated? Furthermore, does such a claim imply a false exclusivism which denies any authentic spirituality to the other faiths and religions of mankind and deprives the majority of the human race to date of the possibility of being saved? As we look at the way in which modern thinkers are grappling with this situation, we shall notice the operation of motifs and assumptions to which Rupp has called our attention.[1] Certain basic questions will confront us. How far is it true to say that some of these thinkers are implying that full knowledge of God and a saving relationship to him in faith and loving trust can in the last analysis be had quite apart from what he has done in and through the person of Christ?

In the second place, what is the concept of God with which these thinkers are operating and whence do they derive it? These matters are

---

[1]George Rupp, *Christologies and Cultures: Toward a Typology of Religious World-Views* (The Hague and Paris: Mouton, 1974).

also tied up with the debate about the doctrine of the Incarnation provoked by *The Myth of God Incarnate* and its sequels.[2] The intent of the original book seems to have been to defend the "decisiveness" and even the uniqueness of Jesus apart from high incarnational doctrine. Some of the contributors seemed to be working with a concept of God which precluded from the start certain dogmatic conclusions, such as the classic doctrine of Incarnation. Another and equally strong motive is the desire to free the Christian faith from its specific claim for Jesus from a religious imperialism which would render impossible creative dialogue, mutual understanding, and peaceful co-existence between the great world-religions.

The idea of God demands our attention first, for it is at this point that the decisive presuppositions are to be found. Don Cupitt, for example, tells us that there is no one, unvarying concept of God from which we can begin. "What counts for God is different in different religious communities."[3] What, then should we do if this is the case? On the level of the history and phenomenology of religion, it is obvious that there is no one, unvarying concept of God. Cupitt admits that he prefers some kind of theism employing the concept of Spirit but hardly seems to go beyond claiming it as a personal preference. Should we, then, drop the concept of God altogether? The retention could only be justified if we can make out a case for the trans-religious sense of the word which would transcend the God-concepts in the various religious traditions, a solution which Panikkar seems to prefer.[4] This, however, is supposed not to be possible because of various influences stemming from the Enlightenment, Kant, and the different forms of modern secularism.

In any case, what would a trans-religious sense of the word *God* mean, to use Cupitt's language, and how could we possibly reach such a sense? As we must ignore the specific religions as the actual channels through which such knowledge might be made available to us, it is difficult to see what we could say about God. One might talk, with Pannenberg, about an all-encompassing Reality but this in itself tells

---

[2]J. Hick, *The Myth of God Incarnate;* M. Goulder, ed., *Incarnation and Myth* (London: S.C.M., 1979).

[3]Don Cupitt, *The Leap of Reason* (London: Sheldon Press, 1976).

[4]R. Panikkar, *Myth, Faith and Hermeneutics.*

us nothing. Certainly no one has been saved in any sense by simply acknowledging such a reality and saying no more about it. On the other hand, if we fall back, as Pannenberg does, on one particular tradition and its history, we are doing what is supposed to be illegitimate. If it is not possible to transcend the absolute presuppositions of our culture and if a religious syncretism is not a viable alternative, then the impasse would seem to be complete. The only other possible solution would be to appeal to some mystical core of all religious experience, as does W. T. Stace,[5] and claim that some basically unknown Reality is being filtered through the symbolic constructions of the human mind. Cupitt uses the phrase, "the interpretative plasticity of the world," to indicate this possibility.[6] Our own view is that the assumptions which underlie this kind of discussion must be radically questioned.

In our view, the question of God needs to be approached once again from the twin bases of reason and faith. Some kind of philosophical or natural theology will have to be rehabilitated if we are to escape from a total relativism. This would not necessarily have to take the form of a demonstrative theism, that is, a theism reached by coercive logical reasoning where logical would mean demonstration in the strict sense as found in pure logic and mathematics. On the other hand, it would need to show the coherence of theism and the reasonableness of its view of God in the light of our human experience. It is well known that some modern philosophers have tended to dismiss this as a possibility, but the end is not yet and the last word has not been spoken. It would also be necessary to show that such a theism gives evidence of its coherence and plausibility without giving a privileged place to any specific religious tradition.

Here again, many notable Christian thinkers have rejected this as a possibility because they believe all forms of natural theology to be both invalid and religiously irrelevant. Furthermore, they are opposed in principle to mixing philosophy and theology and think that all metaphysics is to be eliminated. All of these objections and the

---

[5]W. T. Stace, *Philosophy and Mysticism* (New York: Lippincott, 1960).

[6]Cupitt, *Leap of Reason*, p. 111 (cf. also for a further development of this approach: E. Cassirer, *The Philosophy of Symbolic Forms* and G. Kaufmann, *Outline of Theological Method*).

underlying assumptions are not self-evident and there are signs today that these assumptions are again being questioned and the truth-claims of the theistic hypothesis are again being taken seriously and reconsidered.[7] It is not our intention to pursue this aspect of our theme in this book. We only wish to draw attention to the fact that any claims made for a specific person will be closely related to the conclusions reached in the area of philosophical theology.

The only other way to deal with the problem of norms in religion is to start with the concept of God accepted within a given tradition as authoritative for the believers in that tradition and then try to justify its coherence and reality by its ability to integrate and *illuminate our total experience, including all the other traditions.* This approach would also end in some form of theism and this would necessarily involve a metaphysic of some kind. Its difference from the first type of philosophical theism mentioned would be that it starts from a concept of God given experientially in a certain tradition and then seeks to argue from that to the theistic implications. It is clear that Rupp is trying to do this on the basis of his realist-nominalist-processive version of Hegel. The price he pays, however, is to end up with a concept of God which a Christian can hardly recognize as the God whom he actually worships.

We agree that the problem of religious pluralism should be approached, not in the abstract, but from within a specific tradition. This, of course, is what has been done in the previous chapters of this book. It has been assumed that salvation as a present experience and future hope has been made possible by an act of God in the person of Jesus Christ. The consequences of this for the individual believer is not only the theological issue of faith seeking understanding, although this is an important and legitimate preoccupation. There is also the

---

[7]The following list of books shows that we have moved a long way from the thirties when there was much talk among the positivists about the revolution in philosophy: John Macquarrie, *Thinking about God* (New York: Harper & Row, 1975). R. Swinburne, *The Coherence of Theism* (Oxford: Clarendon, 1977). *The Existence of God* (Oxford: Clarendon, 1979). H. P. Owen, *The Christian Knowledge of God* (London: Athlone Press, University of London, 1969). Christopher Stead, *Divine Substance* (Oxford: Clarendon, 1977). A. Farrer, *Faith and Speculation* (London: A & C Black, 1967). Ninian Smart, *Philosophers and Religious Truth* (London: S.C.M., 1964).

practical question as to whether one should continue in the faith now confessed and what are the implications, if one does, for the attitude to be adopted to men and women of other faiths? Insofar as the faith confessed involves a Christology, then Rupp is correct in maintaining that this will have far-reaching implications for the believer's handling of the problem of religious pluralism both on the theological and practical levels. The crucial issue, of course, is the kind of Christology adopted.

The point has already been noted that religious traditions are not static entities but are themselves involved in fresh interpretations of the tradition which in turn become part of the continuing tradition. The process, however, is continuous and never-ending. Have we now reached a point when the Christian churches and the individual believer must be prepared for a radical change in our understanding of what the Christian faith is and what it implies? The doctrine of the Incarnation is on the line and thinkers who wish to be considered Christian are demanding the liberation of Jesus from the dogmatic superstructure erected by the church's later development of doctrine. This is not exactly a novel idea, as nineteenth century liberal theology has demonstrated. The difference today, however, is that this liberation of Jesus is demanded not simply to make the result more congenial to the Western secular mind. This, after all, might be a transient phenomenon. Rather, it is demanded in order that the issue of religious pluralism might be handled in a more positive and creative way. Is this argument compelling or not?

A number of separate but related questions arise at this point. The claim that Jesus is the Savior in a unique and final sense implies certain answers to certain questions which the thoughtful believer inevitably raises in the modern world. The first is whether we know enough about Jesus of Nazareth to make such language about him appear to be not only true but plausible. As is well-known, the contributors to *The Myth of God Incarnate* argue that the New Testament evidence is ambiguous and that there is not enough compelling evidence that Jesus conceived of his own role in the way which the doctrine of the Incarnation requires. Denis Nineham has suggested in the epilogue to the above book that there may not even be enough evidence to support the reduced Christology of the other writers.[8] It is obvious that no

---

[8]Hick, *The Myth of God Incarnate*, pp. 186ff.

answer to this problem can be given in a few sentences. We have, however, expressed our agreement with T. W. Manson that the quest of the historical Jesus must be continued and that the failure of some nineteenth century attempts must not be taken as a reason for ultimate despair.

It is further to be noted that Don Cupitt has not only criticized exclusivist Christian claims in the area of Christology but has also questioned the universal validity of the Christian analysis of the human predicament as such. To claim Jesus as the Savior, in a unique sense, implies that such an analysis is correct. If it is not, then Christians are in the invidious position of offering a cure for a disease which is not in fact universal. There may be other distortions and other alienations and possibly other saving responses to them. It is arrogant to claim that all men and women, everywhere and at all times, are suffering from the same basic alienation or sinfulness and that Jesus, therefore, is the universal Savior and deliverer from all these conditions. We have already given our reasons for questioning this reading of the human situation.

Cupitt's objections, however, go further and are far more radical. The unique role and status of Jesus Christ cannot be meaningfully expressed in isolation from the special history of which he is a part and that means from the theological interpretation of that history. He means, of course, the biblical history of salvation and the way in which Jews and Christians interpret this sequence of historical events. Yet this interpretation is itself time-conditioned and relative. It can, therefore, make no absolute claim as to its validity nor can it be taken as the only norm for the interpretation of the historical process as a whole. It follows that the uniqueness and the finality of Jesus can only be claimed in a relative sense, but this is to empty such language of any precise meaning. It can also be argued, of course, that the claim to uniqueness and divinity in particular is also inconsistent with the radical Jewish monotheism out of which Christianity itself emerged.

Cupitt is, of course, correct in asserting that the significance of Jesus cannot be divorced from the totality of the biblical history and the assumptions which it makes about the activity of the Creator and Redeeming God in that history. On this point, we must also accept Pannenberg's equally resolute insistence on the transmission of traditions as the necessary setting for the interpretation of the role and significance of Jesus. This, however, does not in itself explain why we should accept the Jewish and Christian transmission of traditions as the normative framework. Cupitt agrees and denies that we can make it normative if this means that no other transmission of traditions (that is, Hindu, Buddhist, Islamic, and so forth) can be an equally valid and saving manifestation of the unknowable Infinite Spirit, or in Pannenberg's language, of the "All-Encompassing Reality."[9]

Are we, then, shut up to complete relativity? Presumably not, for Cupitt wishes to insist that conceptual change is possible. We can select and change our world-view. At this point he seems to be near to Rupp's critical relativism. The crucial question, however, concerns the reason or reasons why we decide either to continue with the world-view we have or decide to select another. The reasons, of course, might be purely psychological or sociological or perhaps in a loose sense temperamental. I change my world-view because the new one is more satisfying to me personally. This makes sense in that it is difficult to imagine anyone embracing a religious world-view or making a religious commitment if it brought no personal satisfaction.

We must then ask what the word *satisfaction* implies. Does it satisfy my feelings and emotions, my intellectual needs, my search for meaningfulness and coherence, my conviction of the truth about whatever we conceive reality to be? If we say that it satisfies in some measure all of these needs, then does it matter how these various elements are combined? Are we not obliged to say that we affirm what we affirm because we believe reality to be of such and such a character? In that case, we believe, even in the existentialist sense of personal trust, because we affirm the authentic reality of the object of our trust, remembering that that object may be a subject if we affirm that God is a personal Agent. In short, we both believe in and believe that because we think the truth has been vouchsafed to us, even if we admit severe limitations on our knowledge.

Now Cupitt is of the opinion that we can break out of relativism by taking Spirit as our fundamental category for all talk about "God" and his relationship to the world. We note also Lampe's use of the same category in his notable Bampton lectures.[10] Spirit is postulated as that

---

[9]Pannenberg sometimes speaks in *Theology and the Philosophy of Science* as if it were his position too. Yet this can hardly be so in the light of his own insistence that the biblical transmission of traditions and Jesus' role in that history is normative for the interpretation of universal history.

[10]G. W. H. Lampe, *God as Spirit*, pp. 115, 117.

which transcends relativity. Whence, then, do we derive this category
of Spirit for its use in this way? Do we derive it from some general
experience of Spirit in human experience as such? Tillich seems to start
from this point in Vol. III of his Systematic.[11] "The question then is,
should and can the word 'spirit,' designating the particularly human
dimension of life, be reinstated?"[12] Does Tillich in his turn derive the
notion of Spirit from Hegel or from German idealism in one or other
of its expressions? The question then arises as to whether Spirit or
Geist in the idealists means what it signifies in the biblical tradition? Or
do we derive the concept of Spirit from a philosophical analysis of
universal human experience prior to any appeal to any normative
divine revelation which then sets the meaning for the term? Everything
then depends on the kind of analysis. If finite substance as experienced
personal agency is seen as reflecting God's nature as infinite Agent and
then applied analogically to God, then the use of spirit in this context
might be justified and meaningful.

There is little evidence, however, that either Cupitt or Lampe are
following either German idealism or the kind of philosophical
theology defended by Farrer.[13] How, then, do we give content to the
term *Spirit*? Cupitt thinks that Spirit as infinite is unknowable and
can, therefore, only be known indirectly in human experience. This
leads us back to the question how Spirit is experienced and why we
select some experience or experiences as more significant or more
normative than others. Cupitt opts for a "theistic philosophy of Spirit"
which alone can rightly balance the claims of society and freedom.[14]
Such a theistic philosophy of Spirit also tends in his view to unite
rather than divide men and women. If we ask how or why, the answer is
that "God as universal unknowable Spirit is a common focus for the
spiritual aspirations of all men."[15] Yet how can an unknowable Spirit
be a common focus in this sense? We may say, presumably, that all
forms of religious experience point in the direction of that ultimate
mystery which is infinite Spirit. The approaches to that Spirit must be

---

[11] Paul Tillich, *Systematic Theology*, vol. 3 (University of Chicago Press, 1963).

[12] Ibid., p. 21.

[13] A. Farrer, *Finite and Infinite*.

[14] Cupitt, *Leap of Reason*, p. 116.

[15] Ibid., p. 117.

pluralistic by the very nature of religion as manifested in diversity of approach. This, however, would seem to lead to an ineffable mysticism characterized as a radical via negativa, that is, by an emphasis on what infinite Spirit is not rather than on what it is.

If, on the other hand, we have to fall back upon some specific symbolic construction or representation of Spirit in order to justify our "theism" or in order to say anything at all, then we are back with religious pluralism in all its bewildering variety. We then have to decide on what grounds we select one symbolic construction rather than another as a truer and more valid apprehension of the reality and meaning of Spirit. If we do not wish to make such a selection, then we have to say that God as pure Spirit is entirely "trans-programmatic," that is, beyond all symbolic constructions. Can we then talk of a theistic philosophy of Spirit, even as a personal blik? In this case, the concept of God seems to dissolve into obscurity.

It is difficult to see how questions of normativeness, finality, and uniqueness could possibly be resolved if this is the starting point. To this it may be replied that this is a good thing because it prevents any one religion from claiming a unique access to knowledge of Spirit. The price to be paid, however, is high. It means that we are left with irreconcilable diversity in our apprehension of Spirit and sometimes with what appear to be absolute contradictions. We shall now return to the more specific question concerning the uniqueness and finality of Jesus of Nazareth when viewed in this kind of context. It is evident from the previous discussion that we are not allowed to make normative claims for the time-conditioned theology of history which is implied by the way in which the biblical writers interpret the history of which they are a part.[16] This would mean that we cannot accept Jesus' confirmation of the Old Testament understanding of God as a necessary starting point for assessing the significance of his own person. It follows that we cannot talk of his finality except in the sense that there is no superseding of the central themes to which he bears witness.[17] But what are these themes?

Presumably God as Creator, His Holiness, Righteousness and Love, the reality of sin and guilt, the need for repentance and faith, the

---

[16]Brevard Childs, *The Old Testament as Scripture* (Philadelphia: Fortress Press, 1979).

[17]Cupitt, *Leap of Reason*, p. 118.

confidence in the ultimate victory of God's power and goodness over all the powers of evil. To this, if we include the New Testament, should be added the resurrection of Jesus, the victory over death as the last enemy, the hope and confidence that the ultimate rule of God will be established in and through the parousia of Christ at the end of the age. These themes are quite specific and come to focus in the figure of Jesus of Nazareth. What, then, is meant by saying that there is no superseding of these themes? Apparently, they cannot be superseded because they raise fundamental questions about our "knowledge" of infinite Spirit and because they point the way to one possible apprehension of that Spirit, an apprehension which is valid for Jews and Christians but which cannot be universalized as necessarily valid for all men and women everywhere. One consequence of this is to play down the importance of the specific human existence of Jesus and in particular his time-conditioned Jewishness or his late Jewish eschatological and apocalyptic mode of thought. The human form through which infinite Spirit manifests itself must itself die and we must die with that death, presumably die to our own limited, finite apprehensions of Spirit.

A somewhat similar idea is expressed by Tillich when he talks of Jesus sacrificing himself to the Christ-principle. "He proves and confirms his character as the Christ in the sacrifice of Himself as Jesus to Himself as the Christ."[18] Again, John Macquarrie says that "it is in the moment of death that the Christhood fully emerges."[19] It is puzzling as to how this language should be taken. If it simply means that Jesus' voluntary sacrifice of his life in obedience to the Father discloses the deepest meaning of his messianic vocation and, therefore, of the character of God as uttermost self-giving for our redemption, most Christians would surely agree. Yet one sometimes gets the impression, rightly or wrongly, from Tillich and even Macquarrie that the death of Jesus is the annihilation of his specific human reality in order that the universal and living Christ may be manifested, freed from the normal limitations of time and space. Again, on this view, the

---

[18]Paul Tillich, *Systematic Theology*, vol. 2 (University of Chicago Press, 1957), p. 123.

[19]John Macquarrie, *Principles of Christian Theology* (New York: Charles Scribner's Sons, 1966), p. 75.

specific humanity of Jesus is not final in one important sense. Needless to say, there is no post-existence of Jesus Christ, a point which Lampe emphasizes.

The traditional belief that Jesus Christ returns to the Father in our glorified humanity, yet still genuinely human as well as divine, must be discarded. This is not a far cry from Cobb's view that the Logos as Christ-principle and as creative transformation can be and must be separated from the specific manhood of the man Jesus. Only in this way can we preserve the universality of the presence of the Logos or the Christ.[20] On this view too, the finality or uniqueness of Jesus can only be affirmed in a very restricted and limited sense. The importance of this view for religious pluralism is that it leaves the door open for other saving manifestations of infinite Spirit which are not tied to Jesus of Nazareth or indeed to any specific historical figure. This seems to be docetism in the sense that the manhood of Jesus must disappear to make way for a universal "spiritual" Christ.

It is not surprising that many Christians are uneasy in the presence of such contentions and are inclined to say with Mary: "They have taken away my Lord and I know not where they have laid Him." It is not surprising also to find Cupitt insisting that we must think of Christ, not in terms of Son and image but of word and witness. Jesus must not be considered as an absolute icon.[21] There is no sense at all in which Jesus can be said literally to be God. He is unsurpassable only in the sense that he witnesses to pure Spirit which is the object of all human spiritual aspiration. An absolute image of God in human form is not consistent with classical monotheism, whether Jewish, Muslim, or various philosophical versions of theism. The relation of Jesus to God is one of faith and witness, not identity. This at one stroke frees us, so it is contended, from the difficulties inherent in the traditional doctrine of Incarnation. It enables us to do justice to the fact that Jesus prays to the Father and never claims to be God. It also frees us from absolutizing the biblical interpretation of the history it records and in particular the eschatological and apocalyptic context of Jesus' witness. Furthermore, it leaves open the door to other ways and other "final" witnesses. Jesus may be for us Christians the unsurpassable witness to

---

[20]J. B. Cobb, Jr., *Christ in a Pluralistic Age* (Philadelphia: Westminster, 1975).

[21]Cupitt, *Leap of Reason*, pp. 129, 131.

infinite Spirit. He cannot be the one and only Lord and Savior through whom all men and women may come to their salvation in an enduring and eternal fellowship.

We began our investigation earlier in the book with the question as to whether a defense could be made for the finality and uniqueness of Jesus Christ in relation to the human quest for salvation. It has been contended that the answer to this question depends upon our definition of salvation, our understanding of the role of Jesus in regard to salvation as defined, and the appeal to experience as validating the claims involved. An attempt has been made to discuss the issues in the context of the religious pluralism which has always been part of the human situation but which has taken on fresh urgency and relevance in the global village we call our world. It has also been argued that the stronger form of the doctrine of Incarnation is still necessary for an adequate conceptualization of the fact of Jesus Christ as witnessed to by the New Testament and experienced ever anew by believers in and through the community of faith. To claim Jesus' unique saviorhood implies also the validity of the Christian analysis of the human situation.

We have examined and rejected Don Cupitt's assertion that Christian anthropology is a purely time-conditioned and culturally-shaped diagnosis of the human predicament. The question then emerged as to the significance of our claim for our attitude to the non-Christian religions and the religious experience of the race in the broadest sense. At this point a second charge against the Christian claim was considered—namely, that it is exclusive in the bad sense because it limits the universal saving activity of God in all of history. This exclusiveness not only does not do justice to the varieties of religious experience and its social as well as personal expressions. It results in an intolerant and arrogant dismissal of all other claims to salvation. Alternatives to such exclusivism were examined but were found to be wanting in the sense that they lead to a confused and ambiguous concept of God and to a reductionist Christology which fails to do justice to the New Testament witness to Jesus Christ, his influence upon the course of human history, and his present significance as known in the community of faith. In these concluding pages, we shall tie the threads together and indicate the direction which the Christian churches should take in the days ahead.

In what sense, to repeat, do we need a Savior in order to be saved? This may seem an absurd question until we remember that many religions and not a few philosophers have in fact also made their exclusive claims. Some forms of mysticism would certainly dispense with the need for a Savior in the specific sense of a relationship to an actual historical figure. Some more recent versions of the Christian faith, whether we describe them as mythical or not, do in fact take a similar stance. Jesus may be the perfect exemplar of certain moral and spiritual values or the paradigm of selfless love but in the last analysis, it is the values which count, not the One who exemplifies them. There is nothing new about this attitude, as all students of history know, but it is being advanced today in a much more sophisticated guise and backed up with an encyclopedic knowledge of other faiths and religions which was not a factor in earlier periods. In this context, John Hick recommends that we move from a "Ptolemaic" to a "Copernican" theology. This means that Christians must no longer use a Christian concept of God, rooted in biblical history and focused on Jesus as the Incarnate Word of God, as the only norm for our understanding of God. Salvation too must not be made to depend exclusively on this norm.[22] All religions must be seen as "different responses to variously overlapping aspects of the same ultimate Reality."[23]

This means that ultimate reality may be conceived and conceptualized in widely different ways: the Yahweh of Judaism, the triune God of Christianity, the Allah of Islam, the Krishna, Shiva, and Vishnu of theistic Hinduism. In these religious traditions, the eternal is conceptualized in personal terms. In another equally impressive tradition (The Brahman of Advaita Vedanta, the Dharma Body of the Buddha in Mahayana Buddhism, and the Nibbana of Theravada Buddhism), the eternal has been experienced and conceptualized in non-personal terms.[24] To the criticism that this involves a fundamental contradiction between personal and impersonal categories as applicable to the eternal and the ultimate, Hick replies that this would be true if we were speaking of a finite reality. We are, however,

---

[22]John Hick, *Death and Eternal Life*, pp. 30ff.

[23]Ibid., p. 31.

[24]Ibid., p. 32.

speaking of an infinite reality and, therefore, our human ideas of contradiction do not necessarily apply. The eternal reality might very well be personal and impersonal. This is similar to the thesis argued by W. T. Stace[25] that in regard to the two basic types of mysticism, introvertive and extrovertive, absorptionist and impersonal categories over against I-Thou or prophetic, personal categorizing of the eternal, there is no contradiction because the human understanding of the law of contradiction is transcended in the mystical experience. There is also a similarity here to Pannenberg's plea for a definition of theology which places the God-concept beyond any specific characterization of God. By this, we do not mean that Pannenberg does not eventually arrive at any characterization because he obviously wishes to do so on the basis of the career and fate of Jesus of Nazareth as the proleptic clue to the meaning of universal history. It does mean, however, that theologically, the taking of Jesus as the clue is a hypothesis to be tested and that the testing need not—indeed, must not—be taken to involve an exclusive and normative claim as over against all other religious traditions.

It must be confessed that this refusal to apply the law of contradiction to eternal reality involves us in enormous difficulties on both the theoretical and practical levels. As we have already pointed out, the very diverse symbolic constructions and conceptualizations of the character of the eternal do not in any self-evident way point to the same reality. If they do, then we must pronounce the eternal unknowable, as Don Cupitt affirms in regard to his Infinite Spirit. In this case, the question as to how much we know and how reliable such knowledge is, which comes to us through any specific symbolization of the eternal, remains an open question. Only a very tentative answer could be given. In no obvious sense are we aiming in the same direction when we pray to the God and Father of our Lord Jesus Christ or discipline ourselves for the attainment of nirvana. Our worship, and in certain ways our ethical and moral behavior, is going to be so different in the two cases as to make it almost impossible to bring them under the same rubric.

The Christian would seem to be faced here with a crucial either-or. For the Christian believer, it is not simply a matter of characterizing

[25]W. T. Stace, *Philosophy and Mysticism*, pp. 65ff. and 260ff.

God in a certain way, namely in such a statement as that "God is love." It includeŝ the further belief that such love has directly acted in Jesus of Nazareth for the redemption and reconciliation of men and women both in relationship to God and to one another. Jesus is not a proxy or an ambassador only, or even in Cupitt's language, an "unsurpassable witness." He is God's presence and his very self in the flesh and blood of an actual historical existence. For the Christian, therefore, Christ is the "image" of God in a far stronger sense than Cupitt and many others would wish to allow.

If the eternal or the Infinite Spirit or the all-encompassing reality is characterized as "The God and Father of our Lord Jesus Christ," then other characterizations must be pronounced to be inadequate and perhaps in some cases false. There is no easy way to bring them all into synthesis with the Christian conception of God. It is clear that the centrality of divine love for Hick derives from his Christian intuitions, a point he would no doubt gladly admit. It is not, however, a characterization of the eternal which follows obviously and clearly from a study of all the religious traditions of mankind. For the Christian, the characterization of God on the basis of a relationship to Jesus Christ must be taken as the touchstone or the norm for the evaluation of all other claims.

Is this sheer spiritual arrogance or "Ptolemaic" in the pejorative sense which Hick gives to the word? Does the Christian hold this view because he has insulated himself against evidence coming from beyond the closed circle of his own experience and theological conceptualizations? It could be so in particular cases. There have been in the past, and no doubt there still are, Christians with absolutely closed minds. It is also possible that a Christian may remain a Christian when he or she has opened the mind and heart to experience and knowledge in the broadest sense and yet still believes that the eternal has made a disclosure in the Word made flesh with a fullness of grace and truth for which there is no real parallel elsewhere. Those we have criticized would no doubt say: *Fine, this is what you believe and it is your prerogative as a free being to adopt the faith which satisfies you. We only object when you go on to claim that yours is the only way, the only truth, and the only life.* It is difficult to respond to this kind of criticism without appearing to fall back into sheer dogmatism. Yet the risk must be taken.

Christ is not and cannot be for the Christian only one among several or perhaps innumerable options. He cannot worship God as if he were in his essential nature possibly reflected in the Jesus Christ of Christian faith and experience, with the implication of other equally complete reflections to be found elsewhere. God has been this kind of God from the beginning and remains such through all the variations and religious multiplicity of our human history.

First, we must repeat again things that have been said several times before in the course of this study. To make such claims for Jesus Christ, and such claims cannot be divorced from a doctrine of the Incarnation and the concept of the triune God, does not mean that no "saving revelation" or action can be found outside Judaism or Christianity. Properly understood, there may be "anonymous Christians" in every time and place, but full weight should be given to the noun *Christian* in this phrase. Such may experience the saving approach of the eternal Word, interpreted in a trinitarian way, even where conscious awareness of the Word made flesh is absent. It is misleading to interpret such a statement as if it meant that such "saving knowledge" is apart from Christ. The eternal Word is the Word which became flesh, not infinite Spirit in the abstract or a merely philosophical Logos with no intrinsic relation with what the Logos was to do for all mankind, past, present and future, in the Incarnation.

We are obviously in danger here of falling into confusing ambiguity in the use of the terms "save" and "salvation." We have already rejected the idea that all non-Christians, merely by being such, are automatically condemned to eternal punishment and excluded forever from any possibility of salvation as a full and blessed existence in Christ in reconciled and eternal fellowship with the God and Father of our Lord Jesus Christ. This we have defended on the grounds that the New Testament does not unambiguously teach that physical death is the irrevocable decision-point in regard to salvation. Final judgment for the Christian believer comes with the parousia at the end of history, and the end is not yet. We agree with Hick, therefore, in his contention that life after death and before the summing-up at the end requires the option of a continuing conscious existence after death from which the possibility of decision and spiritual growth has not been excluded. We differ from Hick in our belief that such growth must be linked in a more definite way than he does with our ultimate relationship to Jesus Christ.

Let us try to consider this question in a concrete case. As a colleague put it to me, *Is Socrates saved?* (The reader may substitute any other historical figure of his choice for Socrates.) The putting of the question in this cryptic way conceals a host of issues which would need to be brought into the open. If the question means, *Is Socrates condemned to eternal punishment in hell?* then the answer must be that God's final decision about Socrates has not yet been made if one is talking about final and irrevocable separation from God. We are not in a position to say how Socrates will respond when he is face to face with the Christ at the end of history. The question, however, may be taken in another way. Does the question, *Is Socrates saved?* mean that because of his intellectual integrity and loyalty to noble moral and spiritual intuitions, Socrates knows God in the fullest possible way and is, therefore, "saved" both in time and eternity? Here again the ambiguity is in the word *saved.*

That he felt himself called to follow the negative leadings of his "diamon," as of a voice and summons from beyond himself, can hardly be doubted. That he pursued truth on the level of practical reason with restless intellectual probing and complete dedication is not open to question. That he faced death with courage rather than compromise his integrity is acknowledged by all. Is he, because of all these things, "saved"? But saved from what and to what? Does Socrates have an understanding and apprehension of God and what kind of God? It may be contended, as by James Beckman, that although Socrates was condemned for his atheism, he was in fact true to a religious vocation. His philosophical way "is a fundamentally religious, though rational and non-supernatural, experience of the world."[26] It need not be contested that Socrates pursued his philosophical way in significant continuity with the Greek religious tradition. As Beckman claims, it may well have been a revitalization of the Greek religious experience and that the "Socratic way was a religious initiation or passage through the philosophical logos to the vision of the Forms as a sublime mystery."[27]

All this is true, but the use of the terms *religion* and *religious* does not directly help us with our problem of religious pluralism. It is, of

---

[26]James Beckman, *The Religious Dimension of Socrates' Thought: A Study of the Greek Experience of Life* (Waterloo, Ontario: Wilfred Laurier University Press), p. 43.

[27]Ibid., p. 175.

course, relevant to our earlier discussion of grace-filled elements and whether Socrates' religion discloses such elements or whether this might be true for the Greek religious tradition as a whole. The nobility of Socrates' vision, which the Christian can and should gladly acknowledge, is not the same as the action of the Creator and Redeemer God who became fully human in order to bring us to reconciliation and faith and fellowship with him in love. There is little positive evidence that Socrates was a theist in a broad philosophical sense. By the nature of the case, he did not believe in a Creator of Heaven and Earth, holy, righteous and compassionate, by whom all things have been made that have been made. One might argue that Socrates' passionate concern for "values," for justice, righteousness, truthfulness, and so forth, might lead to a theistic interpretation or that such values demand to be so interpreted. Yet we do not know whether Socrates did draw these conclusions. We have already noted in a previous chapter Kierkegaard's observation that Socrates saw himself as a midwife for the delivery of truth which the soul already latently possesses.

If Socrates could have understood what a Christian means when he talks of salvation, he would probably have rejected the major Christian premises, namely the reality of sin and guilt and the need for a Savior sent by a personal, transcendent, and loving God to bring forgiveness and establish reconciliation between God and man. Some would no doubt say: *Bravo for Socrates who was not in bondage to the false and pathological analysis of the human situation inherent in the Christian understanding of sin and atonement.* Socrates' courage in the face of death is wholly admirable, but is it the whole truth in answer to the question, *What may I hope?* Is not Socrates' conviction about immortality a pale reflection when compared with hope in a blessed existence in Christ in the eternal communion of saints in everlasting fellowship with the God and Father of our Lord Jesus Christ?

The present writer realizes that to discuss Socrates in this vein is strange, peculiar, and, in some people's eyes, bizarre and perhaps worse. Yet to ask whether Socrates is saved demands this kind of spelling out if we are not to take refuge in the sheer ambiguity of the word *saved*. Socrates is often cited in a spirit of somewhat naive hero-worship. Of course, it will be said by some, *Such a fine person must be saved, whatever you mean by the term saved.* Others will resent even the attempt to foist upon the case of Socrates Christian theological issues and problems. Socrates, it will be said, remains for all time the paradigm of intellectual and moral integrity and the sincere seeker after truth both for life as well as intellect. The very question as to whether Socrates is saved is an insult. Whatever the word *saved* means—and who knows the answer to this—Socrates is saved in the only sense worth bothering about. He remains for all time the shining example of the examined life conducted on the basis of a continuing search for the truth, a search which may have no ending from a human point of view.

To take this stand, if rigorously and logically carried to its conclusion, means that the knowledge of God in Christ can be dispensed with altogether. Not only did Jesus sacrifice himself as Jesus to the Christ in the way earlier considered in the writings of Tillich, but we too can and must sacrifice Jesus both as Jesus and as the Christ, for there are other ways just as valid and profound. Socrates is as fine a model for authentic human existence as any other. Yet the Christian can never admit this in any simplistic fashion. Socrates did not know certain things, a fact he would have happily admitted. If Christians believe they know some things better than Socrates, it is not because they consider themselves morally superior to Socrates or more intelligent. It is because they believe that God in his compassionate wisdom and action has freely shown us the scope and depth of the divine love in a way which Socrates could hardly suspect.

To Socrates, then, can be properly put the question, *Hast thou yet considered the dire weight of sin and its effects? Have you yet seen the measure of a divine love which speaks not only through the inhibiting daimon but through a voluntarily assumed human existence in the life, death, and resurrection of Jesus of Nazareth? O Socrates, with all your splendid integrity, you have not yet seen all the things which God has prepared for them that love him.*

Where, then, have we come out? Do we say that Socrates is not saved? No, we do not say this because it would mean that we have absolute knowledge of all that will happen between now and the end. We would be claiming omniscience in regard to the manner in which every single individual will respond to Christ, whether in this life or in that continuous dynamic growth which follows death and to which the only limit that can be set is the final summing-up of all things in Christ. In the light of our previous understanding of salvation, Socrates is not saved in the full Christian sense on the basis of the sort of knowledge he had in his earthly existence. How could he be? Yet we are not in a position to exclude Socrates from the possibility. Why should it be deemed impossible that Socrates and the Christ will one day meet face to face and that Socrates may find in the Son of man and the Son of God the answer to his own restless search. The Christian cannot dogmatize in terms of logical necessities, but he can without inconsistency entertain the larger hope. If the divine love has in the end no option but the negative judgment of final separation from all truth, life, goodness, and love, then God and God alone can make that judgment. We human beings cannot in the meantime "play God" except at the risk of our own condemnation.

Our conclusion, therefore, is that the claim for the unique saviorhood of Jesus is not inconsistent with a genuine openness in regard to the destiny of those, whether in the past or the present, who have not yet confessed him as Lord. We cannot anticipate the final judgment of God because we lack the complete knowledge of the future which would make such a judgment possible. Nor do we believe that men and women can be compelled by ecclesiastical or any other kind of coercion to confess Jesus as Lord. Nor should Christians wish to use such coercion if they have the spirit of Jesus. This, however, is no reason why Christians should not continue to say, "By none other name shall men be saved." This is not a claim to a self-righteousness or perfection achieved in our own strength. It is a humble confession of the grace of God manifested in Jesus Christ beyond all our merit and deserving.

To the question as to what the Christian has which the Jew, the Hindu, the Buddhist, the Muslim does not have, the simple answer is Jesus Christ. The Christian is not making claims for superior intelligence, profounder philosophy, or even superior moral righteousness. He is simply acknowledging in loving adoration the grace of God actualized in the fact that "while we were yet sinners, Christ died for us" (Romans 5:8). When years ago, the Sadhu Sundar Singh was asked what Christianity had which the profound spirituality of India did not have, his simple reply was, "Christ!"[28]

One can understand that men and women of other faiths have difficulty with this because it often seems to them that they must take

[28]C. F. Andrews, *Sadhu Sundar Singh: A Biography* (London: Hodder & Stoughton, 1933).

Jesus Christ along with his leprous bride the church, to quote the poet Swinburne. Certainly Christians have much to repent of and the church in all its forms needs a profounder renewal than many of us have as yet been willing to face. This, however, does not mean that the Christian can ever remove Jesus Christ from the center of his faith or substitute a new religion or a new philosophy for the Word made flesh. This is not religious imperialism but a humble confession as to where truth and reality are believed to reside. Our personal failures and distortions of the spirit of Jesus cannot finally obscure the glory of God in the face of Jesus Christ. Nor can the Christian deny his conviction that such a Christ will draw all men and women to himself, except where titanic self-centeredness and self-confidence make such acceptance of Christ impossible.

Of course, there will always be pluralism of a certain kind. Cultural, intellectual, theological, philosophical, individual spiritual diversity will no doubt be with us to the end for we cannot believe that God wishes only a dull uniformity. There seems no reason, however, apart from human sinfulness, why such diversity should not find its bond of unity in Christ. "All things are held together [or find their coherence] in him" (Col. 1:17).

Bibliography

Adams, James Luther. *Paul Tillich's Philosophy of Culture, Science and Religion.* New York: Harper & Row, 1965.

Aldwinckle, R. F. *Death in the Secular City.* London: Allen & Unwin, 1972.

_____ *More than Man: A Study in Christology.* Grand Rapids: Eerdmans, 1976.

Allen, Diogenes. *Between Two Worlds.* Atlanta: John Knox Press, 1971.

_____ *Finding our Father.* Atlanta: John Knox Press, 1974.

_____ *The Reasonableness of Faith.* Washington-Cleveland: Corpus Books, 1968.

_____ *The Traces of God.* Cowley, 1981.

Andrews, C. F. *Sadhu Sundar Singh: A Biography.* London: Hodder & Stoughton, 1933.

Arberry, A. J. *Sufism.* London: Allen & Unwin, 1950.

Aulen, G. *Christus Victor.* London: S.P.C.K., 1961.

_____ *Jesus in Contemporary Historical Research.* Philadelphia: Fortress.

Aurobindo, Sri. *Essays on the Gita.* Calcutta: Arya, Calcutta St. Market, 1928.

_____ *The Life Divine.* Calcutta: Arya, College Street, 1939.

Baillie, John. *The Sense of the Presence of God.* London: Oxford University Press, 1962.

Baker, J. A. *The Foolishness of God.* London: Collins, Fontana, 1975.

Barbour, Ian. *Myths, Models and Paradigms.* New York: Harper & Row, 1974.

Barfield, Owen. *Saving the Appearances.* New York: Harcourt Brace, nd.

Barr, James. *Explorations in Theology No. 7.* London: S.C.M., 1980.

————. *Old and New in Interpretation.* London: S.C.M., 1966.

Barth, Karl. *Anselm: Fides Quaerens Intellectum.* London: S.C.M., 1960.

Beckman, James. *The Religious Dimension of Socrates' Thought: A Study of the Greek Experience of Life.* Waterloo, Ontario: Wilfrid Laurier University Press, 1978.

Beidelman, T. O. *W. Robertson Smith and the Sociological Study of Religion.* Chicago: University of Chicago Press, 1974.

Bendix, Reinhart. *Max Weber: An Intellectual Portrait.* New York: Doubleday & Co., 1962.

Benthall, J. (Ed.). *The Limits of Human Nature.* New York: E. P. Dutton & Co., 1974.

Berger, Peter. *A Rumour of Angels.* Allen Lane: Penguin, 1969.

————. *The Sacred Canopy.* New York: Doubleday-Anchor, 1969.

Berger, P. and Luckman, Thomas. *The Social Construction of Reality.* New York: Doubleday, 1966.

Berkouwer, G. C. *General Revelation.* Grand Rapids: Eerdmans, 1955.

Bouquet, A. C. *The Christian Faith and the Non-Christian Religions.* London: Nisbet, 1958.

Bowker, J. *The Sense of God.* Oxford: Clarendon Press, 1973.

Bowman, A. A. *Studies in the Philosophy of Religion,* Vols. I and II. London: Macmillan, 1938.

Brandon, S.G.F. *The Savior God.* Manchester: University Press, 1963.

Brauer, J. C. *The Future of Religions.* New York: Harper & Row, 1966.

Bromiley, Geoffrey W. *Introduction to the Theology of Karl Barth.* Grand Rapids: Eerdmans, 1979.

Brown, James. *Subject and Object in Modern Theology.*

Brown, Peter. *Augustine of Hippo.* London: Faber & Faber, 1967.

Brown, Raymond. *The Birth of the Messiah.* New York: Doubleday, 1977.

Buber, M. *Moses.* New York: Harper, 1946.

————. *Two Types of Faith.* New York: Macmillan, 1951.

Buhlmann, Walbert. *The Search for God: An Encounter with the Peoples and Religions of Asia.* Maryknoll, New York: Orbis Books, 1980.

Bultmann, R. *Theology of the New Testament,* Vols. I and II. Trans. by Kenrick Grobel. London: S.C.M., 1955.

Burn, A. E. *The Athanasian Creed.* London: Rivington's, 1930.

Busch, E. *Karl Barth: His Life from Letters and Autobiographical Texts.* Trans. by John Bowden. Philadelphia: Fortress, 1976.

Butterfield, H. *Christianity and History.* London: G. Bell & Sons, 1950.

Campbell, C. A. *On Selfhood and Godhood.* London: Allen & Unwin, 1957.

Carman, J. B. *The Theology of Ramanuja: An Essay in Interreligious Understanding.* Yale University Press, 1974.

Cassirer, E. *Philosophy of Symbolic Forms,* Vols.I-III. Yale University Press, 1953, 1955, 1957.

Chan, Wing-Tsit. *A Source Book in Chinese Philosophy.* Princeton University Press, 1963.

Childs, Brevard. *The Old Testament as Scripture.* Philadelphia: Fortress, 1979.

Christian, W. A. *Meaning and Truth in Religion.* Princeton University Press, 1964.

Clasper, Paul. *Eastern Paths and the Christian Way.* New York: Orbis, 1980.

Cobb, J. B., Jr. *Christ in a Pluralistic Age.* Philadelphia: Westminster, 1967.

———. *The Structure of Christian Experience.* Philadelphia: Westminster, 1967.

Confucius. *The Analects of Confucius.* Trans. by Arthur Waley. New York: Random House, 1938.

Conze, E. (Ed.). *Buddhism: Its Essence and Development.* Harper & Row, 1959.

———. *Buddhist Texts through the Ages.* Oxford: Bruno Cassirer, 1954.

Cox, Harvey. *Turning East.* New York: Simon & Schuster, 1977.

Cullmann, O. *Christology of the New Testament.* London: S.C.M., 1959.

———. *Salvation as History.* London: S.C.M., 1967.

Cupitt, D. *The Leap of Reason.* London: Sheldon Press, 1976.

Davies, W. D. *Paul and Rabbinic Judaism.* London: S.P.C.K., 1958.

Dawe, Donald G. and Carman, John B. *Christian Faith in a Religiously Plural World.* Maryknoll, New York: Orbis Books, 1978.

De Vaux, Roland. *Ancient Israel,* Vols. I and II. New York and Toronto: McGraw Hill, 1965.

Dillistone, F. W. *Jesus Christ and His Cross.* Philadelphia: Westminster, 1953.

———. *The Christian Understanding of Atonement.* London: Nisbet, 1968.

Dodd, C. H. *The Bible and the Greeks.* London: Hodder & Stoughton, 1935.

———. *The Founder of Christianity.* London: Collins, 1971.

Dunn, J. D. G. *Christology in the Making.* London: S.C.M., 1980.

———. *Jesus and the Spirit.* London: S.C.M., 1975.

———. *Unity and Diversity in the New Testament.* Philadelphia: Westminster, 1977.

Eliade, Mircea. *A History of Religious Ideas.* Chicago: University of Chicago, 1978.

———. *From Primitives to Zen.* London: Collins, 1967.

———. *Images and Symbols.* London: Harvill Press, 1961.

———. *Myth and Reality.* London: Allen & Unwin, 1964.

_____ Patterns in Comparative Religion. Cleveland and New York: World Publishing Co., 1963.

_____ Shamanism: Princeton University Press, 1964.

_____ The Sacred and the Profane. New York: Harcourt Brace, 1959.

_____ Yoga: Freedom and Immortality. Princeton University Press, 1958.

Eliade, M. and Kitagawa, J. M. The History of Religions. University of Chicago Press, 1959.

Eliade, M. and Tracy, D. What is Religion? An Enquiry for Christian Theology. Seabury, 1980.

Evans-Pritchard, E. E. Theories of Primitive Religion. Oxford: Clarendon Press, 1965.

Farley, E. Ecclesial Man. Philadelphia: Fortress, 1975.

Farmer, H. H. Revelation and Religion. London: Nisbet, 1954.

Farrer, A. A Faith of our Own. New York: World Publishing Co., 1960.

_____ Faith and Speculation. London: A. & C. Black, 1967.

_____ Finite and Infinite. Westminster: Dacre Press, 1943.

_____ Freedom of the Will. London: Adam & Charles Black, 1958.

_____ Interpretation and Belief. London: S.P.C.K., 1976.

_____ Reflective Faith. Edited by Charles C. Conti. London: S.P.C.K., 1972.

Ford, Lewis. The Lure of God. Philadelphia: Fortress, 1978.

Franks, R. S. The Work of Christ. London: Thomas Nelson, 1962.

Friedman, Maurice S. Martin Buber: The Life of Dialogue. Harper Torch, 1965.

Fuller, R. H. Foundations of New Testament Christology. London: Lutterworth, 1965; New York: Scribner's. 1965.

Gilkey, Langdon. Naming the Whirlwind. New York: Seabury, 1969.

_____ Reaping the Whirlwind. New York: Seabury, 1976.

Glatzer, Nahum N. The Judaic Tradition. Boston: Beacon Press, 1969.

Glover, T. R. The Jesus of History. London: S.C.M., 1948.

Goulder, Michael (Ed.). Incarnation and Myth. London: S.C.M., 1979.

Griffin, D. A Process Christology. Philadelphia: Westminster, 1973.

_____ God, Power and Evil. Philadelphia: Westminster, 1976.

Grillmeier, A. Christ in Christian Tradition. Trans. by John Bowden, 2nd. Revised Edition. Atlanta: John Knox Press, 1964.

Gundry, R. H. Soma in Biblical Theology. London: Cambridge University Press, 1976.

Gunton, Colin E. Becoming and Being. Oxford University Press, 1978.

Hartshorne, C. and Reese, W. Philosophers Speak of God. University of Chicago Press, 1953.

Heidegger, Martin. *Being and Time.* Trans. by John Macquarrie and Edward Robinson. London: S.C.M., 1962.

Herberg, W. *Judaism and Modern Man.* New York: Atheneum, 1970.

Heschel, A. J. *The Prophets, Part II.* New York: Harper Torch, 1962.

Hick, John, *Death and Eternal Life.* London: Collins, 1979.

—————— *Evil and the God of Love.* Collins, Fontana, 1970.

—————— *Faith and Knowledge.* London: Macmillan, 1967.

—————— *God and the Universe of Faiths.* London: Macmillan, 1973.

—————— *God Has Many Names: Britain's New Religious Pluralism.* London: Macmillan, 1980.

Hick, John (Ed.). *The Myth of God Incarnate.* London: S.C.M., 1977.

—————— *Truth and Dialogue.* New York: Sheldon Press, 1974.

Hick, J. and Hebbelthwaite, Brian, (Eds.) *Christianity and Other Religions.* London: Collins, 1980.

Hocking, W. E. *The Coming World Civilization.*

—————— *The Meaning of God in Human Experience.* New Haven and London: Yale University Press, 1963.

—————— *The Meaning of God in Human Experience.* New Haven: Yale University Press, 1912.

Hodges, H. A. *Languages, Standpoints and Attitudes.* London: Oxford University Press, 1953.

—————— *The Philosophy of Wilhelm Dilthey.*

Howard, Leslie G. *The Expansion of God.* London: S.C.M., 1980.

Hume, R. E. *The Thirteen Principal Upanisads.* Oxford University Press, 1921.

James, E. O. (Ed.). *The Saviour God.* Manchester University Press, 1963.

Jeremias, J. *New Testament Theology:* Vol. I, *The Proclamation of Jesus.* Trans. by John Bowden. London: S.C.M., 1971.

Johnston, W. *The Still Point.* New York: Harper & Row, 1970.

Katz, S. T. (Ed.). *Mysticism and Philosophical Analysis.* New York: Oxford University Press, 1978.

Kaufman, G. *An Essay on Theological Method.* Missoula, Montana: AAR, 1975.

—————— *God the Problem.* Harvard University Press, 1972.

—————— *Systematic Theology in Historicist Perspective.* New York: Scribner's, 1968.

Kee, A. *The Way of Transcendence.* London: Penguin, Pelican, 1971.

King, R. H. *The Meaning of God.* Philadelphia: Fortress, 1973.

Kirk, G. F. *Myth.* Cambridge University Press; Berkley: University of California Press, 1970.

Klein, Charlotte. *Anti-Judaism in Christian Theology.* Trans. by Edward Quinn. Philadelphia: Fortress, 1978.

Koran. *The Meaning of the Glorious Koran.* Trans. by M. M. Pickthall. New American Library, 1953.

Kraemer, H. *The Christian Message in a Non-Christian World.* London: Edinburgh House Press, 1938.

———— *World Cultures and World Religions: The Coming Dialogue.* London: Lutterworth, 1960.

Kümmel, W. G. *The New Testament: The History of the Investigation of its Problems.* Trans. by S. M. Gilmour and Howard C. Kee. Nashville and New York: Abingdon Press, 1972.

Küng, Hans. *Does God Exist?* New York: Doubleday, 1980.

———— *Justification.* London: Burns & Oates; London: Nelson & Sons, 1964.

———— *On Being a Christian.* Trans. by Edward Quinn. New York: Doubleday, 1976.

Küng, Hans and Kasper, W. *Christians and Jews; Concilium: Religion in the Seventies.* New York: Seabury, 1974.

Küng, Hans and Schillebeeckx, E. *Consensus in Theology.* Ed. by Leonard Swidler. Philadelphia: Westminster, 1980.

Lampe, G. W. H. *God as Spirit.* Oxford: Oxford University Press, 1977.

Langdon, Edward. *Essentials of Demonology.* London: Epworth, 1949.

Latourette, K. S. *History of Christianity.* London: Eyre & Spottiswoode, 1941.

Leeuw, Van der. *Religion in Essence and Manifestation.* Trans. by J. E. Turner. London: Allen & Unwin, 1938.

Legge, James (Translator). *The Texts of Taoism.* New York: Dover Publications, 1962.

Lewis, H. D. *Morals and Revelation.* London: Allen & Unwin, 1951.

———— *Our Experience of God.* London: Allen & Unwin, 1959.

———— *The Elusive Mind.* London: Allen & Unwin, 1969.

Lewis, H. D. and Slater, R. L. *World Religions.* London: Watts, 1966.

Ling, Trevor. *A History of Religion East and West.* London: Macmillan, 1968.

———— *Buddha, Marx and God.* London: Macmillan, 1966; New York: St. Martin's, 1966.

———— *The Buddha.* London: Penguin, Pelican, 1976.

Lonergan, B. *Method in Theology.* London: Darton, Longman & Todd, 1972.

———— *The Way to Nicaea.* Trans. by Conn O'Donovan. Philadelphia: Westminster, 1976.

Macquarrie, John. *Principles of Christian Theology.* New York: Charles Scribner's Sons, 1966.

————. *The Humility of God.* London: S.C.M., 1978.

————. *Thinking about God.* New York: Harper & Row, 1975.

Mandelbaum, M. *The Problem of Historical Knowledge.* Harper Torch, 1967.

Manson, T. W. *Ethics and the Gospel.* London: S.C.M., 1960.

————. *On Paul and John.* London: S.C.M., 1963.

————. *The Servant-Messiah.* Cambridge University Press, 1961.

————. *The Teaching of Jesus.* Cambridge University Press, 1963.

McCool, G. A. *A Rahner Reader.* Darton, Longman & Todd, 1975.

Merton, Thomas. *Zen and the Birds of Appetite.* New York: New Directions Book, 1968.

Meyer, Ben F. *The Aims of Jesus.* London: S.C.M., 1979.

Mitchell, B. (Ed.). *Faith and Logic.* London: Allen & Unwin, 1957.

Mooney, Christopher F. *Teilhard de Chardin and the Mystery of Christ.* London: Collins, 1966.

Moore, G. F. *Judaism.* Oxford: Oxford University Press, 1927-30.

Morgan, K. W. (Ed.). *Islam: The Straight Path.* New York: Ronald Press Co., 1958.

————. *The Path of the Buddha.* Ronald Press, 1956.

————. *The Religion of the Hindus.* Ronald Press, 1956.

Neve, J. L. and Heick, Otto. *History of Christian Thought, Vols. I and II.* Philadelphia: The Muhlenberg Press, 1946.

Newbigin, Lesslie. *The Finality of Christ.* London: S.C.M., 1969.

Niebuhr, Richard R. *Schleiermacher on Christ and Religion.* New York: Scribner's, 1964.

Norman, E. *Christianity and World Order.* Oxford: Oxford University Press, 1979.

Ogden, Schubert. *Christ without Myth.* London: Collins, 1962.

Otto, Rudolph. *India's Religion of Grace and Christianity Compared and Contrasted.* London: S.C.M., 1930.

————. *Mysticism East and West.* New York: Meridian Books, 1957; London: Macmillan, 1932.

————. *The Idea of the Holy.* Trans. by J. W. Harvey. London: Oxford University Press, 1957.

————. *The Kingdom of God and the Son of Man.* Trans. by Floyd V. Wilson and Bertram Lee Wolf. London: Lutterworth, 1938.

————. *The Original Gita.* Trans. and Ed. by J. E. Turner. London: Allen & Unwin, 1939.

Outka, Gene. *Agape: An Ethical Analysis.* New Haven and London: Yale University Press, 1972.

Owen, H. P. *Concepts of Deity.* London: Macmillan, 1971.

———. *The Christian Knowledge of God*. London: Athlone Press, University of London, 1969.

———. *The Moral Argument for Christian Theism*. London: Allen & Unwin, 1965.

Palmer, Richard E. *Hermeneutics*. Evanston: Northwestern University Press, 1969.

Panikkar, R. *Myth, Faith and Hermeneutics*. New York: Paulist Press, 1979.

———. *The Intrareligious Dialogue*. New York: Paulist Press, 1978.

———. *The Trinity and the Religious Experience of Man*. London: Darton, Longman & Todd, 1974.

———. *The Unknown Christ of Hinduism*. London: Dartman, Longman and Todd, 1965.

Pannenberg, W. *Basic Questions in Theology*. 2 vols. Philadelphia: Fortress, 1971.

———. *Jesus: God and Man*, Trans. by Lewis L. Wilkins and Duane A. Priebe. London: S.C.M., 1968.

———. *Revelation as History*. Trans. by David Granstou. London: Macmillan, 1968.

———. *Theology and the Kingdom of God*.

———. *Theology and the Philosophy of Science*. London: Darton, Longman & Todd, 1976.

Parrinder, Geoffrey. *Avatar and Incarnation*. London: Faber & Faber, 1970.

———. *Mysticism in the World's Religions*. London: Sheldon Press, 1976.

Pelikan, J. *The Christian Tradition;* Vol. I, *The Emergence of the Catholic Tradition*. University of Chicago Press, 1977. Vol. II, *The Spirit of Eastern Christendom*. University of Chicago Press, 1974.

Pittenger, N. *Christology Reconsidered*. London: S.C.M., 1970.

———. *The Word Incarnate*. London: Nisbet, 1959.

Radhakrishnan, S. and Moore, C. A. *Source Book in Indian Philosophy*. Princeton University Press, Oxford University Press, 1957.

Radhakrishnan, S. and Raju, P. T. (Eds.). *The Concept of Man: A Study in Comparative Philosophy*.

Rahner, Karl. *Foundations of Christian Faith*. Trans. by William V. Dych. New York: Seabury, 1978.

———. *Theological Investigations,* Vol. 5. Baltimore: Helicon Press; London: Darton, Longman & Todd, 1966.

———. *Theology of Death*. New York: Seabury, 1961.

Rahner, Karl and Thusing, Wilhelm. *A New Christology*. Seabury, 1980.

Ramsey, I. T. *Prospect for Metaphysics*. London: Allen & Unwin, 1961.

Redeker, M. *Schleiermacher: Life and Thought*. Philadelphia: Fortress, 1973.

Ricoeur, Paul. *Freud and Philosophy*. Trans. by Denis Savage. Yale University Press, 1970.

———. *The Conflict of Interpretations*. Evanston: Northwestern University Press, 1974.

———. *The Rule of Metaphor*. Trans. by Robert Czerny. London: Routledge.

———. *The Symbolism of Evil*. Boston: Beacon Press, 1969.

Roberts, Louis. *The Achievement of Karl Rahner*. New York: Herder & Herder, 1967.

Roberts, Robert C. *Rudolph Bultmann's Theology: A Critical Interpretation*. Grand Rapids: Eerdmans, 1976.

Robinson, H. W. *Revelation and Redemption*. London: Nisbet, 1942.

———. *Suffering Human and Divine*. London: S.C.M. and New York: Macmillan, 1939.

———. *The Cross in the Old Testament*. London: S.C.M., 1960.

Robinson, J.A.T. *The Human Face of God*. London: S.C.M., 1973.

———. *Truth is Two-Eyed*. London: S.C.M., 1979.

Roper, Anita. *The Anonymous Christian*. Trans. by J. Donceel. New York: Sheed & Ward, 1966.

Rosenstock-Huessy, Eugen (Ed.). *Judaism Despite Christianity*. New York: Schocken Books, 1971.

———. *The Christian Future*. New York: Harper Torch, 1966.

Rupp, George. *Beyond Existentialism and Zen*. New York: Oxford University Press, 1979.

———. *Christologies and Cultures*. The Hague: Mouton, 1974.

Sanders, E. P. (Ed.). *Jewish and Christian Self-Definition*, Vol. I. London: S.C.M., 1980.

———. *Paul and Palestinian Judaism: A Comparison of Patterns of Religion*. Philadelphia: Fortress, 1977.

Schillebeeckx, E. *Christ*. New York: Seabury Press, 1980.

———. *Jesus*. New York: Seabury Press, 1978.

Schleiermacher, F. *The Christian Faith*. Trans. by H. R. Mackintosh and J. S. Stewart. Edinburgh: T. & T. Clark, 1928.

———. *The Life of Jesus*. Trans. by A. Maclean Gilmour. Philadelphia: Fortress, 1974.

Scholem, G. G. *Jewish Mysticism*. New York: Schocken Press, 1961.

Schweitzer, A. *Christianity and the Religions of the World*. London: Allen & Unwin, 1923.

———. *Indian Thought and Its Development*. London: Hodder & Stoughton, 1936.

———. *The Mysticism of Paul the Apostle*. London: A. & C. Black, 1931.

———. *The Quest of the Historical Jesus*. New York: Macmillan, 1961.

Sharpe, Eric J. *Comparative Religion.* London: Duckworth, 1975.

———. *Faith Meets Faith.* London: S.C.M., 1977.

Slater, R. L. *World Religions and World Community.* New York and London: Columbia University Press, 1963.

Smart, Ninian. *A Dialogue of Religions.* London: S.C.M., 1960.

———. *Doctrine and Argument in Indian Philosophy.* London: Allen & Unwin, 1964.

———. *Philosophers and Religious Truth.* London: S.C.M., 1964.

———. *Reasons and Faiths.* London: Routledge & Kegan Paul, 1958.

———. *The Religious Experience of Mankind.* New York: Scribner's, 1969.

———. *The Science of Religion and the Sociology of Knowledge.* Princeton University Press, 1973.

———. *The Yogi and the Devotee.* London: Allen & Unwin, 1968.

Smith, D. Howard. *Chinese Religions.* London: Weidenfeld & Nicolson, 1968.

Smith, John E. *Reason and God.* New Haven: Yale University Press, 1961.

———. *The Analogy of Experience.* New York and London: Harper & Row, 1973.

Smith, W. Cantwell. *Belief and History.* Charlottesville: University of Virginia Press, 1977.

———. *Faith and Belief.* Princeton University Press, 1980.

———. *Questions of Religious Truth.* New York: Scribner's, 1967.

———. *The Meaning and End of Religion.* New American Library, 1963.

———. *Towards a World Theology.* Philadelphia: Westminster, 1980.

Staal, Fritz. *Exploring Mysticism.* London: Penguin, 1965.

Stace, W. T. *Philosophy and Mysticism.* New York: Lippincott, 1960.

Stead, C. *Divine Substance.* Oxford: Clarendon Press, 1977.

Streeter, B. H. *The Buddha and the Christ.* London: Macmillan, 1932.

Suzuki, D. T. *Mysticism Christian and Buddhist.* Macmillan, 1969.

Swinburne, R. *The Coherence of Theism.* Oxford: Clarendon, 1977.

———. *The Existence of God.* Oxford: Clarendon, 1979.

Taylor, John V. *The Primal Vision.* London: S.C.M., 1963.

Taylor, Vincent. *Jesus and His Sacrifice: A Study of the Passion-Sayings in the Gospels.* London: Macmillan, 1937.

Temple, W. *Christus Veritas.* London: Macmillan, 1934.

———. *Nature, Man and God.* London: Macmillan, 1935.

TeSelle, Eugene. *Christ in Context: Divine Purpose and Human Possibility.* Philadelphia: Fortress, 1975.

Thatcher, Adrian. *The Ontology of Paul Tillich.* Oxford University Press, 1978.

Thielicke, H. *Evangelical Faith,* Vol. I. Trans. by G. F. Bromiley. Grand Rapids: Eerdmans, 1974. Vol. II, *The Doctrine of God and Christ.* Eerdmans, 1977.

Thiselton, A. C. *The Two Horizons.* Grand Rapids: Eerdmans, 1980.

Thomas, Owen C. (Ed.). *Attitudes Towards Other Religions: Some Christian Interpretations.* New York: Harper & Row, 1966.

Thornton, L. S. *The Incarnate Lord.* London and New York: Longmans Green, 1928.

Tillich, Paul. *Christianity and the Encounter of World Religions.* New York and London: Columbia University Press, 1964.

————. *Systematic Theology,* Vols. I-III. University of Chicago Press, 1951, 1957, 1963.

Torrance, T. F. *Theological Science.* Oxford University Press, 1979.

————. *Space, Time and Incarnation.* Oxford University Press, 1979.

Toynbee, A. *A Study of History,* Vol. 7B, *Universal Churches.* New York: Oxford University Press, 1963.

————. *A Study of History,* Vol. 12, *Reconciliations.* Oxford University Press, 1961.

————. *An Historian Looks at Religion.* London: Oxford University Press, 1956.

Tracy, David. *Blessed Rage for Order.* New York: Seabury, 1975.

————. *The Analogical Imagination.* Seabury, 1980.

Trésmontant, Claude. *La Métaphysique du Christianisme.* Editions du Seuil, Paris, 1961.

Troeltsch, Ernst. *Writings on Theology and Religion.* Trans. Robert Morgan and Michael Pye. Atlanta: John Knox Press, 1977.

Turner, H.E.W. *The Pattern of Christian Truth.* London: Mowbray, 1954.

Wach, J. *Sociology of Religion.* University of Chicago Press, 1944.

————. *The Comparative Study of Religions.* New York: Columbia University Press, 1958.

————. *The Comparative Study of Religious Experience.* New York: Columbia University Press, 1963.

Ward, Keith. *The Concept of God.* Oxford: Blackwell, 1974.

Whitehead, A. N. *Adventures of Ideas.* Cambridge University Press, 1933.

————. *Modes of Thought.* New York: Macmillan, 1938.

————. *Process and Reality.* Cambridge University Press, 1929.

————. *Religion in the Making.* Cambridge University Press, 1930.

————. *Science and the Modern World.* Cambridge University Press, 1926.

————. *Symbolism: Its Meaning and Effect.* New York: Macmillan, 1927.

Whitson, R. E. *The Coming Convergence of World Religions.* Paramus, New Jersey: Newman, 1971.

Wiles, Maurice. *The Making of Christian Doctrine.* London: Cambridge University Press, 1967.

————. *The Remaking of Christian Doctrine.* London: Cambridge University Press, 1974.

Williams, N. P. *Ideas of the Fall and of Original Sin.* London: Longmans, Green & Co., 1927.

Williams, R. R. *Schleiermacher the Theologian.* Philadelphia: Fortress, 1978.

Wolfson, H. A. *Religious Philosophy: A Group of Essays.*

––––––– *The Philosophy of the Church Fathers*, Vol. I. Harvard University Press, 1956.

Young, R. D. *Encounter with World Religions.* Philadelphia: Westminster, 1970.

Zaehner, R. C. *At Sundry Times.* London: Faber & Faber, 1958.

––––––– *Concordant Discord: The Interdependence of Faiths.* Oxford: Clarendon Press, 1970.

––––––– *Evolution in Religion: A Study in Sri Aurobindo & Pierre Teilhard de Chardin.* Oxford: Clarendon, 1971.

––––––– *Hindu & Muslim Mysticism.* Athlone Press, University of London, 1960.

––––––– *Hinduism.* London: Oxford University Press, 1962.

––––––– *Mysticism and Makebelieve.* London: Collins, 1972.

––––––– *Mysticism Sacred and Profane.* London: Oxford University Press, 1962.

––––––– *The Convergent Spirit.* London: Routledge & Kegan Paul, 1963.

––––––– *Zurvan.* Oxford: Clarendon, 1955.

Zimmer, H. R. *Philosophies of India.* Ed. by Joseph Campbell. New York: Meridian Books, 1956.

Index of Subjects

Index of Authors